Sex, Fetish and Him
How To Cope With Your Partner's Unusual Sexual Fetish

by Jackie A. Castro, MA, LMFT

Cover Layout and Design by Vinnie Corbo
Produced by Vinnie Corbo
Edited by Catherine Gigante-Brown

Volossal
Publishing

Published by Volossal Publishing
www.volossal.com

Table of Contents

How To Use This Book

To get the most out of this book, I suggest you read what I call the opening chapters - those addressing the general things everyone needs to understand about any kind of sexual behaviors considered out of the norm. Then proceed to the chapters which go into individual fetishes.

The opening chapters will give you a good basic foundation and understanding of what fetishes are, how to deal with your emotions and how to successfully deal with your man's fetish.

Once you've established what his fetish is, then you can skip ahead to the chapter which focuses in on his particular sexual proclivity. I've devoted chapters to some of the most common fetishes, which are all arranged alphabetically to help you find them easier.

In the event that there isn't a chapter which discusses your man's fetish, you might find it referred to in the chapter named *A Potpourri of Fetishes*.

Since fetishes are as varied as fingerprints, it's impossible to discuss them all. But I've provided guidelines on how to find out more about your man's specific fetish (and given sample Q&A's) in the chapter called *Gathering The Information*.

Prologue

Many men have sexual fantasies or fetishes that are foreign to the average female. Erotically speaking, men have the ability to create elaborate stories or fixate on specific acts, much more than women do. These special needs begin early on in life. These fantasies are often very different than what society prescribes to be the norm. Many involve acts or costuming that are not "ordained" standard conduct between men and women.

- Maybe you've seen him spending a great deal of time looking at adult Web sites.
- Maybe he's hinted at or even told you outright that he has sexual tastes out of the ordinary.
- Perhaps he's expressed a desire for you to take charge in the bedroom.
- Maybe he has something very specific he'd like you to do but he's too embarrassed to ask.

If you have an inkling that your guy gets aroused by a particular object, body part or unusual sexual fantasy, this book is for you. Even if you don't have a clue what his desires are but suspect there's something he wants but isn't telling you, I urge you to read on.

Sex is the one subject that even the closest of couples have trepidations about broaching. It is difficult to communicate private needs. Even worse, it's painful to imagine disapproval or rejection once you've bared your soul. No wonder why men prefer to have alone time to watch adult DVDs rather than interact with you! It's much safer emotionally. They feel more comfortable masturbating privately to their dirty little secret rather than risk being ridiculed by a judgmental wife or lover.

Many men feel their fantasy is so shameful that they choose not to involve someone they love and hold dear. They often rationalize that they don't want to make their partners feel 'dirty' or drag them down by involving them in these forbidden fantasies.

How sad. How isolating. How damaging to your relationship. Psychologically speaking, it's also very unhealthy. More men than not harbor some type of sexual fetish, and your partner may be one of them.

If your man has a sexual fetish, please understand:

- Sexual fetishes are ingrained.
- Sexual fetishes cannot be erased.
- Sexual fetishes are generally irreversible.

You might wish that his fetish would simply disappear. Many partners mistakenly believe that if they ignore or don't acknowledge their man's fetish needs, they will eventually go away. No matter how much you want to ignore it, this is not the case. The truth is, he could be getting his needs met elsewhere or at the very least, he's contemplating playing out his fantasies with someone else.

You might also think that some kind of behavioral therapy will offer the cure. Some will say that fetish is a 'learned response'. Somewhere along the way, your man interpreted sexual meaning to a non-sexual event. If that's the case, proponents of behavioral therapy will say he can be reconditioned; with practice, desire and dedication, they believe he can learn to attach sexual desire in a more appropriate way.

My experience is different. Time and time again, in working with fetishists, I've seen that fetishistic sexuality is deeply ingrained. Even though many feel ashamed of their desires, they also derive a great deal of satisfaction from their personal fantasies. Reprogramming is damaging, rejecting and highly judgmental. The message he gets is that he's "broken" and needs to be "fixed".

I'm suggesting something more radical and ultimately more beneficial to you and your relationship. I have the key that will provide knowledge, understanding and real unconditional positive regard for each other. My ideas provide you with a holistic, nurturing alternative that is guaranteed to bring your relationship to a deeper, more intimate level.

Why not embrace and learn about an aspect of your man's sexuality which might actually enhance the bond between you and your mate? Why not accept what's been lying dormant inside your partner and join him in a unique but bonding form of sexuality?

Consider this fact. Sexual fetish and alternative sexuality is very deeply rooted. Studies have shown that fetish behavior forms within the first few years of life. So it's almost built into his psyche. Because of this, your partner's fetish is the key that unlocks sexual arousal for him. It's something that guarantees both pleasurable imagery and powerful orgasms. It's also something he'd probably rather learn to manage than give up. If you choose to turn your cheek and deny the core of his sexuality, chances are good that he'll continue the behavior in some form. Only now, he'll do it alone or with someone else.

With that said, maybe it's time for you to put aside society's puritanical prescription for sex and find out what your man is really thinking about during sex. This book will equip you with key questions to ask and also help you to understand that he's not sick, that he's not deviant or a pervert. He's the guy you love. And as his devoted partner, you naturally want to fulfill his sexual fantasies so that you can be truly intimate with him.

You now have the opportunity to become the world's greatest lover in the eyes of your man. This book will help you find out what he really likes and teach you how to do it - and do it well. You'll learn how to do it as best you can without compromising your own values or feeling manipulated. When you do this, I guarantee that your guy will feel so appreciative that he will never leave you, stray or be interested in any woman but you!

Understanding your guy's inner sexuality will draw the two of you closer together. You don't have to participate completely if it makes you uncomfortable, but a little understanding will go a long way.

Fetishists often experience overwhelming feelings of guilt. Your acceptance of his fetish means everything to him. Ultimately it will make your union much stronger than your next-door neighbors.

In this book, I will ask you to:

- Challenge your thinking and toss out conventional attitudes about sex.
- Discover his real sexual triggers, images and catch phrases.
- Find out how to give him permission to open up and talk honestly to you.
- Give him the opportunity to express his inner sexual desires without apology.

I don't view this book as a "how to" guide. Rather, it is a validation of a myriad of human sexual variation filled with suggestions on how you can help him get his erotic needs met. And hopefully, yours too!

Introduction: Crisis Time

Crisis feels immediate. It's a root cause for taking serious action. Chances are strong you recently discovered that your guy's sexuality is unique and out of the norm. So much so that it caused you to search for answers. You are most likely feeling stunned, raw and a little numb. Let's be honest, you've probably had the feeling for some time now that there was some kind of distance between the two of you during sex, and this hunch has recently been confirmed.

- You may have caught him at the computer masturbating to graphic images that are totally out of your realm.
- He may have made a haltingly awkward "sexual confession".
- Perhaps he's been engaging with others in chat rooms.
- He may have even gone to a professional sex worker who specializes in alternative fantasies or fetishes.
- Or worse, he may already be seeing someone else or seriously contemplating having secret sexual encounters.

What's the matter with your guy? Could it be...

- He wants variety;
- He has a special need that he's too embarrassed to tell you about; or
- He's a cheating bastard.

While the answers of A and C might be true, very often a guy looks for extra-curricular sexual activities because he feels something about his sexuality is unusual or out of the norm. He feels embarrassed, silly or guilty for having these feelings. He's tried to push them away or even deny their very existence.

Yet, time after time, at the moment of orgasm...***BAM!*** There's the image or urge right before his eyes. No matter how hard he wishes he fell into society's standards of traditional male/female sexual relations, he's nevertheless incredibly turned on by his own pervasive never-ending fetish, paraphilia or fantasy.

Your guy may have even tried to tell you about it. You might not have truly heard him, realized or understood how significant his confession was, or else you dismissed it with a nervous laugh or a cynical sneer. He might have weakly hinted at it or halfheartedly tried to get you interested in it, but again, you missed the signs.

But today, he finally got up the nerve to tell you. Why today, you wonder? There are many reasons and many possible scenarios.

Why Today?

Reason #1

Today could be the day because he simply can't keep this sexual secret any longer. It tortures him. It gnaws away at him. He hates the way it distances him from you.

He's thought long and hard about telling you. How to do it. When to do it. Why to do it. He's even rehearsed the words over and over in his head with an anxious heart and sweaty, nervous palms, and today, he finally decided to risk it all and take a chance.

Telling you about his hidden sexuality makes him feel extremely vulnerable. It makes him feel scared. He's taking a big gamble of being ridiculed or rejected. Nevertheless, he decided to take the plunge and trust you.

Reason #2

Today might also be the day you connected the dots yourself. Perhaps you discovered that he's been viewing what you consider bizarre and off-color Web sites. These sites are so peculiar and particular, you reason, that no one goes to them by mistake! You're correct in your assumption. People may claim to be "curious" but truthfully, only those who have some type of fetish awareness go to a fetish Web site. These sites rarely have "accidental" visitors.

By making this discovery about his Internet activities, you realize he's into something that you don't know about or share, something that's completely alien to you. To your credit, you've decided to investigate so you can have a greater depth of understanding of the man you love. He'd do the same for you if the roles were reversed. It's the sign of a committed, caring partner.

Reason #3

Another scenario might be that today he confessed that he's been seeing someone else in order to enact his fetishes or fantasies. While he feels badly about betraying you, at the same time he doesn't feel as though he's cheated. Not technically. After all, he hasn't had sex with the prostitute, sex worker or Dominatrix whose services he's hired. She's merely been the vehicle by which he can express his own erotic variation. When he sees her, he feels validated, he feels whole. He finds it a great relief to finally be able to unburden himself and tell another human being about his sexual secrets.

But at the same time, he feels guilty because he's also keeping this very important aspect of himself from you. In truth, he wants YOU to be the partner in his erotic adventures. You're the woman he loves and the one he wants to share them with, not some anonymous hired professional.

Reason #4

Or you might be reading this book because your man bought it for you as a vehicle not only to "come out" and make his fetish "confession" to you but also as a means for you to begin to understand his desires and hopefully, even join him on this exciting journey of discovery.

At any rate, it's difficult for you to hear this kind of acknowledgement. While it might be cathartic for him, it's confusing as hell for you. Some might initially interpret it as "cheating". But before you run out the door, I ask you to consider this:

Seeing a sex worker is as healing, and as shameless, as seeing a psychotherapist. Keeping a huge secret from a loved one can be so burdensome that it affects both the person's physical and mental health. Visiting a person who validates his fetish desires may have been necessary in order to keep him feeling mentally stable.

Please understand that a professional does not have a vested interest in your partner. She is not in a personal relationship with him. She merely did some investigation, learned about your guy's "out of the norm" fetish and enacted it with him to the best of her ability. A clean, business transaction was involved. He paid her money for a service which she provided in a highly-professional manner. It's not so different than someone paying a cleaning lady to do housekeeping for them or hiring a private chef to cook for them. Only this is a type of 'emotional housekeeping'. This pro can easily be replaced, just like another cleaning lady or cook can be hired to do the same job.

However, in this case, the best replacement is you.

What You Can Do

Whether he volunteered the information or you discovered it on your own, either way, you're probably feeling a variety of emotions. The best way to describe them might be as grief or loss.

This is a "loss" experience because something new has been introduced into your relationship. In a sense you have "lost" your old relationship and nothing will ever be quite the same again. You have additional information that directly impacts your intimacy. You can no longer live in denial. Your partner has special needs and you've decided to confront them, embrace them, and hopefully, accept them.

First, I want you to congratulate yourself on being an open-minded, modern woman. You've picked up this book because you have a desire to learn. Discovering something unusual about your partner's sexuality naturally produces emotional upheaval within yourself. You've chosen this book in order to educate yourself and try to make sense out of his sexuality.

However, relationships, as with all partnerships, involve two human beings. Before you delve into investigating him, it's important to acknowledge your own emotions. I'm listing them here in order of intensity rather than alphabetically.

Your Feelings:

Shock

The first emotion you feel is most probably shock. How traumatic it is to discover something which is initially so disturbing! Fetish and the paraphilia associated with it are forms of eroticism that most of us have no prior knowledge of or experience dealing with. Fetish is not taught in high school Sex Ed classes. (But maybe it should be!) Your head is swimming with a million thoughts and questions.

So, take a deep breath and let it out slowly. Try to relax and realize that what you've just discovered is not as mysterious or disturbing as you might think. He hasn't committed murder! As you read further, you'll learn that his avant-garde interests are not so uncommon as you might first imagine.

Partnering with your man at this time will in fact bring a new depth and dimension into your relationship. Enacting fetish and fantasy doesn't have to be dark and scary; it can also be fun. I promise that this book will make it easy, practical and palatable for you.

Anger

Another initial response is also anger. You could feel betrayed that he has "another life" so to speak. Whether he's acted upon these urges or not, he still has to be spending a great amount of time daydreaming about them and obsessing over something he's never shared with you. And this makes you feel mad!

Now he's dumped a big mess in your lap. What are you supposed to do with this information? Who wants to be hooked up with a man whom you may now see as a sexual deviant or pervert?

First, acknowledge your anger. Don't bottle it in. You have every right to feel the way you do. Education, understanding and putting yourself into his shoes can help you work through the initial rush of rage. Then step back and try to imagine telling someone your most embarrassing secret. How would you want to be treated? How would you want them react? Ridicule is the last thing you'd want.

This book will not only give you an understanding, but a variety of ways to manage the fetish within the context of your own personal relationship. You aren't required to do as much as you're required to allow his secret to be "safe" with you.

Fear

This information might also be scary for you. After all, it's out of your realm of experience. You might not even consider it "normal". Sexual deviation might not be in tune with your personal morality. You may even be thinking that this is a deal breaker: "Either he gets rid of this behavior or I'll leave."

But hang in there just a little bit longer. At least until after you finish this book.

Acceptance

Yes, acceptance! Trust me, you'll begin to feel acceptance as time goes on. The more you come to understand about fetish, the less intimidating it will be. You'll even begin to realize that you've actually been given a gift - the gift of a deeper intimacy and unparalleled trust.

You've been given a valuable tool to become his dream lover: this book. It will teach you many ways to use your gift properly.

Joy

It's time for the two of you to embark on an exciting new path. There are no more "pink elephants" in the room, no more 800 pound gorillas that nobody talks about. There are no more secrets between you and wedging you apart. You now have the opportunity to become more involved and more intimate with your man. The more you learn, the more you'll know, and the more eroticism you'll experience. You now possess the key to the switch that is guaranteed to turn him on. You're truly a lucky gal!

The Truth About His Sexuality

And now for a bit of what some might consider bad news: Your man cannot rid himself of a fetish or paraphilia.

But the good news is that he can manage it with your help.

Although religion teaches tolerance and forgiveness, it's also fear-based. We condemn what we do not understand. Give yourself some time to digest the information contained in this book and learn as much as you can about your guy's sexuality. Learn it from him.

Remember, everyone is unique. This book will help you to explore and ask the proper questions in order to gain knowledge and understanding of the person who matters to you most. You'll also learn to acknowledge yourself and be gently guided through ways to take care of yourself and to recognize your own personal boundaries. You have many options laid out before you. Only you can decide how much or how little you will ultimately participate.

In Summary

You've just made a discovery about something that will impact your relationship in a profound way. Whether profoundly good or profoundly bad is entirely up to you. You need to give yourself some time to digest this mind-blowing information. Allow yourself the permission to feel whatever you need to feel.

But remember your emotions aren't always accurate. They are just feelings - and feelings can change, or evolve, just as everything in life does. Think back on the many ways your relationship has changed from the time you first began dating. This is just another step in its evolution.

The fact is that your guy has something unique about his sexuality. Another fact is that you have the opportunity to embrace it and help him manage it in a healthy way.

This book gives you all the tools you need to know to get started on your sexual expedition. The real facts - and answers - will come from him. Ultimately, the two of you will refine your interaction so that it's not just his fetish but part of your intimate lives together.

With any fetish, don't buy into the rhetoric that says fetish removes people from interacting with each other and that the idea of fetish play is distancing. I've found it to be quite the opposite. Fetish interaction brings couples closer together and allows them to bring sexual dreams to life. What unites a couple more than honesty?

Remember, fetish does not define your man. It is only one component of his sexuality and of your life with him. Understanding his fantasy life will succeed in deepening your relationship.

Chapter 1
Understanding Offbeat Sexuality

The technical terminology used in this book is less important than the reality of the definition of what "out of the norm" sexuality means to you. If you want to be correct and precise, your partner's behavior falls under the category of sexual paraphilia with a subcategory of sexual fetish. But personally, I think it's more helpful and healing to just think of his sexuality as being offbeat, unconventional or avant-garde, or to put a more positive twist to it; progressive. Sometimes the terminology you use to describe his interests impacts the way you feel be it positively or negatively.

Take a look at the definition of avant-garde. It means to represent a pushing of the boundaries of what is accepted as the norm or the status quo, primarily in the cultural realm. It can also be used to refer to people or works that are experimental and innovative, particularly with respect to art, culture and politics. Now that's not so bad is it? We're merely extending that definition to include sexuality.

Let's Get The Scientific Lingo Out Of The Way

The technical name for your man's interests is "sexual paraphilia", which describes your partner's proclivities for having an inclination towards unusual sexual preferences. These desires are deeply embedded and define his sexuality in a profound way. It's a personality trait that's very much a part of who he is both as a person and as a sexual being.

We'll go into paraphilia in greater depth in the chapter called *Managing Sexually Compulsive Behavior*, but I'll give you a crash course right here.

A paraphilia is a condition involving sex fetishes where a person's sexual arousal and gratification depend on fantasizing about and engaging in sexual behavior that is atypical and sometimes extreme. A paraphilia can revolve around a particular sex fetish like an object (black fishnet stockings or a rubber apron, for example) or around a particular sex fetish act like cigarette smoking or spanking.

Fetish is the blanket term used in this book. I feel it's a friendlier word and doesn't sound as cold and "clinical" as paraphilia does.

What Is A Sexual Fetish?

In plain language, people who have a fetish, sexualize *something* as opposed to *someone*. That something may be an object, an act or a behavior. A fetishist becomes aroused in a nontraditional way. The fetish can involve the use of nonliving objects such as stiletto heels, leather or latex. Or anything else you can imagine. Even some things you can't!

Fetish can also be about obsessive ritualistic behaviors such as spanking, bondage or costuming.

Roles are also aligned with fetishistic behavior. This book is primarily geared toward male fetishists who enjoy the submissive role. Meaning, the guy who wants his woman to render him powerless and "force" him to engage in behaviors that ultimately evoke sexual arousal in him. And ultimately (hopefully!), in you. Because, let's face it, turning on your man is the ultimate turn-on.

Men who have fetishes need to at least think of their own particular trigger in order to orgasm. Even while having standard intercourse, he calls upon the fetish fantasy to get him excited and relaxed enough to let go.

Where Does It Come From?

The etiology, or cause, of fetishism is not known conclusively. The current school of thought supports the belief that physiological causal is associated with abnormalities in the brain's temporal lobe. In other words, people are born with the fetish gene.

For example, a man who gets aroused by wedgies (seeing people with their underwear "wedged" between their butt cheeks) might recall always being aroused by this thought, and even seeking out wedgie websites on the Internet as a youngster. In fact, one of my clients recently shared his "wedgie memories" with me, and this is exactly what he said.

Whether or not this proclivity gets actualized, or acted upon, is dependent on environmental stimuli and early arousal-causing events. Did a young playmate agree to "wedgie play" during a game of Truth or Dare? Did he see a wedgie by chance?

Scientific research on fetishes is the same as the current thoughts on homosexuality and even addiction. No one really chooses their sexuality or compulsive behaviors. Environmental conditions allow these predisposed tendencies to bloom and fester, sometimes to the degree that the fetish becomes all too consuming. This generally happens when there are associated feelings of guilt and shame. But the good news is that fetish can be managed and incorporated into a healthy sexual lifestyle.

Prior to more recent scientific studies, Sigmund Freud suggested that fetishism is a learned behavior that results when a normal sexual stimulus is paired with a fetish item. The common example used to illustrate how a foot fetish develops goes like this:

> A male toddler crawls on the floor. Inadvertently
> his penis rubs against his mother's shoe. The
> resulting pleasure is then associated with the shoe,
> and a foot fetish is likely to develop.

We've learned a great deal in the field of psychology since Freud was cutting his fetish eyeteeth in the late 1800s. Yes, the young boy rationalizes that it was the shoe that gave him a good feeling. As a result a shoe or foot fetish is established. Today's experts take Dr. Freud a step further and now believe that this little boy already had a predisposing condition or gene that allowed for the association. This is why other little boys would have the very same experience and not develop the fetish.

Most fetishists have no clue as to how or why their fetish occurred. They report thinking about their fetish as young as age five or six. Many claim they don't recall a time when they *didn't* have this fetish. It's like an old friend, a favorite stuffed animal that always seemed to be there to comfort them. However, the fetish was not sexualized at the time since children don't have a conscious awareness of sexuality. Their fetish thought lays dormant during latency (the period between their first fetish experience and puberty) and re-emerges when sexual development begins. In fact, many recall having their very first orgasm while thinking about their fetish.

The fetish image usually occurs spontaneously during arousal. It's not something that can be controlled. As the person develops, the fetish behavior keeps popping up during masturbation or sexual interactions. Depending on the individual's own lifestyle, he may or may not openly engage in the fetish activity. But the desire is always with them, whether acted upon or not. It's dormant and waiting patiently to be realized.

Some people keep their fetish thoughts to themselves and do not choose this as an interactive activity. For many, primal desires emerge as the fetishist grows older. It's very common for men to first act upon their urges when middle age approaches, although the fetish has been with them for as long as they remember.

Sometimes acting upon a fetish happens concurrent with high stress life events such as divorce, job loss and anxiety over getting older. Realizing a longtime fetish helps them cope; it's a comfort to them.

Foreign To Women

Women often have a difficult time grasping the concept of sexual fantasy or fetish. Female sexuality generally tends to be centered around romance and intimacy, not an object. The feminine ideal is often to luxuriate in their partner's arms and "make love."

Another typically female trait is that women usually want to feel as though they are their man's sole love interest. They want to be the only object of his desire. They certainly don't want to compete with a fantasy that has nothing to do with them! Because of this, they interpret the fetish as being the "third wheel" in bed. "The Other Woman," so to speak.

Although these feelings of jealousy are completely valid, ultimately you'll realize that they're incorrect and actually a hindrance in achieving your goal.

So, What's The Goal?

The goal for you is to join with your partner in this erotic journey. The more you understand, the more you can participate with him.

- You can become a part of his fantasy and even the object of his fixation.
- Honesty = Intimacy. Secrets will be diminished between you.
- You'll both feel more relaxed since you'll be working together to have more fulfilling bedroom encounters.
- You can also revel in the knowledge that you are your man's best possible lover because you've taken the time to get into his head and find out exactly what makes him tick.
- You'll discover the words, situations and costuming that correspond to powerful sexual desires, and intense erotic responses. For the both of you.

Yes, it would be far less complicated if he just wanted to kiss, cuddle, and have traditional, Missionary-style intercourse.

However, it could be worse. He could be unfaithful, abusive or a criminal. The sexual fetish that you initially found so intimidating just might be the tool to transform your relationship into something unique, solid and long-lasting. Your knowledge will give you ultimate power both in and out of the bedroom.

A large part of your growth process is to change your belief system about sexuality. Redefining some unrealistic image of what sex *should* be and replacing it with the reality of what *is*. True intimacy isn't really about that elusive experience of joining as one. It's not always a spiritual coming together.

Sexuality comes in an endless variety of sensations, images and depictions. Erotic flames ignite uniquely with every human being. It is our human right to enjoy sexual imagery without judgment or disapproval. Remember, all sexuality is unconditionally "okay" as long as it is between consenting adults.

You are embarking on an exciting voyage to become a participating adult in your partner's unique brand of sexuality. Fasten your seatbelts and prepare yourself for a truly enlightening ride.

What's Required?

I think the two most important requirements are an open mind and a sense of adventure.

When embracing your man's fetish you'll take on different roles and perform acts that are generally not equated with traditional bedroom activity. You'll learn a new language and different techniques in order to be truly intimate with your man.

But trust me, nothing will be too difficult or out of the realm of acceptance. A little will go a long way toward making him incredibly happy. Sometimes being educated and accommodating is all you need to do. In other words, you don't need to learn the "hardware" as much as you need to be open to the cerebral part of your guy's own, unique fetish. After all, you don't have to know the name of every part of the car to enjoy the trip, right?

Making Your Decision

Granted, your man's sexuality belongs to him. Some of the acts that will be described in the upcoming chapters may seem at best, foreign and a bit alien, and at the worst, weird and slightly creepy.

Your first impulse might be to turn away from him and pretend his fetish doesn't exist. You might also hope he'll outgrow it or that he'll give it up if you ask him to.

But believe me, fetish does not go away. It's too deeply ingrained to disappear with a forced promise or the snap of the fingers. Chances are, it was there long before you were. Fetish is an expression of your man's sexuality and it should be embraced. At the very least, you should make an effort to understand it.

Contrary to popular belief, fetish is not inherently a disordered addiction. Unless it is compulsive or disruptive, it should not be considered a sexual addiction and should not be treated as one.

Your goal should be to make your partner feel accepted and comfortable with an aspect of his personality that is not within his realm of control. To truly understand his fetish, it's necessary to explore his feelings of guilt and isolation. It's key for you to learn a way to incorporate sexual fetish into your sexual repertoire as one part and only one part of your overall sexual activity.

Once you discover that your partner has a fetish, you basically have a few choices:

- You can embrace it.
- You can tolerate it.
- You can berate it.
- You can ignore it.

Let's explore your options together.

Why Embrace Rather Than Reject?

Embracing his fetish means that you want to get closer to your man. It means that you understand the shame that goes hand in hand with his confession. It means that you care enough to educate yourself and come to the understanding that fetish behavior is deeply embedded into your man's ability to be intimate.

Fetish is intensely personal, private and yet it is also perceived as somewhat disgraceful to him. That's why he held back about telling you. We still live in a puritanical, judgmental society that supports rigid sexual standards. You can get so much closer to your partner by giving him the opportunity to unburden himself and speak frankly about something he's held inside of him for a very long time. You have the ability to make him feel good about himself and his eccentric desires, and that's pretty incredible.

Women who embrace their partner's sexual fetish are virtually guaranteed a life ticket of devotion. He'll never cheat or lie. He knows there's no reason. He's entrusted you with his deepest, darkest secret and you've risen to the challenge. You are being accepting instead of condescending. You have chosen to *accompany* him on this intimate expedition.

How To...

Truthfully, it doesn't take much to enact a fetish. Something that you'll find pretty effortless (with my help!) will mean so much to him.

Each fetish has its own specific requirements in terms of costuming, props and verbiage. I consider these fetishes so unique and important that each has its own individual chapter. Every chapter will provide you with a broad overview and questions for you to ask your mate. You'll learn how to listen openly and objectively. The result will be a fulfilling experience for him, which in turn will be rewarding and esteem-building for you. I mean, who doesn't want to be worshipped and thought of as a goddess?

The anticipation and language turns on most fetishists to the utmost degree. Just hearing about what you will do to him is often enough to provide him with a great deal of satisfaction. Often, just hearing a buzzword or two will instantly bring him to a state of hyper-arousal.

A good example of working around a fetish that might be distasteful for you but a turn on for him is the "threesome fantasy". Although you may not want to invite another woman into your bedroom, you can still feed his fantasy by simply talking about it. Describe what might happen between the three of you in exquisite detail and take pleasure in his heightened reaction. You see, by acknowledging his fetish, you are participating, albeit passively, accepting and embracing the fantasy without actually doing it.

The same can be true of every fetish and fantasy. You may not want to physically tie him up, whip him till he begs you to stop, pee on his face, pinch his nipples or tie up his testicles but you can at least indulge him by making up a story. By recognizing his fetish, you are validating him, saying silently through your actions that it's okay for him to think about whatever floats his boat. You've given him the freedom to feel comfortable with his fetish and share intimate parts of his psyche with you.

Cons: A Warning To Those Who Choose To Look The Other Way

What happens if you choose to ignore, berate or oppose your guy's fetish? Men who feel alone in their sexuality feel so bad that the most common reaction is for them to retreat. Invariably these men go out and seek erotic relief elsewhere. They often spend countless hours online masturbating by themselves. And what a sad, lonely image this is of someone you love!

This time he spends by himself online may also lead to "chatting" with other like-minded people in specialty chat rooms. This venue is actually a means of self-healing as people with a fetish find themselves feeling alone and separate from those in "polite society." A fetish chat room is an accepting place, somewhere they are the norm rather than the outcast.

Sometimes fetishists also pay professional women - i.e. prostitutes, Dominatrixes or escorts to fulfill their needs. While they find some degree of satisfaction with this type of outlet, they often leave feeling empty. And that's not just because they've emptied their pockets! (And wouldn't you rather he spend the money on you?) They've spilled their soul to a stranger, rather than to someone they love; you. They've turned an intimate part of themselves into a cold business transaction.

Before you know it, an emotional wall is built between the two of you that grows thicker and stronger over the years. Soon bedroom intimacy becomes a distant memory. Your lives are about outside events but not about the two of you.

If you think about it, men have good reason for keeping their fetish a secret:

- They're afraid you won't understand.
- They're afraid you'll be rejecting or negating.
- They're afraid of taking the risk of being seen as "less than" in your eyes.

When men choose not to tell their partner about their fetish, they make a loud-and-clear statement about their union. It says that they don't trust you. They silently pick up on your judgmental vibes. Their silence is the wall that grows taller and stronger as your relationship develops. And from my experience as a therapist, I can tell you that distance is an insidious disease. You don't know it's there until it takes over and destroys your bond.

Take Action

By reading this book, you've already made the decision to change your way of thinking. Or at least to seriously consider it. Rather than seeing his fetish as something that needs to be erased, you're choosing to learn about it and participate in it as best as you can. You are to be applauded for your open-minded attitude and your large capacity to love.

But be prepared because you're also about to embark on a voyage that will lead to intimacy in previously uncharted territory. This book will serve as your guide. It will be a map that will show you the way to learn all you can about your partner's own distinctive sexual fetish.

As leader of this expedition you will feel an enormous surge of empowerment. I'll hold your hand through it all and will show you how to accomplish your goal. Each of "The Fetishes" chapters will teach you the basics of a particular fetish and will provide you with the questions you need to ask in order to bring your man's own inner fantasy to life.

You're on your way to being his best lover ever. Just turn the page.

Chapter 2
Feelings vs. Taking Action

One of the best pieces of advice I can offer it to be careful of your thoughts. It's very easy to consider your man's sexual variation as being "his fault" or think of it as "his problem". At this point, you might feel certain that you can't get involved in his fetish. You could even be harboring angry thoughts because you prefer to be with a "normal" guy. I urge you not to think of it as anyone's fault or even a problem.

The only results these kinds of thoughts accomplish are feelings of negativity which are of no use to either of you. They serve as a wedge between you. Ultimately, they don't help you achieve the goal of having a close, intimate lasting relationship.

You and only you have the capacity to change your way of thinking. The first step toward doing this is to practice empathy. Your man most likely thinks of himself as "perverted" which ultimately makes him feel ashamed.

I want you to put yourself in his shoes for a moment. Let's imagine the fetish from his point of view.

If your partner has a fetish, he most likely feels:

Conflicted

He wonders why he's sexually different than other guys. Most likely he has no idea where his fetish originated. But what he does know is that the fetish is more powerful than his feelings of revulsion. In other words, no matter how much he's tried to "will it away", which I guarantee you, he has, these sexual urges will not go away.

Embarrassed

Some fetishes/fantasies - like submission, forced feminization or cuckolding, for example - cause him to think or behave in ways he perceives to be "less than a man". As a result, they can be very embarrassing to talk about. He would rather die than tell his guys friends. They just wouldn't understand and chances are very good that they'd be critical and judgmental. Similarly, wives have been known to turn their backs on their husbands with taboo desires like these and even worse, to be dismissive of their men's deep, dark secret once he has the nerve to reveal it to them.

Alienated

But most of all, he feels isolated, abandoned, alienated. He would so much like to be able to talk about his feelings and desires with someone but he doesn't dare. The fear of being rejected is just too great. No one wants be considered a weirdo or a freak. Unfortunately extremely derogatory terms have been attached to any kind of sexuality that's out of the norm. And personally, I believe this has got to change in order for fetishists to find a sense of peace within themselves.

Enough About Him: Dealing with Your Feelings

Conversely, your reflexive feelings of being put off by his fetish are completely normal and natural. It's not easy to learn that there's a facet to your man that you never, ever imagined. His sexual difference feels disconcerting, frightening, even off-putting. There's a part of you that would just like his fetish to vanish.

It might also make you feel angry or a bit cheated. Why me you might ask? Why did I have to find out this kind of thing now when everything was going so nicely?

By this time, you've hopefully accepted the fact that your guy's fetish won't go away. As I mentioned earlier, if you choose to ignore it, chances are quite strong that you'll have a man who strays. Even if he doesn't stray physically, he'll stray mentally. He'll "cheat" in his thoughts and be forced to slink around in a sneaky, secretive manner because you refuse to embrace or even "try on" his fetish for size. Eventually, you'll notice him spending more and more time alone at the computer. Working, he might tell you, but instead, he'll be skulking away to download pornography, visit online chat rooms, seek out the services of a sex worker or worse, he'll form a "kinky relationship" with another woman.

It may feel like an unfair choice to you: accept his fetish or risk losing him. But those are the choices you have. Like it or not, this fetish is a prime ingredient of your man's sexual makeup. You can opt to join in and create a happy, harmonious relationship. Or you can elect to reject his fetish and distance yourself from your partner. The choice is yours.

Confused

I understand your initial doubts and feelings of ambivalence. This is not what you originally signed up for when you and your man met and began dating. It's confusing to learn about an interest that strays so far from what we were brought up to believe is "normal" sex.

Most of us learned that intimacy is all about kissing, hugging, caressing, fondling and other types of socially-acceptable foreplay that lead to "vanilla" sexual intercourse. We want the sex act to be all about us—and our vaginas. We don't want it to involve diapers, a smack on the bottom or dangerously-high stiletto heels! When we find out differently we have a knee jerk reaction which may be negative and harmful to our relationship. But let's explore that thought process.

Should You Listen to Your Feelings?

It depends upon whether or not your thoughts are based on fact.

- Is it a fact that men should be dominant and women should be docile?
- Is it a fact that sex needs to conform to the societal norm?
- Is it a fact that he must think romantic thoughts at the moment of orgasm?

Try and be honest with yourself and rationally figure out "deal breakers" in your relationship. For example, would you leave him for betrayal, cheating and untrustworthy behavior or would you walk out because he thinks differently than you do? My guess is that you'd opt for a guy who's loyal, honest and faithful. Private thoughts and fantasies take a back seat to overt acts of deception. Think of it this way: the moment of orgasm lasts less than a minute. Are those few seconds really that important in comparison to the remaining 1,399 minutes in a day?

When you harbor thoughts that your husband's fetish is weird, wrong or unhealthy, you naturally start to feel bad about yourself. You might try to convince yourself that you chose your mate poorly and that you lacked foresight or judgment in your union. Your thoughts also might make you feel angry because his "out of the norm" sexuality requires that you get up off your butt and take action.

Upon learning the intricacies of his fetish and what it might involve—scripting, costuming, etc.—you might initially think of all the work it involves. True, some fantasies do require your active participation and some "work" on your part. Participation requires education, creativity and planning. That's a lot more work than most women have to do in the bedroom. It's more involved than lying on your back and looking pretty. But if you do it right, fetish fulfillment can be much more rewarding.

However, if you think about his fetish as being more trouble than it's worth, it's easy to begin to feel weary, angry and very alone. You might ask:

- "Why me?"
- "Don't' I have enough to do?"
- "How could I ever have gotten hooked up with such a freak?"
- "I can only imagine what my friends or family would think of me if they knew!"

See where this is leading? I bet just reading these phrases are bringing up strong emotions in you. But that's not entirely a bad thing. I want you to notice what you're experiencing in your body right now. Chances are that your breathing is shallow, you feel knots in your stomach and your energy level is low.

But the good news is that you have the ability to control your thoughts. You can change your way of thinking to include helpful, positive and soothing self-messages.

Listen and take heed to these kinds of thoughts:

- "I have the opportunity to be helpful to my man."
- "I can show him how much I care."
- "I want to create a wonderful experience so we can bond and be closer."
- "The only opinion I care about is my own."
- "It's nobody's business what goes on in our bedroom."

I'll bet that when you read these statements something changed in your body. Your breathing became calmer, your stomach felt better and you probably grew more relaxed and confident.

I can't stress enough how strongly thoughts influence feelings. Change your thought-pattern into words that reflect acceptance, positivity and empathy. You'll feel happier, tranquil and more capable. You'll also realize that your guy is worth the effort.

Some women cook huge meals for their mates. They'll tell you that it's an expression of love. Accepting your man's fetish is very much the same thing. It's a declaration of love.

But just like you need to prepare for a sumptuous meal ahead of time, you'll also need to plan for a fetish episode—get the "ingredients," prepare the meal, then make the big presentation.

And I'm willing to bet that he'll be more agreeable to cleaning up the bedroom than he'd be cleaning up the kitchen!

Be The Initiator

Some women do all the fetish research and then wait patiently for him to make the move. When they do act out the fetish scenario, it's with an underlying attitude of resentment. They do it solely to please their partners but with an "I can't wait to get it over with" manner. Or else they just go through with the scene so he'll get off their back. Their attitude is half-hearted and be-grudging, and worst of all, their partner can sense it. Almost as bad as not taking part in the fetish at all!

Again, my advice is to keep an open mind. Never make him beg for fetish play. That's something that he'll find off-putting and cause him to harbor resentment.

It's key for you to be an enthusiastic participant. Initiate fetish games when you're feeling energetic, loving and really want to do something special.

Remember the analogy of a fetish scene being like cooking an exceptional meal? You don't need to do it every night but when you do, take pride in doing it right. Fetish interactions aren't meant to replace the sexuality you already have in place. Fetish play is meant to enhance and expand your bedroom repertoire. You don't wear the same shoes every day, right? Why should you wear the same old, tired roles in bed?

In Summary

In my therapy practice, I've helped thousands of men achieve a sense of acceptance about their sexual variations. Each of these men had to work hard to gain self-acceptance. Their final stumbling block was always the challenge of incorporating the fetish into their existing relationships. So many of these men gathered the strength to tell their wives or girlfriends about their fetish only to be met with disdain, disinterest or contempt. It just about destroyed them emotionally and sometimes, their relationships.

You don't want to be one of these women. You want to change your own belief system to include unconditional, positive regard and acceptance. If you didn't, you wouldn't be reading this book.

Before you do anything else, you'll look at your own thought process and examine the beliefs you personally have about human sexuality. You'll think back and remember what your parents, school and religion taught you about sex. You might discover that your introduction to sex is laden with rigid values and beliefs. You'll come to understand that the original ideas instilled in you about sex are not the final word about human sexual interactions. As an adult, you have the capability and intelligence to make your own decisions about what sexual relations are really about.

Remember that sexuality is fluid, not definitive. Sexual relations can flow and expand in many directions over time. I'm asking you to focus in on what your goals are in this relationship you cherish. Prioritize these goals and make sure what you really want is in sync with your actual behavior. If you do this, you'll have a new outlook on participating in your man's sexual fetish. But only when you are clear about your own sexual belief system.

Are you ready to begin?

Chapter 3
Preliminary Quiz: Your Sexual I.Q.

By the time we reach adulthood we all have very strong ideals when it comes to sexuality. Society, parents and religious doctrines all help shape our sexual sensibilities. We have an inherent belief about what should or should not take place in our bedroom.

It just so happens that you were dealt a "wild card" when it comes to your guy's sexuality; he deviates either a lot or a little from the norm.

Before you embark on your journey of exploration, it's helpful to understand where you're coming from so you can better deal with your man's proclivities. This is the purpose of the following quiz.

It's ideal if your Sexual I.Q. rates in a category that reflects flexibility and open-mindedness. If it does, that will make your quest a great deal easier. If you don't rate in this category, that's okay too. This just means it's something for you to be aware of and work on. Think of it as the same as having to learn anything new; like an unfamiliar appliance or an alternate way of doing things. Some of us are naturals at reading the instruction manual and comfortable with the new apparatus right away. Others are apprehensive about change even when ultimately we know the new machine or new method will be better for us in the long run.

This short quiz will help you hone in on your own beliefs and standards when it comes to sexuality. I suggest you take the quiz now, before you continue reading the book. You'll also find the very same quiz at the end of the book. It might be very interesting (and telling) to see if and how much you've changed.

I guarantee that you'll be pleased with the change I know will occur in your belief system after reading this book. I also feel certain that your change in attitude will bring about a more confident you and a more cohesive relationship between you and your partner.

Your Sexual I.Q.

Select a number below each question to indicate how strongly you agree or disagree with each statement. When you're done taking the quiz, tally up your score. And don't peek at the answer key at the end!

1) Do you feel there's something sexually "wrong" with your man?

> 3 - Not at all
> 2 - Somewhat
> 1 - A little
> 0 - A lot

2) Do you feel upset about the possibility that he enjoys sexual acts that are foreign to you?

> 3 - Not at all
> 2 - Somewhat
> 1 - A little
> 0 - A lot

3) Does the future of your sexual relationship feel hopeless?

     3 - Not at all
     2 - Somewhat
     1 - A little
     0 - Very

4) Do you feel *he's* the one who has the problem so *he's* the one who has to change?

     3 - Not at all
     2 - Somewhat
     1 - A little
     0 - Well he's the one with the fetish

5) Do you have a favorite sex position?

     3 - I enjoy them all
     2 - Most of them
     1 - Sometimes I'll get on top
     0 - Missionary only, thank you

6) Do you find sexual activities such as oral sex distasteful?

     3 - Not at all
     2 - Somewhat
     1 - A little
     0 - Very

7) Do you mind dressing up for your partner when you're having sex?

     3 - Love it, I have lot's of outfits
     2 - I have one or two costumes
     1 - Sometimes I'll wear lingerie
     0 - Is this really necessary, I have enough laundry

8) Have you and your partner ever experimented with sex toys or other props?

    3 - We have a closet full
    2 - We have a few toys we enjoy
    1 - Once or twice on special occasions
    0 - Are you nuts, get that thing away from me!

9) Do you have any objection to using certain phases or erotic buzzwords to help stimulate your partner?

    3 - Not at all
    2 - Sometimes
    1 - Potty talk belongs in the potty
    0 - A lady never uses such language

10) Do you believe that your partner should focus his attention only on you during sexual interaction?

    3 - Not at all, fantasy is healthy
    2 - What goes on in his head is his business
    1 - I'd prefer if he's focused on me
    0 - He'd better be focused on me

11) Do you wish he could take a pill and be "cured" of his unusual sexual proclivities?

    3 - Not at all
    2 - Sometimes
    1 - How much is this pill?
    0 - Call the pharmacy now

12) Do you believe that anyone who is turned on by sexuality out of the norm is perverted and needs to be cured?

    3 - Not at all
    2 - Somewhat
    1 - Maybe
    0 - Absolutely

13) Do you worry that his sexual predilections could be the demise of your relationship?

     3 - Not at all
     2 - Sometimes
     1 - I can't help but worry
     0 - I'm sure of it

14) Are you willing to be flexible and learn to participate to some degree in his fetish?

     3 - Bring it on
     2 - If it keeps us together
     1 - If its his birthday and I'm in a good mood
     0 - Hell no

15) Would you be willing to share something about your own sexuality with him?

     3 - I love to tell him my fantasies
     2 - I'll tell him some, but not all
     1 - A girl has to have some secrets
     0 - Mind your damn business

Your Sexual I.Q. Quiz Results

0-4
Established
You have rigid beliefs when it comes to sex. This came from the way you were brought up and reflects strong messages from your parents, schools and church. You ideally believe that sex should take place between married couples. Right now you are encountering a problem that you strongly wish would disappear.

5-10
Conventional
You are a slightly open-minded but prefer conventional, married, "vanilla" sex. Ideally it's your hope and belief that sex is all about the bond that brings you together as man and wife.

11-20
Borderline Traditional

You recognize that his fetish is something that affects you both. You would prefer to have a traditional sexual relationship but you are willing to entertain other ideas. You're curious and willing to explore other possibilities in order to help your relationship.

21-30
Getting There

You have opened your mind to the possibility of change. You're pretty certain that your man has something different and/or unusual about his sexual tastes but you're open-minded and want to explore the possibilities of getting involved with his fetish

31-45
Congratulations!

You're on your way to being your man's best lover. You're willing to find out what he likes and then "go for it" the best you can. You are inwardly confident and know your capabilities. You will do only what you honestly feel is right for you. You have the inner strength to say no but will do what it takes to acknowledge his fetish and fulfill it to the best of your capabilities.

Chapter 4
Managing Sexually Compulsive Behavior

Let me assure you once more that having a sexual fetish or strong sexual fantasy does not mean that your guy is an addict. He merely has a preference for a sexual act that is out of the ordinary. It's as simple as that. As mentioned previously, in clinical terms this means he has a paraphilia, which is a technical way of describing a group of persistent, intense sexual fantasies that are atypical and often extremely detailed. This means that although he can and will engage in pedestrian sexual activity, he might need to call upon his paraphilia in order to climax.

Many would argue that having a strong sexual fetish takes away from the intimacy of sex. The fact that he's dependent on inanimate objects, articles of clothing, or ritualized fantasies certainly can be upsetting or off-putting to a partner. It might feel like he's abandoned you in favor of his own imagery. While that might be true for the 30 seconds or so he takes to ejaculate, is it really such a tragedy? Does that really ruin the entire sexual encounter for you?

We've already established that most women have a romanticized image of sex. We want the focus to be on us! That's why we light candles, wear sexy lingerie, anoint ourselves with perfume and perhaps even sip a glass of wine to set the mood.

But with a paraphilia, we're suddenly being asked to set the mood in a different way! Wear latex instead of satin. Be bossy instead of cuddly. Act out a specific fetish that doesn't fall into the standardized, socially-acceptable category "romantic." But in reality we are still setting the mood when we partake in a fetish scene. Just a different type of mood. Leather as opposed to lace. What's the big difference. Why not think of it as another type of erotic costume?

If you happen to be with a guy who has a strong sexual fetish, you can run from it or embrace it. You can label it as sick behavior and ignore it, or you can view it a challenge. Something different, exciting. White bread, rye, pumpernickel or multi-grain...which is better? It's simply a matter of taste.

The choice is yours; you're the one in the driver's seat. But be aware of the possible outcome. Strong paraphilia never, ever go away, so acceptance is the healthier, more grown-up response.

Sure, some behavioral therapists claim they can change sexual orientations. There are clergymen who preach that the Lord can intervene to save someone's soul. But does someone's soul really need saving just because they like to wear women's panties? I think not.

The truth is that sexual paraphilia is a part of your man as much as any part of his anatomy is; his arm, his pinkie toe or that cute, little mole behind his left ear. I believe you have an obligation to provide him with an atmosphere that is accepting and supportive.

The other side of the coin, rejection, is negative and non-nurturing. It's emotionally harmful to provide him with a home which supports and feeds his damaging feelings of guilt. Remember that guilt is a lethal, destructive emotion. It can produce more seriously damaging behaviors such a sexual addiction or compulsivity.

The Lethal Nature of Guilt

It's a vicious cycle. Guilt will lead your man to try and repress his fantasies. Repression will create anxiety because a deep need of his is being squelched. Eventually the pain of denial will become more than he can bear. He'll soon become angry and resentful. That's where even larger problems develop and how sexual disorders and addictions are born.

Yes, that's correct. Sexual addictions are often the result of feelings of rejection. They're grounded in the fact that a man inherently knows he's sexually different than other men. To compound his self-imposed negative feelings, society supports the "deviant" label wholeheartedly. Nobody wants to be labeled abnormal, so this man now exerts a great deal of effort to conceal his secret sexuality.

As his wife or lover, you're the one he should be confiding in, but because his dirty, little secret was scorned by you instead of accepted, he's spending a great deal of time and effort to hide his proclivities from you. The more he disavows his fetish, the more it builds up inside him.

This is especially painful and difficult for him because fetishes are often tied into everyday events or occurrences. Imagine having a foot fetish and taking a trip to the beach where there's a smorgasbord of bare feet to gaze at. It would be incredibly difficult to contain one's feelings in that kind of foot free-for-all atmosphere.

The same is true of almost every fetish. Events, articles of clothing or attitudes can easily trigger the fetish image no matter where the man is. Sometimes the fetishist is aroused by something as subtle as an open button on a silky shirt, glossy red lipstick or everyday leather wear. The world is literally his sexual oyster. It may seem initially thrilling but ultimately it is very painful.

Imagine the angst of stepping out into the world. For him, it's the equivalent of entering a strip club or nude beach. What does he do with his feelings of arousal? How can he hide, manage or handle an overt erection? These are the difficulties that one who has an intense paraphilia faces daily. He feels embarrassed, out of control, anxious.

Clearly he needs your support. He needs to learn how to handle and manage his powerful desires. Repressing them is not only difficult but emotionally unhealthy. If you allow your guy to share his reactions with you, they will lessen and diminish.

However, if he has to squelch them, eventually he'll channel the energy into places where you don't want him to go.

The Pitfalls of Deprivation

The feelings people experience when they try and "white knuckle" a fetish is similar to the way you feel when you decide to go on a strict, crash diet. You know you want to lose those pounds, so you make a solemn vow to stay away from chocolate, pizza, pasta or any food that really satisfies your culinary desires.

While it's possible to stick to this harsh dietary regimen for a while, even for long stretches, you often find yourself feeling angry or cheated. Since you do have to eat in order to survive, eventually you need to make peace with your food. The best way to manage your weight is to manage your eating habits. This means not giving up food completely, but learning how to eat correctly and restricting fatty foods to smaller amounts and infrequent ingestion.

Making a change in your eating habits works best in a caring, affirming environment. This change needs to come from you, but you also need your partner to support you in your efforts. You never, ever want to feel like this change is being forced upon you. It's much more successful if you approach eating healthily in a relaxed, easy fashion. Change can, and does, occur slowly in small steps.

To lose weight, you don't have to deprive yourself completely of the rich foods you like. You just make the decision to eat good foods more often and reward yourself with little portions of fattening treats once in a while. As soon as you feel discouraged or berated, you'll notice that you reach for bad foods out of rebellion or anger. That's because you're harboring feelings of anxiety on top of the difficulty of changing your diet.

I've found that managing a sexual fetish is very similar to dieting. When you express contempt for your guy's sexual fetish, you support the feeling of humiliation that's already deep inside of him. He'll try to either hide or deny his fetish - just like people sometimes hide the fact that they're gorging themselves on sweets. This secretive behavior takes energy. Energy that unnecessarily spirals into obsessive-compulsive behavior patterns.

By struggling to hide his fetish, your man's focus is now split. While he's concentrating on getting his needs met, he'll also come up with creative ways to deceive you. He'll be plotting and planning to get his "next fix"- alone time so he can sneak online and view pornography without your knowledge.

As I mentioned in the previous chapter, the general pattern is then seeking out Internet chat rooms and message boards. When non-physical contact isn't enough, then he'll most probably sneak out to attend fetish parties or even hire a skilled Dominatrix who can help fulfill his unique sexual fantasy.

All of this will be done behind your back because he knows you don't approve of his fetish. The more he feels your disapproval, the worse his behavior gets and the more he'll be drawn to participating in illicit activities without your knowledge. He'll be cheating on you emotionally, so to speak, without having intercourse with another woman, but by sharing fetish intimacy, which is almost as invasive.

How You Can Help Him Manage His Paraphiliac Behavior

Acceptance is the key to successfully managing paraphilia:

- Give him the opportunity to explain what
  he enjoys and listen with an open, curious mind.
- Don't judge or express your opinion.
- Never analyze.
- Learn how to participate to the best of your ability.
- Encourage him to seek out an open-minded
  sex therapist if he needs help with impulse control.

Remember, your job as a supportive mate is to provide an atmosphere of acceptance so that he can talk and describe to you in detail what's going on. He'll share only if he feels like you're listening non-judgmentally. As soon as he gets an inkling of any kind of disapproval or contempt he'll clam up, guaranteed. You may never get the rare opportunity to talk to him about this again. Instead of being a confidant, he'll view you as a threat to his desires and his defenses will quickly build up.

Listen openly and be neutral. By neutral I mean that you shouldn't make quick responses or offer any kind of promise or threat. You need time to process what he says. Be aware that he's feeling very vulnerable because he's divulging a secret he thought he'd take to the grave.

Be curious. Be interested. Ask him the open-ended questions found in this book and allow yourself to be in the moment with him.

I guarantee you that if you acknowledge your man's fetish and do your best to follow the suggestions I've laid out here, his anxiety level will diminish. He'll begin to relax knowing that you've accepted him, despite whatever quirks he happens to have. He will no longer fixate on how to get his needs met or hide them from you. It's just like the dreaded diet. When you think of the chocolate cake as a special treat you can have every so often, you'll experience a sort of relief knowing that the option is there when you really want an indulgence.

Your unconditional, positive regard of his fetish will insure that your man doesn't feel frustrated. He'll know he has options and this feeling is quite sustaining and validating. His thought process will change along with the sense of urgency he has about his fantasy. Once you've accepted it:

- He will stop feeling alone, deranged and abnormal.
- He'll internalize self-acceptance that you are relaying.
- He'll feel loved and cherished by you.
- His anxiety level will decrease and so will sexual compulsive behavior.

When anxiety is contained, sexual compulsivity is greatly diminished.

Specifics on Managing Over-Indulgence

Communication and acceptance is your first step to managing over-indulgence. Now that the two of you have been honest about his interests, you need to figure out a way to establish boundaries if the fetish is taking up a disproportionate amount of his time.

Only the two of you can figure out what is acceptable and what is not acceptable behavior. Although, there are no specific guidelines, the general rule of thumb is that a behavior is addictive when it interferes with relationships, work or leisure time. If his fetish is getting preferential treatment, you need some tools to get this under control. And here they are:

Time Management

How much time is too much time? Is he online instead of spending meaningful time with you, your family or friends? Is he opting to spend time masturbating instead of engaging with others?

Time parameters must be established according to what works for each individual and their personal relationship.

If it's obvious to you that he spends an excessive amount of time with online Web sites, chat rooms or pornography, you can help him to diminish this time by showing interest. Never threaten to take anything away or give him ultimatums.

Instead of threats, you can encourage him to schedule some "fantasy time" alone. Despite your best efforts to join in, he may still want to keep up with his own private masturbation time. After all, it's probably been a comforting ritual for him for many years.

And solo fetish time is perfectly okay, just as long as you do something equally as self-indulgent. A hot, steamy bubble bath with a touch of body oil in just the right places is a good compromise. Hey, if he can have a private stroke-fest, so can you!

Boundaries

Figure out what behaviors are harmless and what behaviors can lead to trouble. Generally speaking, it's safer for him to view anonymous photos than to make direct contact with real people.

Recognize the things that would make you feel comfortable versus the things that would feel hurtful to you. For example, you might be all right with him chatting up someone via the Internet, yet you'd feel tenuous about him picking up the phone and actually speaking with that person. You could be fine with letting him see a professional Dominatrix, yet you wouldn't be cool with him meeting another fetishist face-to-face.

The two of you must set very specific guidelines and then adhere to them. When he knows exactly what he can and can't do there will be less room for slip-ups, misunderstandings or mistakes. And if he does cross a line, he'll do it with full knowledge that he's violating a boundary. Your boundary.

Flexibility

Remember, you need to be patient and flexible in your thinking. Understand that change doesn't happen overnight. He'll need to make a shift in his own feelings about himself in order to get to the point of understanding that whatever he thinks or feels sexually is normal and natural for him. He needs to embrace rather than fight his fetish. And what a lucky man he is that you're there to help him.

If, after a good chunk of time, you notice that he's still being secretive, or indulging in risky or dangerous behaviors, you will then have to consider seeking outside help. Find a therapist who's unprejudiced and knowledgeable about alternative forms of sexuality. There are plenty great therapists out there. Try Googling with key words pertinent to fetish. That's how many of my clients have discovered me, I'm told.

Beware of counselors who are rigid in their belief system. Also make sure the therapist doesn't automatically assume sexual addiction is the same as drug addiction. In other words, you're looking for someone to help you manage the fetish; not tell him to abstain.

Time for Concern

Behaviors that are dangerous or illegal are definitely a concern and require immediate professional help. As responsible adults, we know the sexual behaviors that are illegal (like rape and pedophilia, for example) and they are out of the scope of this book.

The fetishes and fantasies described here are all geared toward consenting adults. Fetish behavior becomes dangerous when someone is coerced into participating. There's a big difference between pretending to be forced to do something than actually being forced to do something. True dangerous or illegal sexual acts have devastating results if acted upon.

When Is A Sexual Paraphilia Unhealthy?

The general rule of thumb is that sexual fetish becomes disordered when it takes precedence over other activities, relationships and careers. It is also problematic when given monetary priority. For example, if someone goes into deep debt to feed their fetish, it's a big warning sign.

The way a fetish colors some people's lives and sexual thoughts is pervasive. It's all-encompassing and omnipresent. However, there's no rule of thumb about frequency. You have to rely on your gut instinct on how much is too much.

Similarly, masturbation is highly personal in terms of frequency. Some people can function quite well self-pleasuring themselves every day, while others claim they need several times a day to feel "right". However, if your guy, like some men I treat, can't control their impulse to masturbate no matter where they are, that's a strong indication of a problem that needs to be handled immediately by a professional.

In Summary

According to the American Psychiatric Association's Diagnostic and Statistical Manual of Mental Disorders (Fourth Edition), in the absence of distress over the fetish behaviors, the activities are not considered to be in need of treatment, but are simply an attraction. Over-indulgence is often used to offset feelings of shame and guilt.

Fetish behavior can be easily managed within an atmosphere of acceptance and communication, starting with you.

Chapter 5
Gathering The Information

At this point, you probably have a pretty good idea that your guy has something unique about his sexuality, but you need to find out some specifics so you both can make the most of his fetish. Then you can truly begin your wonderful erotic journey of discovery and fulfillment.

Communication

Your man's the one who possesses the key to his fetish. I'll take a wild guess and venture that all of his knowledge had been bottled up inside him for years and he's been aching to share it with someone special like you. Chances are he's often dreamt about the day he could tell you all about his desires and has some very specific ideas of how they can be fulfilled.

Because of this, no book, no movie, no website can explain his fetish to you better than he can. That's because each person fantasizes uniquely. Every fetishist conjures up their own particular turn-ons, erotic triggers which are distinctly theirs.

So, while I will guide you through modes of communication and suggest pertinent questions to ask, ultimately, it's you and your guy who need to communicate to pinpoint the nuances that make up his particular fantasy or fetish.

For this reason, it's not enough for him to paint broad pictures of his fetish. As they say, the devil is in the details. Even the grandest projects depend on the success of the smallest components. Him making the blanket statement, "I like feet," doesn't tell you much. What does he like about them? Does he like toes as well as feet? Painted toenails? If so, what color? And so on. See what I mean?

Even vague buzz words like domination, submission, female superiority, feet, tickling, cross-dressing, leather, latex and smoking are not specific enough. Especially for a newcomer to the world of fetish like yourself. This is why you need to guide him into being very precise and descriptive about his desires so you can tailor them to his fantasies and ultimately reenact the scenario he sees in his head. If you do it right, the very act of him revealing his fetish to you will be a great arouser for him. And hopefully, for you too, when you see his reaction.

Okay. Now it's time for you to put on your "detective cap" and go after the details. Don't be afraid to jot down notes so you won't miss a thing. You can always refer to them later if you need to clarify something.

Ask Open-Ended Questions

The best way to learn about his fetish is to ask open-ended questions. The reason? Open-ended questions will never get a vague yes or no answer, even if he's a bit shy about revealing his secrets to you at first. Open-ended questions also encourage him to elaborate. They provide a forum for him to go into detail.

An example:

Closed question: Do you like to be tied up?
Answer: Yes or No

Open question: What is it about being tied up that gets you excited?
Answer: He might tell you that he likes the idea of being rendered helpless and therefore likes tight rope bondage. Or, he

might say that being bound allows him to give up control and relax. But no matter what his response is, this kind of question motivates thoughtfulness on his part.

Do you see how the open-ended question invites him to think and explore his own feelings about bondage? It encourages a deep, probing discussion of the topic. Think of yourself as a talk-show host and him as your slightly shy guest.

Active Listening

Active Listening goes hand-in-hand with asking open-ended questions:

- When you listen actively, it helps you stay focused on your partner and put your own thoughts aside.
- Concentrate on listening. You shouldn't be thinking about what you want to say or ask next.
- Make sure you heard him correctly by reframing or repeating what he said.
- You may also want to ask follow-up questions that relate to what he's revealed.
- Remember, when you listen actively, you don't respond, make a rebuttal or refute what he's said with your own agenda.
- Do your best to listen objectively. The goal is to take in, understand and process the information he's conveying.

A Word On Communication

Communication is constantly taking place. Communication even happens when people are silent.

When you sit down with your man to learn about his fetish, observe his body language.

- Can he look at you directly?
- Does he look down or look away during particularly personal parts of the communication?
- Take note of his breathing. Shallow breaths indicate anxiety or tension while deep breaths convey confidence or key ideas.

- Notice his facial expressions, the way he sits and his hand gestures. All of these body movements are clues as to how he feels about the material he's presenting to you.
- Always remember that active listening requires you to ask open-ended questions, reframe his questions and be present "in the moment" while he's speaking.

Setting the Stage

The discussion needs to take place when you're both feeling amicable, relaxed and ready to talk. Avoid having this talk when either one of you are tired or stressed out over work or any other part of your lives. Be aware that you're embarking on sensitive territory. Reassure him that you have a sincere interest in learning, being supportive and want to be a part of this aspect of his life.

Learning about fetish takes time. Don't expect to find out everything you need to know in one sitting. Be patient with yourself and give yourself a big pat on the back for being such a supportive partner.

Revealing Questions

The following questions will help steer you to the right chapter(s) of this book so that you can discover even more details about his fetish. What follows are general fact-finding questions to help get you started in your more in depth discussion about his fetish.

These questions are intended to establish rough guidelines. You don't need to ask every single one. Here, I've designed a series of queries that will help you get the ball rolling to pinpoint his fetish. Feel free to improvise in order to gather the information that will get you started on the road to being his perfect fantasy lover.

Sample Q&A:

If I were to star in your fantasies, tell me what image I'd convey.

Listen for words that describe attitude or demeanor. Be tuned in on details that might convey images of a sophisticated goddess, a sexy super-heroine or a slutty cheerleader, for example. He'll probably talk about clothing, hair and make-up. By describing his "dream girl", he'll also be revealing such things as possible leather, latex, shoe and Dominant/submissive fantasies.

What would I be doing to you when I'm dressed like this?

Now you'll get some real meaty answers that will supply the information you seek. He might respond that you'd be taking the lead in bed, tying him up, whipping him or dominating him.

If he answers that you'd be dominating him you'll need the follow-up question:

How would I be dominating you?

His answer will guide you to his specific area of interest, the key that unlocks the door to this book's correct chapter. He might use terms like spanking, whipping, tying up, tickling, cross-dressing, etc. If so, you'll know exactly which chapter to skip ahead to.

While masturbating, what do you think about at the moment of orgasm?

This can also lead to very revealing information. Ask this when you sense he's feeling comfortable and ready to talk frankly. It can be a very vulnerable subject, so you must respect his vulnerability!

When did you first know that your sexual tastes dabbled outside the norm?

A true fetishist will remember early childhood experiences and perhaps even the defining moment he realized something aroused him. Like being tied up while playing Cowboys and

Indians, for example. Encourage him to tell you his earliest
fetish memories.

Have you ever acted on these fantasies? If so, tell me about it.

He may recount experimenting with girlfriends, co-workers or
even strangers. Remember to listen actively and keep your own
emotions out of the way. For now, at least.

What are some of your sexual triggers?

Think of the five senses: seeing, hearing, touching, smelling
and tasting. Each has an extremely important role in fetish. Have
him go into detail about what turns him on. Ask about favorite
buzzwords and images. Remember that even if you can't actually
enact his fetish, you can always talk about it when you're
pleasuring him.

Do you own any adult material that will help me understand your fetish more clearly?

He may or may not have hardcopies of racy magazines. These
days, everyone "owns" their own adult bookstore online. Make
time to sit down at the computer beside him and ask him to share
some of his favorite Web sites with you. A picture's worth a
thousand words. You'll get a crystal clear understanding of his
fetish by going online. Bookmark the pages (if he hasn't done so
already!), as you'll probably want to go back on your own so you
can digest and explore the material when you have some time to
yourself.

If you were soliciting the services of a high-ticket prostitute or a Dominatrix, how would you communicate your needs to her?

This might be the only question you need to ask because it
encompasses all aspects of his fetish. Since he would be paying a
great deal of money for a pro to enact his fantasy, he'd feel
compelled to communicate clearly to get the most bang for his
buck, so to speak. He'd need to describe his fetish in minute
detail in order to ensure she could do the session to his liking.
Also, he'd need to tell her what to wear, how to act, what to do,

etc. Listen carefully and be sure to ask lots of questions. Imagine yourself as a seasoned professional who takes pride in her work.

Are there any phrases or buzzwords that get you going?

I'm willing to wager there are! One fellow I know likes to hear the words "jack off" from his wife. Others quiver when they're told,

> "I will spank you soundly!"
> "I'm going to gouge out your eyeballs!"
> "Down on your knees!"
> "You belong to *ME*!"

There are literally hundreds of trigger words and phrases associated with each fetish. You're the detective. Find out his special phrases. And use them!

Describe a favorite sexual story or fantasy.

Remember Penthouse Magazine's famous "Letters" section. Well, this is your man's own private sex column come to life. Asking this question will encourage him to give details. Instruct him to paint you an erotic picture with words. His words.

How does it feel to talk with me about this?

Here's where you get to don your therapist cap and be empathetic and understanding. Put yourself in his shoes and imagine how difficult it is for him to tell you things he's probably never told anyone else before. Listen closely for any feelings of shame or guilt. Try your best to offer him unconditional acceptance.

When the Q&A session is over, whether or not you want to respond to his information is entirely up to you. I suggest that you listen openly during the first conversation. Period. Give yourself ample time to think and to process what you've learned before you respond to any of his revelations.

If you decide that you'd like to discuss it further, arrange for another time to discuss your response to his fetish.

Confidentiality

Immediately after your Q&A, you might be feeling a bit freaked out. You might feel that you need someone to talk to about this, and understandably so.

Unfortunately, you can't phone your best friend. What your man has just revealed to you is private and has been told to you in the strictest confidence. Although she'll do her best, your BFF probably won't understand and won't give you the kind of support you need.

Your best bet for the moment is sit quietly with the information:

- Think about it with an open mind.
- Focus your attention on the positive results of showing him that you love him.
- Congratulate yourself for giving him the avenue to open up to you and deepen your relationship even more.
- If you feel like you absolutely have to talk with someone in order to help you process all of this information, employ the help of a therapist who is open and knowledgeable about alternative sexual lifestyles.

If You're Still Upset

You've just learned something new, unusual and even monumental about your man. Maybe some of your worst fears have been validated. Maybe you think it changes your relationship drastically. Initially, you might even feel that his fetish is wrong, sick or perverted. You're wondering if you'll ever be able to enact his fantasy or get into role. In a panic, you might even consider leaving him.

Stop worrying and take a deep breath. Worry won't help you achieve the goal of being the best lover you can be. Ending the relationship won't change anything or solve anything.

The best way to soothe yourself is to take action. Be a victor instead of a victim.

Based on the results of your initial conversation with him, turn to the chapter that pertains to his fetish. Choose a time when you're not rushed, but relaxed. Make the decision to read the chapter with an open mind. This way, you'll be able to continue your conversation with him and increase your learning curve.

Some suggestions:

- Imagine yourself in the role he described and create a scenario where both of you are having fun.
- Go shopping in your head and think about what you'll want to wear when you enact his fetish.
- Think about some of the props you'll need and the things you want to learn.
- Go online and start surfing the plentiful websites that are dedicated to his fetish.

But most of all, praise yourself on being an objective woman who is sexually secure and confident in her abilities.

Think proactively and you'll immediately feel differently. Again, don't get bogged down with what he's just told you. Instead, be liberated by it. Feel incredibly good that he's entrusted you with something he's held inside the entire time you've been together...and even before that. This initial conversation with him laid the groundwork for deeper understanding, fact-finding and taking positive action.

What's Next?

This is just the beginning. You have broken important ground here. His secret fetish in no longer a secret. It's out in the open. The two of you will have the pleasant task of figuring out how you will (or won't) incorporate it into your lives. Even if you choose not to act on the fetishes together, at least he doesn't have to sneak around when he visits his favorite Web sites. His inner desires are accepted and acknowledged by you. This in and of itself is a precious gift.

Both you and your man need to seriously consider how you're going to proceed. Plan on having several more heart-to-heart discussions. The following chapters will help you to hone in on his fetish and ask more specific, telling questions.

There's a distinct possibility that his unique fetish is so specialized that it isn't covered here. That's okay. The open style of asking questions I've described in this chapter and in the fetish chapters is interchangeable. It provides you with a template to formulate a game plan for you and your guy.

The following chapter, *Dominant and Submissive Roles* explains a bit about the power exchange mindset. It's important to read it before flipping to the chapter about your man's specific fetish since more often than not, a great many male fetishes incorporate the idea of female supremacy.

A chapter toward the end of the book called *A Potpourri of Fetishes*, gives a quick overview of many of the more uncommon fetishes to help you on your voyage of discovery.

Chapter 6
Dominant and Submissive Roles

The element of power exchange is at the core of the majority of fetishes discussed in this book. I strongly suggest you read this chapter before diving into the one devoted to your man's particular fetish. It will help you better understand the basics of your man's specific predilections.

Within the context of Dominant/submissive play (D/s), one person fundamentally gives up their rights to a "higher power". The person in control is referred to as the Dominant. The person who relinquishes control is the submissive. In the D/s scene, Dominant is always written with a capital "d" while submissive always appears with a lower-case "s" to symbolize the relationship even in writing.

For the most part, you as the female will be taking on the Dominant position. This is often called a power exchange because traditionally it's the male who's the aggressor in the bedroom - and in many aspects of life. D/s play allows the woman to spread her wings and run the show.

A Dominant has a very important, substantial role: she is the protector, teacher and lover to the submissive, or sub.

- As the lover, the Dominant allows her submissive to please her when and how she deems appropriate.
- As the teacher, she instructs and guides her submissive to do the things that please her.
- As the protector, she adheres to the idea that the submissive is her "property". He belongs to her and she can do whatever she pleases to him. But she also has the weighty responsibility of ensuring his safety, especially when administering corporal punishment.

The role of the submissive appears to be somewhat simpler, but in actuality, the submissive plays a very large part in shaping the D/s relationship. Though his role is to please, in reality the submissive establishes the guidelines. A good Dominant will do what you are doing right now—she gets inside the head of her guy and finds out what makes him tick. She then cleverly uses the information she's culled to take charge and control.

Every submissive is there because he *wants* to be in that role. The Dominant is there to facilitate the submissive's needs but at the same time she attains fulfillment herself. These roles are therefore not as clear-cut or rigid as they appear to be. A good D/s relationship takes everybody's needs into account.

D/s and Building Self-Esteem

Many women feel reluctant to take on a role that is customarily male. A majority of women are still brought up with the notion that men are supposed to be the ones to make the first move and take charge when it comes to sex. I acknowledge that the idea of having a man relinquish control and allow you to do as you please may feel foreign to you at first. You might not even have a clue what to command him to do. Plus you also might feel that this is all a little contradictory since you're essentially exploring your mate's sexuality, not your own.

Let me assure you that there will always be room for you to mold the scenes so that you can derive pleasure from them yourself. You'll actually have the opportunity to focus on getting your own needs met from a position of power and control. As it turns out, there's a great deal of benefit you can experience from being on top.

Here's how it works. You are now investigating and exploring your man's most privately-held sexual secrets. This fact alone gives you more intimacy and closeness in your relationship. You might very well be the first and only person he's with whom he's shared these dark, sexual secrets. With my help, you will then execute and bring these fantasies to life. Again, this makes you an invaluable partner, someone he will stay with and cherish forever. He certainly won't feel the need to sneak around or seek comfort elsewhere. Your position in the relationship is infinitely increased. The bond between the two of you is strengthened profoundly.

At first, you may feel strange taking on this new role. After all, this is not the way most women are brought up. Certainly, sexual role reversals and fetish behaviors are not something we were schooled in when we first learned about sex. For you, this may even go against some deeply-held morals or religious beliefs. You'll need to rethink your views about sex and even reexamine the parameters of the union you have with your man.

Even though you might not be a woman who's used to taking charge, these empowering feelings will help you in all aspects of your life. You'll suddenly feel more able to compete at work, develop clearer boundaries with your children and naturally be more assertive in relationship with friends and family. By overcoming some initial inhibitions and insecurities, you'll ultimately experience a sense of true accomplishment. These behavioral changes will make you feel empowered, guaranteed.

Changing a behavior often leads to an innate change in the way you feel about yourself. Ultimately, this new sense of authority will enhance your ability to achieve and strengthen your feelings of self-esteem.

Within the context of D/s relationship there are some very essential basics you need to find out from him off the bat. It's important to get the information straight because these questions are the very foundation of what you need to know to get started on the right track.

Q&A:

Are you looking for a Mistress/slave relationship?

A Mistress/slave relationship is the deepest and most profound union in the fetish world. In this exchange, you are the ultimate Goddess he wants to worship and adore. A true slave wants to relinquish all control and do whatever he's told. He doesn't have an agenda other than pleasing you and trying to fulfill your every need.

It's a very pure relationship that is based on love and adoration. Technically, he would only want to receive pain if it gave you pleasure. He would want to be whipped only to show you that he's willing to accept pain in order to prove his devotion.

The Mistress/slave relationship is the sub's ultimate fantasy. It implies a lifestyle where you would always be the one in control, but it's actually very unrealistic within the context of normal everyday living. However, the roles can be developed for specified periods of time. In other words, you could conceivably have a Mistress/slave Day on a specified point in time. On that day, he would be at your disposal to do your bidding. You could have him do household chores, take you shopping or service you in bed for hours on end. It's all up to you. This is the one time where you'd be in complete charge of everything.

In my experience, very few men really want to be a true slave. Underneath their desire to be a slave, there's an agenda. You still need to do your homework and find out what he imagines the relationship will look like and how he wants to serve you. The general mindset is that you are the Queen and he is the servant. It can be a great deal of fun and allows you to get creative. It's also a good opportunity for you to learn to state your own wants and needs.

Are you looking for a Dominant/submissive relationship?

This is more likely than a Mistress/slave relationship. D/s is actually a more current term for what used to be called a Mistress/slave relationship. It's almost the same thing except I interpret a Dominant/submissive relationship to have more flexibility and communication between partners.

You'll find that I generally use the term D/s in this book, though in reality he might use the words Mistress/slave or S/M (Sado-Masochistic) to let you know that he wants a relationship where you're the one in control. Within the context of a D/s or S/M relationship, the two of you might be taking part in bondage, cross-dressing, foot worship, role-play and the myriad of fetishes described in subsequent chapters.

Are you looking for a disciplinary relationship?

This expression is generally used to describe play that's more corporal punishment-oriented. You play the role of a disciplinarian who sets specific guidelines and boundaries while he's more of a "naughty boy" or a brat. Understand that he isn't submissive in the usual way, but that he's simply being "punished", i.e. corrected for misbehavior either real or imaginary.

For more depth on this attitude, please see the chapters on *FemDom Domestic Disciplinary Relationships* and *Spanking*. The mindset of a bad boy is extremely different than the mindset of a submissive or slave.

What do you like to do when you're in the submissive role?

The word submissive is a very broad term. There are a host of sub-fetishes that go hand-in-hand with being submissive. Each sub has their specific laundry list of likes and dislikes.

He might say he enjoys being submissive and then ask you to tie him up, whip him, force him to cross-dress or torture his nipples or genital area. Or he could say that he's submissive and that he enjoys worshipping your feet, legs, bottom or breasts. He also might say that he wants you to force him to be submissive by humiliating him and pushing him to do acts that he'd otherwise find reprehensible. This is the time to ask details about fetishes, turn-ons, buzzwords and specifics.

What kind of clothing would you prefer that I wear?

Generally guys who want a Mistress, like women to wear some kind of leather or latex outfit. FemDom attire will allow you to wear more business clothing like suits, tight skirts or even old-fashioned girdles or corsets. Some guys will be very specific communicating their "outfit needs" to meet their fetish desires. Others will be less specific and just want you to feel comfortable and sexy.

Do you imagine this relationship to be full-time, part-time or just once in a while?

Here's where we get into lifestyle choices. Some guys fantasize about being in role 24/7. I personally find this to be unrealistic and unhealthy. It's also a fantasy that is usually abandoned after it's tried. D/s and fetish play are largely sexual acts. You have to be in a sexual mood or turned-on in order to participate. It's very unrealistic to think of doing this on a full-time basis. It's also unfair to you as a newcomer. My advice is to stick to small increments for starters. Session time can increase as you feel more comfortable in your role as Dominant.

Is D/s something you need in order to get aroused?

This is most likely the case. Here's where you'll have to figure out how to make this work for you. Clearly, you will probably not be happy providing fetish entertainment for him every time you make love. You need to find out how strong his D/s and fetish needs are and then proceed from there.

You'll discover that I talk a great deal about the power of verbiage throughout this book. Oftentimes uttering his favorite buzzwords are enough to get him going. Still, you might feel like this is an imposition every time you have sex. You'll have to discover his needs to devise some kind of compromise that works for both of you.

Describe your ultimate D/s scene for me.

Listen carefully. Here's where he'll tell you details about his specific fetish or interest. Ask him to be as precise as possible. When he's said his piece, proceed to the chapter that most closely mirrors his desires and ask the questions you'll find listed there.

General Things to Know About a D/s Relationship:

Communication

The more you communicate, the better your interactions will be. Right now you're at the exploratory stage of your budding fetish relationship. You're finally hearing secrets that he's kept buried for years and years. This investigation is a process. He might tell you everything at once or he might reveal it to you slowly but surely. Trust is the key. If he feels accepted, he'll be willing to share more. If he feels judged, he'll sugarcoat the real fantasy and you'll never totally get where he's coming from.

Be gentle with yourself. You might hear information that's disturbing. Remember that fantasies are like dreams; they reflect certain emotions, moods and memories but they're often metaphoric and should not be interpreted at face value. Listen to what he says without bias, but remind yourself that you never have to do anything that makes you feel compromised, disrespected or uncomfortable.

Always talk before or after a scene. Be clear about what you're about to do. When the scene is over, talk again and listen to feedback. Ask what he enjoyed most as well as things that could be eliminated or improved upon.

Safety Words

When you're in the middle of a scene, using a safe or safety word allows for communication so that the mood isn't broken. A safety word or signal allows him to nonverbally communicate some kind of disconnect during a scene. Maybe you're whipping too hard or tying him up too tightly. Maybe he suddenly has to go the bathroom. By establishing some kind of signal, you can both stay in role but he still has the opportunity to communicate his needs.

Most commonly the submissive would say:

- Mercy
- Red light
- Or squeeze your leg for a non-verbal sign.

Safe words are essential for new players in the fetish scene. It allows you to stay in touch with each other and it's a cardinal rule in developing safe, consensual play.

Lifestyle D/s Relationships

Lifestyle D/s Relationships are parallel to Domestic Disciplinary Relationships. Both imply that one person is always the Dominant and the other person is always the submissive. These unions establish that the roles extend out of the bedroom and sometimes even out of the house. Again, many guys fantasize about living this kind of life but ultimately they don't work. You and he are both adults. Essentially, one adult can't control another adult. As the Top, you'll feel exhausted. As the bottom, he's bound to rebel.

What You Need to Get Started

Your guy is your best source on where to begin. He'll know about the kind of props you need and he can also show you how to use them. Never be intimated about asking for help. The great part about being on top is that you now have the power to ask for anything you want, even assistance.

It's also okay to ask him to buy you the necessary equipment and clothing to enact his fetish. Sometimes bondage gear is confusing to use. You can tell him to buckle himself in or teach you to tie knots. You are still in control; you're merely giving him orders and commands. Remember, the submissive enjoys meeting your needs. You have a need to learn. Your wish is truly his command.

In Summary

D/s power exchange is the foundation for a great number of the fetishes and fantasies found in this book. The core need is based on a desire to relinquish control. What you will do once you are in role is something that will be defined, refined and implemented as you learn from each other.

It's important to listen and understand the symbolic meaning of what it means for him to hand over the power to you. Is it a gesture of love, control or the desire to experience some kind of physical sensation? Listen and gather as much information as you can.

Now you can proceed to the chapter which discusses his specific fetish...and enjoy!

The Fetishes

Chapter 7
Adult Babies and Infantilism

Let me guess...you were probably extremely surprised to learn that your grown male mate pleasures himself by donning diapers, playing with a rattle, sucking his thumb and pretending he's a baby. He finds it soothing, relaxing and sexually exciting. What's so terrible about that? Until now, he's indulged in this play alone but by telling you about it, he's invited you to participate.

Perhaps your first reaction was panic, and maybe even disgust. You don't know where to begin or even if you want to take part. I'm here to demystify infantilism for you and to explain how this can be a very healing, nurturing fetish.

People who identify as "adult babies" have a strong urge to regress back into the first few years of life when they were cared for, coddled, comforted, and didn't have a care in the world.

Please take note that this fetish is not to be confused with any kind of pedophiliac activity because the focus of infantilism is strictly on the individual, not on others.

Understanding Infantilism

Who would imagine a male adult wanting to be treated like a baby? Yet, your man does - and many men do. Infantilism is a fetish characterized by the desire to revisit the infancy stage. Among the many activities Adult Babies self-indulge in are using diapers instead of the toilet, wrapping themselves in soft blankets and playing with toddler-type toys.

This fetish is often enjoyed as a solo activity. The fact that your man has divulged his secret to you is huge, monumental. It demonstrates an enormous amount of trust in you because shame is a very common byproduct of infantilism. He's told you about this desire because he feels an overwhelming need for acceptance. He'd probably also find it validating to have you join in and share this fetish need with him. After all, babies do need Mommies, and by admitting his fetish to you, he's asking you to nurture, care for and play with him when he's in his baby state.

Diapering and being changed is a strong component in the Adult Baby enactment. Psychologically, infantilism is a manifestation of D/s play but in a more domestic arena. Instead of being the Dominatrix you're the Mommy. There's no doubt about it, you're the one in control in this role. You may be called upon to be a nurturing, strict or indulgent mama or your role might simply be to facilitate or bear witness to him wearing diapers, sucking on a pacifier and sporting a baby bonnet on his head.

Again, I want to remind you that this fetish fosters guilt because it's considered by society to be very extreme and way "out of the norm". Even Adult Babies have trouble explaining how wearing a diaper sparks an erection and masturbatory activities. No matter how much they analyze it or try to change their behavior, deep-seated or visceral sexual desire takes over the intellectual desire to stop the infantilism fetish and "be normal". That's why it's extremely important for you to put aside your feelings and demonstrate a positive regard toward his proclivity. Plain and simple, he needs your validation.

A major plot point of the mainstream movie *Shoot 'Em Up* revolves around infantilism. There's a scene in a bordello with a special "baby room", complete with multi-colored baby bottles and a crib. Breast-feeding is also involved. If you'd like to add to your learning curve about this fetish, you might want to rent the DVD. But be aware that this is a sensationalized Hollywood representation of the Adult Baby and might not even remotely mirror your man's interests.

Handling Your Feelings

I understand that your knee jerk reaction to this fetish might be negative. Your initial repulsion stems from the fact that you have an ingrained view of how men are "supposed" to behave. As women, we imagine our guys as strong, capable and protective, not as infants! Classic female fantasies have to do with a man overtaking us, rescuing us or being virile on some level, not changing his Pampers.

Remember the chapter *Feelings vs. Taking Action*? There, I explained that it's your choice to feel whatever you choose. Be aware that no matter what your reaction, your man's fetish remains.

The truth of the matter is that your guy sometimes likes to be diapered and treated like a baby. Chances are good that he's been indulging in this by himself for years. Wouldn't it be nice for him to finally have a companion so that he doesn't feel so alone? Wouldn't it be wonderful to give your man the gift of unconditional acceptance? Consider the difference this would make in his life. I guarantee that your willing participation will insure greater closeness and a trusting bond between the two of you. You alone have the ability to provide your man with a lifelong, unfulfilled need. And how wonderful is that?

The Origins of Infantilism

Infantilistic behavior expresses the need to let go and regress to an earlier, simpler time. Chances are excellent that this fetish is helping him work through some kind of deficit from his past. An event, feeling or association stimulated his subconscious mind to equate babying, diapering or infantile activities as an erotically-charged feeling. This feeling later became interpreted as arousal.

Specific incidents may have occurred during childhood that were the catalyst for his sexual association with diapers. It may have been bedwetting and a subsequent feeling of safety in diapers. It may also have been the loss of a parent during a critical point of development. It could even have been sparked by some kind of disciplinary action that was taken which involved the wearing of diapers as punishment for bedwetting or childish behavior. Whatever the case, your guy experiences a feeling of stress relief when role-playing as a baby.

The origin of the fantasy is not as important as the execution of enacting the fantasy itself. Your enthusiastic participation will ultimately be healing for him. Here are some questions you'll need to ask to deepen your knowledge:

Q&A:

Have you been engaging in your fantasy by yourself?

This is something that might be very, very difficult for your partner to admit. However, his needs are so strong that he probably realizes there will be great relief in finally divulging this top-secret area of his life to you. When he begins talking, chances are he won't be able to hold anything back because a huge weight of shame is being released from his being.

Have you ever done this with another person?

He may have gone to visit an adult fantasy worker or a Dominatrix to realize his infantilistic fantasy. Many sex workers offer "babying" as part of their services. Some Dominatrixes even have their own baby rooms complete with bottles, playpens and a changing station, as portrayed in the film *Shoot 'Em Up*. Your guy might have experienced a fetish "session" at some time in his life. If so, inquire about how the session was for him. What did he like about it? Is there anything that could have been improved upon?

Would you like to share this fetish with me?

Find out whether he wants to keep this as a solitary activity or if he indeed wants to make you his "Mommy". If so, have him describe his ideal Mommy. Ask about the attitude he envisions you having: stern or loving. Chances are he'll want you to be nurturing, but he might also want you to be a little strict, especially if he needs a spanking.

As Mommy, what are my duties?

Mommies of Adult Babies can do many things depending on the needs of the mate. You can coo, cuddle and fuss over him as you would a real baby. Play "Peek-a-Boo" and other infantile games. Read him a story, shake a rattle and use other toys. Feed him baby food, bottles and even do some breast-feeding. If he's an Adult Baby who wears diapers, you might have to change his mess but this task should be optional and negotiable. After all, in the end this is a pretend activity, and this aspect of his fantasy can remain fantasy if you find it stretches your personal limits.

What props will we need?

I'll bet he already has many of the necessary accoutrements to enact his fantasy, but always double check. You might need to stock up on adult diapers and plastic changing mats. Add some rattles, pacifiers and other baby toys to your collection. Some Web sites offer specially-made cribs for adult babies. It might be fun for the two of you to shop together. The "forbidden" aspect of the fetish can add to the excitement.

Do you like to be breast-fed?

I'm guessing he does but always double-check. Now would be the time to instruct him on how to best suck on your nipples, rather than when you are in the midst of a scene.

Do you prefer this to remain a solo activity?

He might want his privacy. That means you'll need to give him space and be okay with the alone time he requires to satisfy his desires. At this point, he may still feel embarrassed and ashamed of his fetish confession to you. Perhaps over time, he'll feel comfortable enough to bring you in on the interactions. The more accepting you are the more he'll want to let you in.

Having a caring, flesh-and-blood participant in his fetish will ultimately be very cathartic for him. Start with one activity and see how you both feel. For example, you can feed him a bottle and then tuck him in for a nap. Later on, you can talk about what it was like for him to be seen as a baby. Explore your own feelings as well. It might actually be enjoyable for you to tap into your motherly, nurturing side with the man you love.

Do you characterize yourself as an Adult Baby, a Diaper Lover or both?

This question has to do with terminology. I'm willing to venture that he's done some research on the topic and has placed himself in a category. There's a distinction between an Adult Baby and a Diaper Lover. Technically speaking, an Adult Baby enjoys being fussed over and allowed to have the sensations of an infant. He likes being mothered, cuddled and cooed. Adult Babies may also be Diaper Lovers. That means as a baby he also indulges in wearing diapers. Sometimes he may even make a mess as an expression of his total lack of control.

What does it mean for you to be a baby?

He may talk about being the center of attention and the object of your adoration. He may also discuss the freedom to let go of all responsibilities. A real baby is at the complete mercy of his caretakers. He can do absolutely nothing for himself. Your guy might revel in the experience of allowing himself be cared for. He might also talk about the idea of seeing the world with new eyes. A baby has a natural curiosity about everything including his own body. Your baby might want to suck his thumb, play with his penis or suck on a pacifier. All of these acts are done with the idea of creating pleasurable body sensations.

How significant is diaper play?

Some Adult Babies enjoy wearing a diaper but it's not the core part of their particular fetish. If your guy likes to wet and let go, he also has a diaper fetish. Find out about the significance of wetting or messing a diaper. Does he do it because he enjoys the sensation? Or is he doing this to get a rise out of Mommy and get punished? In either case, he probably enjoys the sensation of being changed like a baby.

Do you enjoy being "seen"?

Many Adult Babies have an exhibitionist streak. They like to be observed by others. To this end, they enjoy being dressed in a bonnet, rubber pants and given a bottle. Adult Babies have their own small but organized community. They even have their own Web sites and events. The events give Adult Babies the opportunity to meet others, share ideas and be further educated about their fetish. These events also provide an opportunity to be displayed and fussed over by many. Gatherings are good for both the Adult Baby and his partner to experience because you'll see that you're not so alone in this fetish. There are plenty of Adult Babies out there. You just have to know where to look.

What's going on inside of you when you regress?

His answer to this question is integral in your understanding of his psyche. It will give you a sense of the core elements of his unique needs. You'll get a better handle of what being a baby means to him on an emotional level. It might be that your man is in a high-stress position like the military and sees this as a relief. Perhaps he came from a background where his family moved about often and because of this constant upheaval, he wasn't given the level of care he craved. This would explain some of the feelings he's after when he goes into baby mode. It's hinged upon giving him permission to experience the feeling of being cared for.

Is humiliation part of your infantilism fetish?

Some guys experience infantilism as a form of humiliation. There's an embarrassing element about being dressed and diapered as a baby. But here, the feeling of humiliation carries with it a sexual charge. Embarrassment and sexuality are linked closely. Being made fun of or shamed often carries with it a sexual feeling.

Do you prefer to be "forced"?

The idea of forcing happens with other fetishes such as feet, cross-dressing and bisexual acts. Your guy perceives his fetish as something he doesn't really *want* to do but he'll do it in the context of some kind of power exchange. I.e. he does it because you want him to do it. He doesn't necessarily want this, but he gets off on having his limits tested. Those who identify with D/s exchanges are likely to be ones that fantasize about infantilism coupled with humiliation.

Do you see this as a form of D/s play?

Here, Mommy replaces the Dominatrix. On its most base level, the Dominant's persona links directly to the source: mother. With most of us, Mom is our first experience with rules and boundary-setting. She was the first authoritative figure in our lives. In this kind of fantasy role-play Mom might incorporate other D/s kind of play such as bondage, tickling or spanking.

Do you like to incorporate spanking when we're doing a scene?

Many lovers of spanking also enjoy some age-regressive interaction. E.g. your guy might wet his diapers in order to motivate you to administer a spanking. As the Mommy you would have to teach your "baby" a lesson by removing the wet diapers, spanking his bottom and then re-diapering.

What kind of diapers?

Again, you need to get specific in order to successfully bring his fantasy to life. There are disposables, cloth and rubber underpants.

Are you a "sissy baby"?

Sissy babies mix gender play with infantilism. Some cross-dressers like to couple their female dressing with regressive age play. Your guy might enjoy being dressed as a little female baby. If so, you'll need to get out the frilly panties, dresses and anything pink.

Is your cross gender dressing coupled with humiliation?

Sometimes being dressed like a sissy girl is viewed as punishment. In this case, your man wants you to derive pleasure out of making him dress as a female infant for some kind of real or imagined wrongdoing. Get inside his head and establish the exact guidelines of his fantasy. Is he seeking a feeling of being controlled, dominated or stretched to do something out of the norm to please Mom?

Does Mommy ever administer an enema to her sick baby?

Enemas can sometimes be associated with this fetish. It's another thing that Mom might do to care for her offspring. The enema might be given for purposes of healing but it could also be given to an "older baby" for purposes of punishment. He might also have thoughts about expelling in the diaper. You decide how that will be done and my suggestion is to make sure the baby grows up in time for "clean up." See the chapter on enemas for more information on attitude and practical tips.

Enacting The Infantilism Fetish

You'll bring the scene to life based on your fact-finding exploration. Pretend he really is your baby. Get into a nurturing, maternal headspace. Infantilism is a sweet fetish based on the idea of providing unconditional love and safety. Be sure to use any buzzwords he may have communicated to you like: "There's a good boy" or "Momma loves her dear, sweet baby." The more into his fantasy you get, the more pleasure both of you will derive from it.

In Summary

Infantilism brings your man back to a vulnerable place. In it, he is revealing to you a heightened emotional state laden with deep meaning, expressing a need to be nurtured or to be disciplined. Be supportive, active and empathic in your shared exploration of infantilism and Adult Babies. As with any fetish, have fun with this.

Chapter 8
Ass and Anal Play

It's funny how society is completely fine with describing a male as a "tit man" or an "ass man", but throw in the word "fetish" and some people get bent out of shape. The reality is that the phrase "ass man" could actually be the precursor toward acknowledging a sexual fetish. There's already unconditional acceptance that some men fixate on certain parts of the female anatomy. A fetish just takes this fixation a step further.

When does an ass man turn into a fetishist? What's the difference between a guy who simply gets aroused when he's walking behind a woman in snug pants and a guy who harbors images of female bottoms when he climaxes? The difference lies in the extent of the need.

When a man enjoys seeing, touching and/or tasting his partner's derriere as one component of the overall sexual experience then that guy is a regular old butt man. It's only when the ass becomes the sexual experience that we'd label it as fetish behavior.

Characteristics of The Ass Fetish

The ass fetishist is indeed preoccupied with the female bottom. He fully enjoys the visual and tactile experience. That experience may include touching, smacking or inserting objects into the anus. He also may like attention paid to his own bottom as an acknowledged personal erogenous zone. For example, he might want you to touch, smack or insert toys into his own anal passage.

If your man is indeed an ass man, you probably didn't need to conduct an informal investigation to discover this. Chances are very good that he's given your bottom a resounding smack or pinch on more than one occasion. You've probably also witnessed him ogling women at the mall or on the street. I'll wager that he enjoys seeing you wear clothing that accentuates your nether parts.

But what you probably didn't know is that the anal region is the key to unlocking your man's private, most powerful sexual fantasies.

Origins

Most ass men have shown this preference all their lives. The association with strong sensations and the bottom occur countless times in our lives. Think about it, babies' bottoms are lovingly diapered, powdered and wiped. Kids hit each other's butts playfully and give each other wedgies. Young boys often witness a girl being taken out of her wet bathing suit on the beach or get a glimpse of panties underneath a skirt as their female pals climb the monkey bars at the playground.

The man who possesses the predilection toward an ass fetish will unconsciously store these powerful sensations in the subconscious mind and draw upon them later. His sexuality is then skewed in the direction of whatever he found stimulating during his formative years. In your guy's case, the association for pleasure is linked with the buttocks and anal region.

Your Investigation

You're reading this chapter because you already know your man's got an ass fetish. While that's a good jumping off place, you still have some homework to do because in reality, an ass fetish can encompass a variety of acts and interests. In order to really grasp the details of his particular backdoor fetish, you need to do further investigation. Here are some questions to help get you started.

Q&A:

What do you like about the buttocks region?

Some guys will explain that they like the butt cheeks. Others will say that they like the asshole. Still others like the "taint". You know what the taint is, don't you? That's the region between the anus and the vagina. "'Taint quite pussy and 'taint quite asshole," as the old joke goes. Still not sure where the taint is? Your man will be more than happy to show you!

Is your fetish about things being done to your ass or do you prefer to do them to me?

I'll bet it's a little of both. Ass men generally love to see and touch your bottom. Your man would probably find it erotic for you to caress his bottom and anus too. This is something he may have only dreamed about and never done in reality. Most women are a bit shy about touching their partners' ass and even more reluctant to venture between the cheeks. Bottoms are often a highly neglected erogenous zone from both a male and female perspective. If he's an ass man, it may be time to set aside inhibitions, open your mind (and your butt cheeks!) and start making some explorations.

Have you ever tried having anal sex?

Many men consider anal sex to be the ultimate fantasy. By acknowledging his desires, he's psychologically entering "the forbidden zone".

Physically, the anal region is tighter and therefore more stimulating to a man's penis. However, the actually fulfilling this fantasy for him is entirely up to you. It's simply a matter of personal preference. Some women really enjoy it, while others find it extremely painful and uncomfortable. You might decide to try it once or twice before you flat-out say, "No way!"

Another option might be for him to slide his penis between your oil-slickened butt cheeks. Many ass men find this as satisfying as actually penetrating a bottom.

At this point, you're merely asking investigative questions. It's important for you to learn what he likes. You don't have to actually indulge in anal sex if you choose not to. Merely acknowledging his fetish and talking about it in explicit detail might be enough for him. If you decide that your anus is out of bounds, be sure to visit the chapter titled "Bedroom Talk" to facilitate fulfilling his fantasies verbally rather than physically.

What about tonguing or rimming the asshole?

Your anal region is actually cleaner and dryer than your vaginal area. Many men enjoy the sensation of pleasing their woman in this way. Some guys like to lick their woman's butthole because it's psychologically perceived as being nasty, naughty and slightly deviant. Other ass fetishists simply like the smell and the taste.

Don't be frightened. Remember, it's only a fact finding mission at this point. You might be one of many women brought up to believe that this area is off limits because of its excretory function. However, the bunghole is also an erogenous zone. If you put your inhibitions aside you might actually find it enjoyable to "sit on his face" and have your bottom worshipped. A nice, warm bath beforehand will get you relaxed and smelling sweet. Leave the rest up to him.

But for now, just find out if backdoor sex is one of his desires. The specifics and negotiations can take place further down the road.

Do you enjoy ass worship?

Ass worship is part of a general D/s scenario. In it, the submissive is literally "kissing your ass," which can be quite pleasurable. When you are the Top, or the dominant, you have total control over what he does or doesn't do. It's good to know first if he enjoys "rimming" (tonguing the asshole), but ultimately as the Dominant, you decide how much, how deep or if you want him to insert his tongue.

As part of the D/s scenario you'd order him get on his knees and show homage to your buttocks region. You can demand that he kiss, lick or caress your bottom either over your clothes, over your panties or permit him contact with your bare bottom. It's up to you and totally dependent on what you feel your "slave" deserves at the moment.

What about forced ass worship?

Forced ass worship connects with the guy who is conflicted about his desire or believes ass worship is a form of humiliation or punishment. The act of ass worship is the same but the context of the scene is commanding or disciplinary. In this scenario, he doesn't "want" to stick his tongue in your ass but is "commanded" to perform the act by his Superior, you, his Mistress or Top.

The idea of him being commanded to do the act takes away his power. You see, he has to lick your ass whether he wants to or not. It's a variation of the old "The Devil made me do it." You'll notice that many fetishes have a "forced" component, however, the "owner" of the fetish is the one who lays down the groundwork and the specific details of the fetish.

For example, if a man hires a Dominatrix to "force" him to do certain acts, he's really the one calling the shots because the scenario is all arranged beforehand between him and the Dom. At their core, these fetishes are consensual because ultimately the submissive is being urged, or permitted, to do the very act he fantasizes about.

Is face-sitting or smothering part of your sexual repertoire?

Face-sitting means that you order him to lie face up and actually sit yourself on top of his face. Before sitting down, you can straddle his face and give him a ringside view of your shapely globes. This just adds to the agony/ecstasy of the act.

Smothering is similar to face-sitting but it entails sitting square over his nose and thereby cutting off his air supply with your buttocks. Obviously, you can't stay there too long, so in between smothering intervals you can squat over his face and order him to apply light kisses to your butt cheeks.

Face-sitting and smothering are easy ways to drive an ass guy totally wild. Some of them have never even heard of these acts, so this is something new and wonderful that you can introduce him to yourself. He'll be lying helplessly beneath the place he likes best.

Remember, sexy smothering and face-sitting is all about the tease. Since you're the one in control, don't be afraid to voice your own desires. A little cunnilingus tied in with the bottom play won't hurt!

Is face-sitting or smothering done within the context of a D/s scenario?

Both can often be utilized within a general Dominant/submissive scene. Rather than have the scene turn sexual (and involve penetration), you can actually use the face-sitting episode to demonstrate your power and control over him.

When you cut off his circulation you are obviously in charge of his breathing, therefore in charge of *him*. That's a very powerful vantage point. You can learn to be seductive from a more powerful place. Permit him to smell but not to taste, if the mood strikes you. Remind him that he belongs beneath you, that he is your sitting stool, that he lives to see your bottom. He'll love it.

What about farts?

Believe it or not, if he's a true ass guy he might also like gas. Don't despair. Again, this can be something you acknowledge in terms of bedroom talk if you find the very idea of this embarrassing. Or you might actually find it fun if you give it a whirl.

Guys who like farts like them for a variety of reasons. First and foremost, most men have never seen their women fart. We've all been taught that flatulence is unladylike, so chances are you've learned to fart quietly or run to the bathroom when the need arises. Most men are curious creatures and farting is one thing that some find arousing. Ask if your guy harbors these sorts of fantasies.

Farting generally goes with face-sitting, so some ass guys get aroused by the very idea of you passing gas on their face. Ask what his particular fantasy position would be. Most likely, he'll describe the face-sitting position and imagine that you are squatting over his face.

Sensual or forced farts?

His response will be indicative of his attitude about the farts. Sexy bedroom play or part of a D/s scene?

Is there any special verbiage you prefer?

Find out what kind of words he enjoys hearing when it comes to farting. What are his own private buzzwords? He may want you to describe the fart – juicy, smelly, nasty, windy. Or he might only want to hear you "threaten" him with a fart. The talk may be graphic but remember, it's only talk. The more you talk about it, the more you yourself will become desensitized.

Eventually you may gather the courage to actually fart in his face. If so, you can assume the smothering/face-sitting position and then let loose. Remember to verbally build him up to it. If this is an area of interest for him, he's probably been daydreaming about it for a long time. Try to make the "trip" as enjoyable as the actual act. In other words, get him aroused to the utmost and make the farting a part of a larger smothering or D/s scenario.

Do you like to spank?

Find out if he merely likes to smack a bottom or if he wants to give you a full-blown spanking. If so, ask exactly what his spanking scenario entails. Does he want to spank you? What does he want to use—a hairbrush, a paddle, his bare hand?

Many butt men don't like to spank. There's an entire chapter devoted to spanking. However, this chapter is focused more on the guy who is so zealous about butts that he can't hold back from smacking them every now and then.

Getting spanked is an idea you might initially reject, but before you rule it out, please remember that these acts can be adjusted to accommodate your own comfort level. Think of spanking as a spectrum. There's a wide range of spanking styles, from love taps to vigorous thrashings that leave marks.

Men and women who are true spanking fetishists can take quite a hearty spanking. That's because they're sexually aroused by the act and their bodies are releasing endorphins—chemicals that convert the pain into pleasure. If you're not a spanking aficionado, you obviously won't have this reaction. Therefore, you'll feel each and every spank. You might want your partner to take it lightly the first time you give spanking a whirl.

Just because you might not personally be into spanking doesn't mean you can't participate in your man's fetish. As an "ass man," he probably likes spanking because he likes looking at your bottom. He likes the way it jiggles when it's tapped. He'll understand that you don't like pain aspect of spanking. I'm suggesting a pleasurable alternative here.

I'm willing to bet that he'll be just as thrilled if you lie across his lap and allow him to give you some light, sensual slaps on your panty-clad or bare behind. Put on some music and let him tap out the rhythm on your bottom. Squirm, writhe and react favorably while you're over his knee. You might actually enjoy these light taps on your behind.

Remember that the buttocks are an erogenous zone. As the spanks cause blood to flow to that region, you'll begin to feel a flush of excitement. The over-the-knee position is extremely stimulating if you position yourself so that your clitoris makes subtle contact with his knee. The harder he spanks, the more you shudder.

Do you like to get spanked?

There's a good chance he does. Try to find out more about his spanking fetish, then proceed to the "*Spanking*" chapter.

Do you enjoy anal play?

Find out his private definition of "anal play." It varies from person to person. For example, does he want to give or to receive? Obviously anal play can go both ways—on his or hers. Some enjoy anal play using fingers. Others prefer toys such as butt plugs, beads or dildos.

If this is something he imagines doing to you, find out his level of experience. Anal play can be very stimulating but it has to be done gently and proficiently; especially if you are a "virgin" in this area.

He may want you to be the initiator. Attitude is everything here. Are you incorporating anal play as sensual bedroom tease or are you taking on the role of Dominant? As Dominant, the anal play might be "forced", depending on his fantasy. Perhaps it's his fetish to pretend he doesn't necessarily want to do it, but he'll have no choice because you're the one in control. Only in reality, he's the one who's orchestrated every detail about enacting his fetish.

What about wedgies?

Some ass guys enjoy seeing/giving/having a wedgie. For them, it's usually all about reenacting episodes from their past—seeing somebody get a wedgie, the helplessness, the embarrassment, the way it looks. The wedgie question is just another road to explore to complete your investigation. Wedgies are also covered in the chapter "A Potpourri of Fetishes."

Doing Your Own Scene

You now probably have a sharp, clear picture of what your man's ass fetish encompasses. While you discuss his likes and dislikes, take note of his attitude, the purpose and make sure you understand exactly what you'll be doing. Be prepared with lubrication, butt plugs, dildos or any other necessary accoutrements.

Safety and cleanliness are major concerns in a backdoor episode. Dildos, fingers and penises are generally safe to insert into an ass, as long as you make sure to use plenty of lubrication and not to "lose" the object when it's inserted. Seriously. It has happened.

If you're using a finger always wear a latex glove and remember to use a water-soluble lubricant. With him on his back, slide your palm-up finger in all the way. Insertion in that position will probably hit his prostate and drive him wild!

Don't be afraid to try a strap-on dildo. If he enjoys anal play, I suggest you try it at least once. Some women feel a sense of power with a strap-on protruding from their pelvis. Now you get to do the fucking. Wield your complete and total power and have him suck your strap-on before you use it on him. Dildo play can add to his sense of erotic humiliation and also be a turn-on. It's your chance to experiment with role-reversal and other sexy scenarios.

You can even incorporate face-sitting, smothering or farting into your anal erotic scene. There are so many possibilities. But before you begin, first have him tell you what he envisions as his ultimate anal scene. Then do your best to replicate it. And remember, have fun!

Clothing

Ass men generally like tight clothes that accentuate the bottom. Dresses are out, unless they're particularly clingy, like Spandex. Tight pants are in. The tighter the better is a good rule of thumb. He may also enjoy seeing you wear full-back panties, g-strings, pantyhose, old-fashioned girdles or body shapers. Just ask him. I'm sure he has a clear-cut image of you wearing his dream outfit. Unless he has a particularly strong preference (which might then constitute another fetish) wear whatever makes you feel sexy and flatters your own derriere.

In Summary

The nether parts are the catalyst for a myriad of sexual experiences. When your guy describes himself as an "ass man", that could mean a number of things. It's your job to elicit as much information as possible from him so you can understand and also bring to life his secret sexual ass fantasy.

Discover his turn-ons and chances are great that you'll discover your own buttocks are an untapped territory for pleasure. A once-taboo body part can now bring a new dimension to your relationship. It may expand your capacity for intimate sexual bonding and in addition, be the ultimate erotic experience for your man.

Chapter 9
Bedroom Talk

Let me be the first to give you the great, big "'Atta Girl!'" you deserve. Seriously though, you should be very proud of yourself. After all, you've done a thorough investigation of your man's offbeat interests and now have a clear understanding of his fetish.

Perhaps you're here because your man has voiced an interest in dirty talk or Bedroom Talk, as I call it here. Or maybe you're here because you've decided that for whatever reason, you can't enact your man's fetish and have made the choice just to indulge in fantasy talk about it.

To your credit, you've read the *Feelings vs. Taking Action* chapter and you're confident you're not allowing incorrect thoughts to motivate negative feelings about his fetish. You also understand that you don't necessarily have a moral or emotional disconnect to his fantasy. The simple truth is that you don't wish to engage in behaviors that you personally find abhorrent. E.g. you've made the decision that you don't want to engage in any activity which involves excrement, degradation or physical pain.

You're also very firm about the fact that you don't wish to involve yourself in the act of giving or receiving any real physical torture.

No matter how you much you want to fulfill his fantasies, no matter how great your desire is to please him, you simply cannot (physically and/or mentally) bring his sexual fetishes to life in real time.

So, how do you fulfill his fetish fantasies, then?

There is a solution... Bedroom Talk. Let's call it BT for short.

BT doesn't mean that you'll necessarily do everything you say. It's all about weaving a verbal fantasy about things you know he desires and thinks about in private. In essence, your words become your man's custom-made fetish Web site. Remember the story of Scheherazade and her 1,001 Arabian Nights? Well, think of BT as your own naughty version. Or more closely, 1,001 Fetish Nights.

BT allows you to demonstrate your acceptance of his fetish without having to actually enact the aspects that might make you feel uncomfortable. By talking about it, you're validating his fantasy and giving the message that it's okay with you. BT gives you the opportunity of being together and sharing the titillating thoughts he used to entertain when he was alone.

When it's done right, BT is an intimate sexual activity. Your words can lead him to the same earth-shattering orgasm he'd have if you were actually physically engaging in his fantasy.

In fact, sometimes words are more intense than the act itself. All sorts of things can go wrong when you're physically partaking in a fetish scene. For example you could be all thumbs in bondage games, the ropes can be too tight or you might lose the key to the handcuffs. (That can really dampen the mood!) BT is a foolproof way to go deep inside the dark, pleasurable, forbidden recesses of his sexual mind. Your voice is the instrument which gives him permission to let go and share his intimate, sexy secrets with you.

Many fetishists find the description of the act to be just as stimulating as the act itself. In BT, you use the buzzwords which fuel his fire and describe the scenarios that get him going in painstaking detail. The idea is to talk while you're touching, caressing or masturbating him. Trust me, BT is guaranteed to produce very positive results.

Bedroom Talk is something you can do as an added dimension to your existing sexual repertoire. There will be times when it won't be practical to play out his fetish scene; like when you're spending the night at his folks' house. Or else, his scene might be too elaborate to enact when time is an issue.

BT can then be used as a form of foreplay or it can be a way for you to participate in his masturbatory fantasies. When you acknowledge his sexual thoughts verbally, they are no longer a secret shame. He'll feel relieved and unconditionally accepted. And who wouldn't love and cherish a woman who did that? Wouldn't you like that cherished woman to be you?

Benefits of Bedroom Talk

Bedroom Talk is an excellent alternative if your man's fetish is one that can't be reenacted on your own. In other words, his fetish might be too complicated, too involved or impossible to recreate. For example, if it involved an entire sports stadium. It also might be an act you're uncomfortable participating in. That's your own personal choice and your private decision. Ultimately, you owe it to yourself to only take part in acts you feel secure about.

This book will never suggest you do anything which you find personally repugnant. However, not *doing* something doesn't mean you can't *talk* about it. Try putting your own feelings aside and describe scenarios he daydreams about. It's easier than you think.

BT is perfect for those times when you're menstruating or just don't feel like having intercourse. Your guy can let his fingers do the walking while you do the talking. Remember to caress and touch him while you describe his fantasy acts. This adds an additional layer of intimacy. From a psychological viewpoint, these fantasy talks also strengthen the bond in your relationship.

To shake things up a bit, you might even want to reverse roles one day. Perhaps you have some of your own secret sexual thoughts you'd like to reveal. Who better to tell than your life partner?

Even If You Can't Say the Words...

Sometimes it's difficult to verbalize acts you might find off-putting or confusing. Try as you might, you could still feel like you're not capable of orally expressing his fetish.

One way to get around this dilemma is to create a fictional character that represents your alter ego. This is the woman who will perform all of these acts with your guy, not you. But it's not technically another woman, but more closely, it's a woman who represents a part of you.

- Go online and do some research.
- Gain an understanding of what really turns him on.
- Describe the things and situations he's shared with you.
- Take him on a sexual fantasy journey.

The words you use, the very sound of your voice will jump-start his motor. It's way of sexually joining with him. He'll soon associate the sound of your voice with the fantasy. This is truly a viable way of partaking in the fetish without physical participation.

Talking about the fetish will also help to normalize it. The more you talk, the more desensitized you'll get. Over time, the words and the fetish will have less power over your own personal sensibilities and will be less adverse to you.

How to Do Bedroom Talk

Either of you can be the initiator. Think of BT as a nice gift to give your guy before bed. Treat him to a soothing backrub then turn him onto his back. Gently use your fingertips to stroke him all over. Take your time before working your way to his genitals.

As you start to touch him erotically, tell him things you'd like to do to him. Remember to use his own personal buzzwords and pet phrases. You can ask him questions while you stroke him. Pay close attention to his answers - and to the change in his breathing. Hearing how turned on he is will be a turn-on to you. Now...repeat his own words back to him. He'll love hearing you say things that came from deep within his sexual soul.

Continue to tease and please him, but all the while, keep talking. If your guy enjoys domination, BT is a good way to control his orgasm. Tell him he'll need permission to climax. Your permission. As you keep talking, watch his arousal level skyrocket. Notice the phrases that get his penis particularly excited.

One of my girlfriends swears that her husband stands at attention at the mere mention of the phrase "blow job". Although this same friend is not a fan of anal sex (she's tried it several times) she's has however, discovered that just talking about it while they're making love brings her husband to explosive levels of satisfaction. Inadvertently, she found that her husband responds to auditory stimulation. She was clever enough to use it to her advantage.

Take note of the exact moment he ejaculates. Remember what you were saying at the time and make a mental earmark of it. Chances are he'll release when he's the most turned on. His orgasm is your key to knowing his ultimate sexual popping point and the words and phrases that bring him there.

In Summary

Bedroom Talk (BT) is a useful addition to your sexual tool kit. BT can be used as an alternative to engaging in acts that are out of sync with your comfort level. BT is also handy when time is an issue and you are engaging in a "quickie".

In addition to being arousing, BT provides you with additional information about the specifics of your man's fetish. He'll talk more freely when he's relaxed and sexually aroused.

Your investigation is never done, though. There's always more to learn and new facets to be revealed. Take mental notes. He'll tell you more as he gains more trust in you. Remember that he's sharing thoughts he originally thought he'd take to the grave. Your sexual investigation takes time and patience. Listen openly without judgment. And remember, you don't actually have to physically engage in his fetish in order to become an involved, enthusiastic fetish partner.

Chapter 10
Bondage

So, he likes to be tied up. Unlike some of the other fetishes discussed in this book, this proclivity is probably not all that confusing or repugnant to you. Bondage is something that is relatively common and almost mainstream. Movies like *9 1/2 Weeks*, *Crimes of Passion* and *Black Snake Moan* have made it almost commonplace.

It's actually pretty simple. You take some silk scarves, render him helpless and then have your way with him. Right? Relatively straightforward. Or is it? Bondage can be as simple as putting a leash around your man's neck or as complex as creating a web of beautiful, meticulously-tied knots.

When he says he likes bondage, it can also mean a great deal more than a square knot or two. Bondage might only be the clue he gives that he wants something more. He may crave being your "slave" or "sex toy" within the realm of a Dominant/submissive relationship. He might also be hinting that he wants the bondage introduced into your relationship for purposes of discipline. In other words, he likes a dose of Discipline with his bondage; he wants to be reprimanded as well as restrained while you whip, spank or paddle him.

Bondage is both literal and symbolic. Physically, he's made to feel immobile with some type of material like a rope or chains. Symbolically, he can be in bondage because of the submissive position he would like to assume for you. Restraints are used as a prop because he would remain submissive to you even if the ropes were untied.

Bondage As A Fetish

Many aspects of bondage may be at the core of your man's fetish. Some people are straight-up bondage enthusiasts. For them, it's all about the tying - doing the tying or being tied up. Sex is not necessarily involved. The very act of helplessness or the visual of seeing someone tied up helplessly is the key to his arousal. Some guys just love the feeling of rope against their bodies. It's the concept of being rendered helpless or immobile that's at the root of the fetish.

As with most fetishes, a real attraction to bondage can be traced back to childhood experiences. We've all played with rope in one form or another. We've played with jump ropes or have climbed the rope in gym class. Children still play variations of "Cowboys and Indians". In it, "the bad guys" get tied up when they're captured or the "bad guys" tie up the "good guys". For some, these innocent games trigger the "fetish gene" that lies dormant until puberty. And then, *BAM!*, out pops their fetish like the goddess Athena from Zeus's head.

Many bondage fetishes have reported to me how innocent childhood "tie-up" games were their epiphany, their moment of realization. They even say how they would try on purpose to be the one who was getting caught, running extra slowly so the mad "cowboy" would catch them and lash them to a tree.

As an adult, when your guy becomes sexual, thoughts of bondage creep out from his subconscious mind. Seeing a movie may have triggered him. (Remember those silent films depicting the fair damsel tied helplessly to the train tracks?) Or perhaps a random thought popped into his head during masturbation as a youth.

Whatever the case, your man likes bondage. Your fact-finding mission needs to be quite extensive with this fetish since it encompasses many different acts, fantasies and stimuli.

Here are some questions to ask so you can get a greater understanding of what your man's bondage fantasy entails:

Q&A:

How did you first come to discover that you enjoyed bondage?

Most fetishists can trace back their need to be tied up to a very young age. Some even remember tying themselves up when they were kids or playing wresting games (which involve restraint, an element of bondage) with their friends.

When did you first begin to sexualize the act of bondage? Most fetishes are latent until puberty strikes. There's a good chance he became "bondage aware" when he started to masturbate.

Have you ever tied yourself up? If so, how did you manage it? What did you do when it happened?

Listen carefully to his answer. If he tied himself up to be very immobile and liked the idea of staying there, he enjoys the actual feeling of being rendered helpless. It might make him feel safe, like being in a cocoon. If he ties himself up and leaves one hand free (for...guess what?), he's probably more sexual about his bondage preferences.

What does bondage mean to you?

You'll note that this question is deliberately worded in a very open-ended fashion to make him think about and elaborate upon his answer. We already know that bondage may be used in conjunction with whipping, cock and ball torture (CBT), nipple torture (NT), tickling, spanking and cross-dressing. Listen for those other fetish components in his response.

Also listen closely to see if he is a bondage "purist." In other words, he's fixated on the concept of being rendered totally helpless. Find out what material he prefers you to use. Discover what he imagines being restrained with and how tight he likes to be tied.

Do you like being tied tightly or do you like to struggle to get free?

For some, it's the challenge of being able to loosen the bonds. They like to squirm, decipher how tightly they're tied and then wriggle to get out. Psychologically, for others it may feel comforting to know they're not able to break free and are totally at your mercy.

Is bondage something that goes along with sex?

Men are action-oriented creatures. They have issues about *allowing* themselves to be pleasured. When a man is rendered helpless he has no choice but to lie back and enjoy the experience. Bondage is actually freeing in that it allows him to let go. One client explains it very clearly and succinctly: "Sometimes you just want somebody else to do the driving."

What's your ideal bondage scene?

Some guys imagine bondage within the context of role-playing games. Common bondage scenarios include but are not limited to: inquisitions, robberies, prison or hospital type settings. Discover your guy's scene with this question.

What about straightjacket bondage or mummification?

These are special kinds of restraints. Straightjacket bondage is pretty self-explanatory. It's when people enjoy their arms encased, like in a straight-jacket. Mummification means tightly wrapping the entire body with material such as Saran wrap, rubber, or leather.

What about being tied and teased?

Tease and denial is a sexy bedroom game with many variations detailed below. If this is his interest, you can use rope or silk scarves to bind. Get even more creative and employ your fingertips, a feather duster or a light leather flogger to tease.

Do you like the idea of being rendered helpless and then being left alone for a period of time?

Some people find bondage to be a solitary activity. They like to be tied tightly and left totally alone. However, you have a big responsibility in this kind of a role. They are never truly alone because you as the responsible partner is always close by. Check in on him periodically to make sure he's alright and don't leave him alone for too long.

Okay, I've got the answers. Now What?

Once you've gathered your basic information, you need to plan for the actual scene. I've detailed it for you here:

Bondage as a Part of a D/s Experience

Your investigation reveals that your guy likes bondage in conjunction with a typical Dominant/submissive scene. What's your next step?

Bondage is symbolic of the power you have over him. Make the most of it. Get into it. Revel in it. First, a few possible scenarios:

Scenario # 1:

- Tie his hands behind his back and have him get on his knees.
- Order him to kiss your feet and legs and anything else you desire.

Scenario # 2:

- Insert a hook in your ceiling. (Call in a professional to do it. If you're embarrassed, you can say that you're a sculptress and want to use it to create art...in a sense, you are.)
- Tie his hands above his head.
- Do some basic whipping to him in this position.
- Anywhere, any way you like. But establish safety words beforehand. (See the chapter on "Spanking" for more on safe words.)
- If you feel compelled, use nipple clamps or a cock ring when he's in this vulnerable position. Refer to the chapter on "Cock and Ball Torture" and "Nipple Torture" for more.

Most of all, remember that the bondage is only a part of the overall scene. It's the sugar in the cake but not the whole dessert.

It's Bondage and Nothing Else

If he's a straightforward bondage boy, you might need to get some rope-tying lessons in order to sufficiently enact his fantasies. Don't hesitate to ask him to do the honors. Chances are good he's already "experimented" on himself and has otherwise done his bondage homework. Let him teach you and then practice on your own ankles or on a doll. Make sure you're confident in your rope-tying abilities before you do a bondage scene with him.

Some enjoy bondage purely as an art form. Japanese-style bondage is so lovely and intricate, it's similar to macramé. If you're crafty, you may discover a whole new outlet for yourself.

Saran wrap is another easy way to render someone helpless. So is duct tape but it's generally used for more extreme kinds of scenes and advanced players. Look in your kitchen or your junk drawer for inspiration. Items like twine and blind pulls might also do the trick.

Latex is another material that's currently associated with bondage. It's more difficult to use since it's so thin and easy to tear. If latex bondage is his thing, I suggest enlisting his help in obtaining it and learning how to use latex properly.

When You Execute the Scene...

Tie him as tight as his needs require. Admire him in bondage. Set up a long, tall mirror so he can see himself in gear. Touch him. Use your body to rub up against him. Do sexy things to him. Remember, he's very turned on when he's in this vulnerable state.

If bondage is more of a punishment activity for your guy, proceed (with gusto!) with the spanking or whipping. Get out your nipple clamps or other "stimulating" pieces of equipment you've bought for the occasion. Be creative. He's yours. Don't be afraid to use normal household items like wooden or plastic clothespins.

If you're tying him and leaving him, choose an appropriate room. The bathroom might be an interesting choice! A walk-in closet works, too.

Important: Remember to always check in on him. Never, ever leave the house and leave him tied up. That is *not* cool. As the dominant or "Top," in addition to his pleasure, you have a great deal of responsibility for his general state of well-being.

Sexy Bondage

One of the most liberating parts about being tied up is that responsibility is taken away. Many men (and women) enjoy a light form of restraint in the bedroom. This way they can literally just lay back and receive, guilt-free. No using their hands. No reciprocity in sex. Nothing at all is asked of them. They can just enjoy, enjoy, enjoy.

This is the time for you to put on some sexy, silky lingerie and tie his arms comfortably to the bedposts. The silken scarves are more figurative than literal. They remind him that he's not allowed to do anything to you or for you. His only role is to revel in your touch and in the pleasure you give. Or don't give!

Once you lightly tie him up, do whatever you wish. You can be sexual or non-sexual. Kiss, lick or suck him, wherever you choose. Now's the time you use the tips of your fingernails to gently caress him all over.

Take your time. Touch his shoulders, arms and the insides of his legs. Watch his response. The key is for him to be pleasured. Gently caress his body. Pay extra attention to his nipples - for many men this is an erogenous zone. Slowly work your way to his groin area. This kind of bondage can lead to sex...or not. Sometimes the ecstasy is in the agony of not climaxing. That's completely up to you. It can be foreplay or the play itself.

Tease and Denial

This is a variation of sexy bondage. The goal here is to work him up and then prolong the pleasure (or the pain), depending on your POV, by not allowing him to orgasm.

Remember that your voice is as important a tool of arousal as your hand or any fetish tool is. Tell him what you will do to him as you're doing it. Make your voice sound as creamy as velvet, brimming with power and desire.

If you desire, apply some lubricant to his penis. Masturbate him until he's about to explode. Then stop. Make him say "Mercy", "Red Light" or a phrase of your choosing if he's on the brink of orgasm.

Prolong his state of arousal by removing your hand from his penis. Caress it with your hand, a single feather, a feather duster or a light, soft whip. Then return to his penis and stroke it until he's about to ejaculate again. Tease and denial is highly arousing and can be played for as long as the two of you desire.

This kind of interaction is a good way to actually be in total control of his ejaculation. Again tease and denial can be done just by itself or in conjunction with more traditional D/s play.

Cum or Else!

Another fun bondage activity is to restrain one of your man's arms and have the other arm free. The scenario goes something like this:

- He's told that he has to masturbate and "cum on command".
- You can give him a certain amount of time to accomplish this task. Three minutes, for example.
- If he doesn't climax within that time, there will be a consequence.
- For the punishment, you decide what would be appropriate in your own situation.

I personally like the idea of having a pair of dice or deck of cards on hand for the punishment. He chooses a card or rolls the dice and also chooses the number of strokes he will receive from a paddle or your hand.

Another good option is to have him pick a number and you climb onto his face for the allotted amount of time.

Relax Cum Relax

My husband coined this phrase and refers to it as an RCR for short. This is another take on intimate bondage play. Render him helpless. Massage and relax him. Give him an exquisite hand job until he climaxes. Then massage and relax again. This is a very nice way to send him off to sleep.

Of course, RCR is also something you might enjoy yourself!

Mental Bondage

Sometimes ropes or scarves are not at hand. When you're traveling or are a guest in someone's home, for example. You can enact the activities I've described above by decreeing "mental bondage". In it, your man must imagine that his hands are tied and that he can't move. Proceed as above, giving him orders, pleasuring him, etc. It's convenient, enjoyable and just as effective when you don't have lots of time or the energy to deal with the knots and other embellishments.

And Speaking of Knots

Some of us are former Girl Scouts and might have earned a Merit Badge in knot-tying. Others are all thumbs when it comes to ropes. The intricacy of bondage is entirely up to you. You can learn from your mate, books or videos or even the Internet. I have mastered a few basic ties but bondage has never been my forte or my passion. I have therefore learned some easy tricks of the trade, which I'll share with you below.

Bondage Made Easy:

- Use very soft, pliable rope. Not too thick, not too thin. Wash it to get it even softer. Double the rope and loop it. Tie it around a few times and then make double knots. Believe me, it works.
- Get utility hooks and boat hooks from the hardware store and have a pro install them. Chains can work well with the hooks and this way, you don't have to tie knots.
- Purchase some leather-type restraints, which

are easily found online. You'll see that there
are many easy-to-use, effective bondage devices
which are quick, simple and no hassle. Like
premade nipple nooses, for example. Click
and explore.

Bondage Tips

In bondage, as in every other D/s activity, please exercise care and caution. You're dealing with a human being, someone you care deeply about, but someone whose passion might get in the way of their personal safety. It's your responsibility as the Top to make certain they stay safe.

No matter how tight they may beg you to tie them, always be sure that your partner's circulation is not being cut off. If you bind wrists or ankles, there should be enough room to slip a finger in. Watch for any evidence of the fingers or toes turning bluish. If so, unfasten immediately and turn to a gentler form of play.

Rope bondage is the most common type. This includes rope, scarves, neckties, belts or any other multi-purpose item that can be used for restraint.

Usually, the hands are bound together, but they can also be bound to the thighs, waist, behind the back or above the head.

Your guy can also be bound to another object such as a chair, shower curtain rod, a hook in the ceiling, and many other places where you can tie off a rope. Their feet can also be bound together, or apart. I can't stress enough never to leave someone unattended in bondage for more than a couple of minutes.

And if your partner's hands are tied behind his or her back, do not allow a sudden change of position that puts pressure on the arms, as it is easy to dislocate a shoulder that way.

What's In It For You?

Fulfilling a deep-seated fantasy/fetish for someone you care about raises your own self-esteem because you've proved your ability to be open-minded and the best lover you can be to your mate. And what's more empowering than that?

What's more, you've successfully done your investigation and were instrumental in bringing his bondage fantasies to life.

This provides you with a fulfilled, satisfied partner who will be yours forever.

Consider the erotic aspects of bondage for yourself as well. After all, you deserve a break too! He'll probably jump at the chance of reciprocating the experience of your very own erotic bondage games.

In Summary

Bondage has many meanings and works in conjunction with a variety of fantasies and fetishes. It can be used with a number of D/s activities or can be a fetish in and of itself. Bondage can be punishing, pleasurable or a combination of the two. As an intricate, multi-faceted fetish, it requires extensive information gathering, equipment and active participation. But because it's so involved, it can also be deeply fulfilling.

So grab a rope and your guy and have a blast!

Chapter 11
Cock and Ball Torture (CBT) and Nipple Torture (NT)

What in the World Are CBT and NT?

CBT and NT is the terminology used to describe men who
enjoy a particular kind of stimulation to their genital and nipple
area. CBT and NT are slightly different than other fetishes since
they don't involve a non-sexual object, obsessive fantasy or
specific role play. These predilections usually go hand in hand
with a Domination or bondage scene but they can be used alone
as bedroom foreplay.

If your guy likes a lot of attention to his nipples and/or genital
region he's either extremely sensitive in these areas or the act of
"torture" could represent a sub-category based on a broader
masochistic type of mindset.

Giving nipple stimulation to their man is often a surprising
concept for women to grasp. We tend to think of nipples as part
of the female anatomy, though obviously males have them as
well. Most gals are shocked to learn that nipples can be an
erogenous zone for men too. But think about it, if ours are
sensitive, why shouldn't theirs be?

CBT is another shocker. We usually think of male genitalia as being very sensitive, even tender to the touch. So it's tough for us to conceive that some guys actually like their testicles squeezed, whipped, stomped or smacked.

During your Q&A session, you may find out that your guy enjoys receiving a dose of pain to his nipples or genitals. Or he may not have even mentioned this but you still have some suspicions. If you have a feeling he may be interested in this type of strong stimulation, then CBT and NT are actions you can initiate during a D/s scene or even during "vanilla" sex. It's something to do when you dominate him or even when you're taking the lead in bed. Employing light CBT and NT can easily be initiated on your own.

Give It A Try!

As you know, I strongly suggest verbal communication before enacting any kind of fetish. CBT and NT are exceptions to that rule. You can try it out if you already know he likes S/M or D/s. Experiment with some mild nipple or cock and ball stimulation when you're in your dominant role. Watch closely for non-verbal cues expressing signs of pleasure or displeasure. If you observe positive responses, then you can explore with the questions provided further along in this chapter.

NT and CBT might be something he's never tried but ends up enjoying. It's like eating sushi for the first time. Who would imagine that raw fish could be so delicious? Yet just one taste often produces a convert.

Sensual sexy nipple play can also be a foreplay activity. Cuff him to the bedposts and stimulate his nipples as a way to tease and sexually dominate him. If he's truly "into" pain, he'll have an intensely stiff reaction.

Simple Nipple and Cock Play

This is something you can do as part of foreplay or when he's tied up and completely yours.

- Use your fingertips to very lightly encircle or graze his nipples.
- Watch how his body responds for non-verbal cues.

- If he seems to enjoy your touch, go a bit further.
- Take your tongue and lightly lick his nipples.

Most likely a man will get erect as a positive physiological response to the above. This is your opportunity to ask if he's enjoying the sensations. If his response is "Yes," then pursue your exploration further with more intense sucking, light pinching and even some nips with your teeth.

You can pursue his cock and balls in a similar fashion.

- Instead of rubbing your hand up and down along his shaft, work your way to his balls and give them a firm but gentle squeeze.
- If he doesn't freak out, go a little further.
- Try flicking your thumb and middle finger against his scrotum.
- Still no complaint? Lightly and I mean lightly tap his balls.
- Take note of his response.

If you ascertain that there is indeed an interest and /or positive response when you employ nipple and/or cock stimulation you can proceed further. He may have already indicated an interest in NT or CBT. Once again, this fetish can take many forms and be realized in many different ways. Let's investigate!

Q&A - NT:

Are you aware that many men enjoy nipple stimulation?
It's always reassuring for anyone to know they're not alone. Many guys are a little embarrassed about their preference since it's considered by many to be feminine. Your knowledge and acceptance of it will get him to relax and divulge more information.

When your nipples are stimulated what feels best?
Find out if he likes being touched with your hands, your tongue or both. Sometimes guys like a light, feathery touch. Others want it firm, leading to more heavy-duty pain. Let him

touch you in the way he wants to be touched himself so you get a clear idea of the type of stimulation he seeks.

Do you like your nipples sucked? If so, how?

This is another instance of actions speaking louder than words. The best way to find out what he likes is for him to demonstrate on you. Some men like a mouth completely covering their areola area. Some want just the nipple sucked or flicked with the tongue. There are so many preferences and varieties. Discover his.

Hopefully, his demonstration will feel good and you can both enjoy some reciprocal nipple interaction. But don't let your own enjoyment get in the way of your investigation. Focus on what he's doing so you can really understand and give him the kind of attention he craves.

Do you enjoy pain with your nipple play?

At this point, you can stop having him demonstrate on you unless you're feeling very brave, or like a dash of pain with your pleasure. Encourage him to start describing what he likes verbally. Find out if he wants you to pinch his nipples. If so, take your fingers and squeeze until he cries "Uncle."

Does he prefer that you nip or bite? If so, how hard? Go ahead and give it a whirl until he's close to his limit. "Hands-On" experimentation will give you a great deal of information.

Have you ever tried nipple clamps or weights?

If he replies affirmatively to this question, I'll bet he has a few nipple clamps or clothespins stashed in his dresser drawer. If he doesn't own any but wants to give it a whirl, all you need to do is Google "nipple clamps" on the Internet and you'll be amazed at how easy it is to find and order these devices right online. Or better yet, run out to your all-night grocery store and pick up a bag of regular old wooden clothespins. They work just as well and add a nice low-tech touch.

As a beginner, you might want to loosen up the tension of the clip before playing. Ask for his help in the initial application. Once again, everyone has a different preference for the way the clamp is applied and a different threshold of pain. The first time let him put them on himself and show you the best fit for his own nipple size and shape.

Weights are recommended for more advanced players. Again, they come in all shapes, sizes and varieties. Hardcore extremists like the idea of stretching the nipple.

Do you think about having your nipples pierced?

This is very advanced nipple play and you probably won't be exploring it. However, there is something called "play piercing" which you might want to at least know about. Play piercing entails actually taking very slender needles and inserting them through the nipple area. It's called "play piercing" because there's no jewelry inserted and it's only temporary. The sharp, intense sensation of being pierced is what practitioners of play piercing seek.

Although the very concept might make you squeamish, it's important to understand the spectrum of this nipple fetish. Obviously piercing is the extreme. If you engage in even a little play piercing, make sure to cleanse both his nipples and the needles you use with alcohol to prevent infection.

What is your fantasy around nipple torture?

Some guys report that they like the sensation. Others seek the sensation within the context of a D/s scene. These are two different mindsets requiring you to behave very differently.

Nipple Torture In The Dungeon

NT incorporated into D/s interaction requires you to take the dominant role. You choose the clamps. You position, place and decide where you want to take him. Your decisions aren't random, however, but based upon your knowledge of his personal needs or desires.

As a Dominant or Top, it's your responsibility to push, but not exceed, his limits. This is a delicate balance that comes with experience and lots of communication. When he's in a submissive state of mind, he wants to sustain pain for you. Submissives do not necessarily enjoy pain but they do like to "suffer" for their dominant partner as proof of their love and devotion.

Everyone experiences the pleasure of pain differently. Similarly, everyone has different limits. Only through experience combined with communication can you understand exactly what your guy means when he says he enjoys nipple torture.

Q&A - CBT:

What is it about cock and ball torture that turns you on?

He may talk about sensation. He may also discuss the psychological aspect of male inferiority within the context of a D/s relationship. But whatever his response, listen closely and learn.

A man's penis is often his most prized possession. This is the appendage that has provided him with pleasure for years. Most males discover their penis within the first few months of life, some even in utero. It's something to play with and hold. The fondling is soothing to them and provides relief from stress. It's like an old, dependable friend, always there, always ready.

Your guy may simply like more intense stimulation. Perhaps there's some guilt around masturbation. Maybe he feels a need to be punished. Other submissive men believe in female superiority. It then makes sense that cock and ball torture is about sacrifice. The penis symbolizes his male inferiority. The pain the female inflicts upon him symbolizes her superiority over him.

Investigate what kind of mindset your guy has around cock and ball stimulation. Find out if he likes his cock teased, tortured or humiliated. Each of these three aspects of cock play is specific and requires you to take very different approaches.

When you say you like CBT, are you talking about cock, balls or cock and balls?

This distinction is very important. Though some men like both the penis and testicles to be played with, many have a specific area of preference. You need to find out what he is seeking.

Is it pain that turns you on?

This is a very sensitive query and you need to be delicate in the asking— and sure of yourself even if he says he likes pain. Some guys like being kicked in the balls. I personally think this is entering into a dangerous zone, physiologically speaking. It's too easy to do permanent damage with a well-placed kick.

Instead, I suggest you begin with some simple ball squeezing or flicking your fingertips on his penis and scrotum. You might also try some intense ball sucking or biting if he likes that.

Does this have to do with fear or trust?

CBT requires him to entrust a very important organ to you. Sometimes fear turns into sexual excitement. Be curious and try to unearth what's behind his interest.

What kind of fantasy goes along with your interest in CBT?

Some men like CBT because it meshes perfectly with their D/s fantasies: he is literally handing you his balls. They now become *your balls*. The extreme fantasy is to be castrated so he no longer has balls. This is the ultimate to a CBT guy.

The other fantasy extreme is to wear a chastity belt so he can no longer have access to his own organ. Again, these thoughts are extreme but they often fit into the CBT mindset.

Listen carefully to his response and take note of the exact words he uses. Remember to repeat some of his fantasy buzzwords back to him while you're playing. Some guys are into verbal humiliation and crave talk about their "small penis" (even if the size is just fine to you).

Others have extreme fantasies such as castration you can verbally threaten to do so, or talk about the supposed castration that will take place in the future if he doesn't behave. Talking is always stimulating and can be almost as much of a turn-on as the act itself.

Do you have a small penis?

Howard Stern loves to make fun of his small penis. None of us have any idea of how it measures up in reality, but this Shock Jock always knows what to say in order to get a rise from his listeners.

Guys who get sexually aroused by verbal humiliation generally initiate talk about their small penises when they are deep in the arousal zone. They want you to laugh and make fun of their "small dick." They want to hear about bigger cocks you have seen and have had relations with.

This is strictly a verbal humiliation fantasy. I included it here since we are talking about the penis. These days you can't talk about physical abuse without mentioning emotional abuse as well. With this fantasy, abuse is only a fictional state of mind. Please remember that everything I am proposing here is between two consenting adults.

Are you open to CBT devices?

There are many cock rings on the market. Some fit on the testicles and others tie around the dick and balls. Chances are he may already have his own stash. If not, you can always go online for a CBT shopping spree. These devices are easy to find and order.

If you seek something immediate, you can always tie his balls with soft rope, twine or a leather string. Let him show you the mechanics that will work with his body type. I'll bet he's experimented before, alone, without you even knowing it!

What about cock bondage and whipping?

If he expresses interest, you should know that the scrotum responds well to the flogger. Tie his penis in such a way that it will pull on the ropes as it flinches from each stroke of the whip.

Do you consider Tease and Denial to be part of CBT?

Tease and Denial may or may not fit into the category for him but it's certainly a way of controlling him through his penis. You might want to incorporate the delicious torture of flogging and stopping, flogging and stopping again. For more on Tease and Denial, see the section in this chapter.

CBT How-To's

CBT can be effortlessly incorporated into a Dominant/submissive scene. After all, he's tied up and helpless. You can:

> • Squeeze his balls or smack them with your hands.
> • Suspend his arms above his head and use a cock ring.

- Tie a rope around his balls and lead him around the room on all fours like a good doggie.

CBT is definitely a component of a D/s session. Always remind him that his balls are now your balls. You own and control them.

You can also control him with something called "Tease and Denial."

Tease and Denial

This can be used in a D/s scene or it can also be used for sexual domination. You might even want to experiment with a cock ring (a ring that fits snugly around the base of the penis; it can be purchased in sex shops or online.) Cock rings actually make the penis harder and keep blood engorged in the shaft. Or you can fit a cock ring around his testicles. It's more difficult for him to orgasm with his cock and/or balls tied tightly. Now you can have some real fun with him.

- Restrain him with rope or have him put his hands beneath his head and lay face up on the bed.
- Use lubricant and masturbate him until he's very hard. He'll want to orgasm, but only you can decide when - and if! - that will happen.
- Keep masturbating him but take care not to let him explode.
- While he's at this most vulnerable place, tease him physically and mentally.
- Run your fingers along his body and pay close attention to his nipples if that's another of his hot spots.
- Graze your body against his.
- Talk dirty to him. Tell him all the things you plan to do to him.
- Stress that you own his body and that you also control his ejaculation. Remember the unique sexual fantasies he shared with you.
- Use his favorite verbiage and buzzwords.

Now you will truly understand the strong connection between the brain and the erection. Your words and your knowledge can keep him in a highly aroused state for hours. Tease and Denial is a powerful way to incorporate many aspects of fetish and domination into your play. You can utilize it from a position of dominance or a position of being sexually controlling.

Remember, with Tease and Denial, you have the power to decide when he orgasms and how it happens. I guarantee that you'll help facilitate one of the most explosive orgasms of his life. That's a gratifying pay off for you and a sure fire way of gaining his unfaltering devotion.

Who knows, when you see his powerful response, you might want him to employ some T&D tactics on you as well!

In Summary

Many men have a strong desire for attention to their nipples or genital region. Some simply like the sensations. Others feel that this kind of interaction adds to a feeling of powerlessness or submission.

A great deal of the male population is unaware of their nipple sensitivity and exploration in this area opens up another pleasure avenue. Nipple play is something you may want to initiate as a way to assert power or spice up your sex life. Go slow and observe his body language when you try out these techniques.

Both nipple and cock play can be used in conjunction with bondage and D/s scenes. They are great stimulators and enhance your knowledge and control of his body.

Chapter 12
Cross-Dressing

- Is your guy a little more into fashion than he likes to let on?
- Has he raided your closet and put on your bra in jest when he's had a few too many cocktails?
- Have some of your panties disappeared recently?

If your answer to any of the above questions was "Yes," then your man might be a cross-dresser.

Upon further investigation, you might discover that your man likes dressing up in women's clothes. (No wonder he didn't mind all those trips to the shopping mall!) Is he gay? Probably not. Is he a sissy? Definitely not. Your guy merely likes to dress up in female clothing once in a while. Plain and simple.

You'll be surprised (and relieved) to know that cross-dressing is very common fetish. Supposedly, former FBI director J. Edgar Hoover was a staunch cross-dresser. More guys like to dress up than you can imagine. Some have a preference for wearing silky panties underneath their three-piece suit while others enjoy undergoing a total transformation—stockings, high-heels, bra, panties, dress, make-up and hair.

Cross-dressing is actually accepted and embraced in many cultures, especially Latin American cultures. Think of the scores of pretty cross-dressing males during Rio de Janeiro's carnival.

Thankfully, society's idea of what it is to be a man is changing and we are allowing men to be more expressive than ever before. Men are now taught that it's okay to show their emotions, shed tears and even help with the housework. They are learning to tap into their "feminine selves" and allow their softer, creative sides to shine through.

However, when it comes to fashion, men have a long way to go in the realm of self-expression. The men's department still features the same array of drab grays, tans, blacks and browns. If they're lucky, they can find funky neckties and socks, but that's about it. There's little variation between work and casual attire. No wonder your guy might be curious to find out what it feels like to wear some satiny panties, a tight girdle or dress up in pretty, colorful clothing.

Origins of Cross-Dressing

The cross-dressing fetish is much more complex than just wanting to try on your wife or girlfriend's clothes. Like all fetishes, this also originates in childhood. Many cross-dressers report having mothers who wished they'd had a daughter instead of a son and made no secret of hiding this desire. Some mothers even went so far as to put their boy in a dress as a joke or just to see how cute he looked. These guys grew up to be confused about acceptable male/female behavior and may still want to dress as a girl now that they are older. By her actions, Mom gave cross-dressing a "seal of approval". And who doesn't want to please their Mommy?

Other men remember impulsively dressing up when they were young because of their innate curiosity about the opposite sex. Panties are forbidden items of clothing associated with female privacy. Little boys are discouraged from going into their mom's or sister's panty drawer. They're told it's private, personal and off limits.

Understandably, this forbidden aspect of feminine underthings draws a mischievous lad into the very place he's told not to go. Of course the little boy then wants to rifle through the panty drawer and find out what the secret's all about.

When he does look in the secret drawer, it's like Pandora's box but filled with soft, frilly undergarments instead of evil spirits. He picks up the silky, brightly-colored undies and examines the female articles very closely. He takes note of everything: the scent, the appearance and feel of the wispy material.

Naturally, this may lead to actually trying on some of the articles of clothing and making believe he's having some kind of interaction with the "female" he sees in the mirror. How can his body *not* react to contact with all of the silky-softness? Understandably, it leads to masturbation. This is how the link is established between wearing female clothing and arousal. By wearing the clothes and masturbating, he gets into the mindset that he is making love to a woman; himself. The ensuing pleasurable feelings lead to a positive connection between dressing and sexuality.

Genetically, the cross-dressing enthusiast most likely has a predisposition to this kind of behavior. Triggers will always be needed to get the fetish started, but biologically only certain people inherit this yet to be thoroughly understood "fetish gene".

Men who like to cross-dress do it for many reasons. You'll have to discover what this is for your guy. Many adult men report to me that dressing up helps them relieve stress as a fun, harmless diversionary activity. Dressing up is like going on a mini-vacation. Some cross-dressing guys enjoy the act of shopping for their attire in stores, while others prefer buying clothing and make-up anonymously from online shops or catalogs.

Still other guys say that dressing enhances their sexuality. One very handsome, extremely masculine-looking gentleman confided in me that donning a petticoat was the equivalent of Viagra for him. Wearing the frilly skirt, he stayed hard endlessly and could make love for hours. Without it, he could perform but not quite as enthusiastically. Of course, he had trouble finding a lady who could get past the visual of a muscle-bound guy in a lacy slip! But once he found that special someone, he cherished her.

For this fellow, the very feel of the material against his skin was an aphrodisiac. It simply got him in the mood. When he finally did meet a woman who was accepting of his fetish, he married her and they have a wonderful, caring life together. The petticoat only comes out on occasion. It turned out that what he really needed was acceptance. Once he had acceptance, the petticoat was only a "special occasion" thing.

I know that sometimes it's difficult to get past the visual image of what you want your guy to be. You think, 'I don't want this life! If he really loved me, he would just burn those clothes.' You perceive that a man dressing up as a woman is deviant, sick and distasteful.

You're entitled to your opinions and can certainly think this way if you choose, but will this mode of thought help you strengthen your relationship or destroy it? Will this mode of thinking change the sexual make-up of your man? Absolutely not on both accounts.

Instead, consider it this way. Your guy did not choose his fetish; it chose him, in a sense. For him, dressing is a way that he learned to cope with the daily stresses of life. Cross-dressing doesn't harm anyone. It's not dangerous to his health or his well being. It's simply a part of him and a card that's been dealt into your relationship. He doesn't have to dress up all the time. What he needs is your acceptance so that he can feel good about himself and he doesn't have to sneak around to satisfy his fetish.

Cross-dressing couples actually report that they have loads of fun together. They can go shopping as a pair. He then gets to play a dual role - your guy transformed into your girlfriend! And think of this: while shopping together, he'll be more likely to be extra generous in purchasing clothes for you as well as for himself.

Cross-dressing is such a widespread fetish that many "dress up" events are held throughout the world. Not only can you travel to gorgeous places but you can meet other like-minded people and expand your horizons by embracing his hobby and fetish.

And most importantly, you demonstrate a real, deep loving commitment when you choose to embrace his sexuality solely because you want him to feel confident and happy about himself.

There are many variations and nuances to the cross-dressing fetish which involve men who like to wear female clothing and what they want to do once they are "dressed". Here are some basic investigative questions devised to give you greater understanding of your guys' cross-dressing proclivities.

Q&A:

Do you like to be fully dressed?

Discover what kind of clothing he likes to wear. Some men prefer slutty outfits. Others choose to be more matronly or "prim and proper". How he dresses is a window into the soul of his alter ego. Good girl or bad girl? Party girl or office attire? Or maybe he's versatile and has different outfits for different moods.

Also, find out where he buys his clothes and how he'd ultimately like to look. Some guys have a vision of their female self but don't have an inkling on how to achieve that look. Offer your help in choosing the correct colors and styles that flatter him.

Do you have a name for your alter ego?

Many cross-dressing guys have a female name. If your man doesn't have one, it might be fun to help him name that part of his persona.

Do you like hair and make-up?

Cross-dressers who do their hair and make-up are generally more hardcore. Many take the time to scour fashion magazines and figure out how to apply make-up. In fact, some can do this better than the average gal on the street. These fellows generally opt for heavy-duty pancake make-up to cover their beard stubble. The preference seems to be for colorful eye shadow, thick glossy lips and long, false eyelashes. The hairstyle/wigs they choose will again be indicative of the kind of woman they imagine themselves to be. Some will go for more conservative, short do's while others like long, sleek blonde hair. Again, your input on helping him do this tastefully will be greatly appreciated.

Do you prefer to dress just partially?

He might like to only wear undergarments. Find out what partially-dressed means to him. Is it just panties or does he also like wearing bras or stockings? Is it garters and stockings or pantyhose? You'll discover that he has a definite preference.

When do you generally wear these undergarments?

Some guys like to wear feminine underthings beneath their business suit. Again, they find that it relieves the stress of the workplace and also provides some "naughty but fun" feelings of distraction. Others will wear female clothing within the context of fetish play like bondage, spanking or whipping.

What do you do when you're dressed?

Some men like to dress and go out in public. It's a turn-on for them to go into shopping malls, buy clothes and "pass" for a woman. Other fellows prefer to dress up in private. They find it relaxing to do while home alone. For them, it's similar to listening to music or reading a book; it helps them unwind. Still others prefer being dressed up when having sexual relations. Which one is your man?

Do you view cross-dressing as a humiliating activity?

Guys who think about cross-dressing within the context of embarrassment or humiliation have a completely different mindset. For them, cross-dressing is not done as a hobby or stress reliever but it's seen as a punishment. Refer to the chapter on "Humiliation" for greater insight into this aspect of cross-dressing. I'll touch upon it here, though.

If your guy is into humiliation, for him part of the thrill is being made to feel "embarrassed" about being dressed. When he's dressed he wants you to call him names like "pantywaist", "sissy pants" or something similar. Ask about his own buzzwords. And use them!

If your guy likes to be humiliated by getting dressed, the out-fit will probably be just a pair of panties or maybe some stock-ings. Nothing too elaborate. The point is to put down his mascu-linity by making him wear "girly" clothes. You need to get into his head and ask him what he means by humiliation. Find out how he views dressing as being a humiliating activity. Uncover what aspect of cross-dressing feels embarrassing to him.

Do you need to be forced to cross-dress?

Forced cross-dressing and humiliation are very close and almost interchangeable. If he likes forced cross-dressing, it's a form of punishment and humiliation. You provide the clothes and force him to put them on as penance for a real or imagined wrongdoing. Find out more about what "forcing" means to him.

Some guys are into being forced to wear just panties. Others want to be forced to dress up like a whore. There's a term commonly used called "petticoat punishment." It means being forced to wear something frilly and girlish, and generally, getting spanked in that outfit. Ask him about "petticoat punishment" and if the term has any meaning for him.

Do you get into a submissive mindset when dressed?

For some, feminization is an expression of true submission. Some cross-dressers enjoy the idea of being subservient when they're dressed. They imagine donning a maid's outfit and doing housework. Or they want to do something special for you. How can you resist something like that? Getting your house cleaned while feeding into his fetish is a win-win situation.

Enacting The Fetish

Now that you've done your investigation, you'll know where you fit into his fetish.

Privacy

If your man likes to dress up as a means of relaxation or simply enjoys wearing panties under his work clothes, you really don't need to do much. Just let him do his thing. Maybe buy him a pair of plus-size undies or a sexy thong as a surprise gift once in a while. You've opened the door to communication. There doesn't have to be any more secrets between you. He no longer has to sneak around or live in fear that you'll somehow find his private stash of women's clothing.

Also, you won't have the pain of one day finding a pair of panties in his bedroom and assuming they belong to another woman. You'll know they belong to him and that he really, truly belongs to you because he's trusted you with this information.

Being a supportive woman will score points with him in many ways. Who knows, eventually you may even get him to feel comfortable enough to explore the fetish with you more deeply. This would demonstrate a great deal of trust and will create a deeper bond between the two of you. When a guy feels that comfortable with his woman, rest assured he'll never stray. Where would he find another woman as accepting and loving as you?

Dressing In Secret

Cross-dressers will go to great lengths to make sure their needs are met. I know of several who have actually established separate apartments just to have a place where they can have some privacy and dress when the mood strikes them.

I also know one married man who dressed alone for more than 25 years. To enact his fetish, he hired a "professional" as often as his budget allowed. He even maintained a separate residence to house his extensive wardrobe. Imagine the money he could have saved (and spent on his wife and family) if he had a partner, like you, who is willing to be accepting.

On the other hand, I personally know cross-dressers who are able to share their fetish with their wives. These couples have unusually strong relationships and are close with each other because they don't have a secret wedging between them.

Playing Dress-Up With Your Man

Don't expect him to want to cross-dress all the time. For most guys, dressing is the same as a vacation; it happens once in a while. You'll want to set up special days for "girl time" with him so he can enact his fetish. Just like you set up dates for dinner or the movies.

Consider it this way: you've made a new friend. Do the things you like to do with girlfriends. Start with simple shopping trips. Help him buy clothes or make-up. Depending on the situation, allow, and even encourage, him to wear undergarments beneath his male clothing.

And if you're feeling adventurous, go ahead and help him dress like a female. Apply makeup for him. Fuss with his wig. Take him out someplace, to the movies or a club. You'd be surprised at the kind of reactions you get.

Or you might simply choose to stay home. Your guy might be the type who wants to serve you when he's dressed. If so, have him wear a maid's outfit and find some simple chores for him to do. He might also like giving you a pampering manicure, pedicure or a relaxing massage. The choice is yours. You may enjoy doing the same for him. Two good girlfriends hanging out at home, having fun.

Dressing as Part of a Scene or Bedroom Activity

Other times Cross-Dressing is combined with a domination scenario. To play the part, you'd get dressed in one of your Dominatrix outfits and head for the bedroom. Plan out a scene where you'd dominate him and order him into an outfit.

In this scenario, after he's dressed, you'd put him into some kind of bondage with ropes. Many cross-dressers like to be tied very tightly while dressed in female clothing. The combined sensations of strict bondage and restrictive female clothing such as girdles or form-fitting material feels very erotic to them.

Sometimes the Dominant/submissive cross-dressing scene is done with the idea of turning your guy into a "slut". Many very straight-laced guys enjoy assuming a trashy alter ego in this role. When they're ordered to dress in sexy clothing combined with an alluring wig, they feel free and liberated from the constraints of masculinity.

When your man dresses up, he allows himself to lose his inhibitions. Your job is to foster this alter ego by having "her" do the kinds of things that he normally would never do on his own. The orders you spout give him permission to open up and let go.

Make him your "slutty girlfriend". Tell him to worship various parts of your body. You're the one in control. This is a big perk of being a Dominant. You can say and do things you might not ordinarily do or say. As women, we're taught to be polite. As a Dominant, you have permission to do things you don't ordinarily do in the "Vanilla World".

Thankfully, your slutty girlfriend also has "lesbian" tendencies. If you feel like having oral sex, as a Dominant, you have the license to be very specific in your instructions. Most men admit they have no clue about cunnilingus. Now you have the opportunity to speak openly and freely about what feels good to you.

As you grow comfortable in your role as a Dominant female, add a strap-on dildo to your bag of props. He'll probably enjoy getting on his knees and performing oral sex on your "penis". Have fun with this role reversal. You can now tell him to "suck my dick" any way you like. Have him kiss it, lick it and deep-throat it if you so desire.

If you're feeling especially adventurous, have him get on all fours and present you with his ass. Ever wonder what it feels like to be a man? Now is your chance to experience intercourse as the one who inserts. You can make him really feel like a woman by fucking him in the ass. You'll feel empowered and he'll feel liberated. But remember to use plenty of lube and discuss this concept with him well before it's actually introduced into play.

The Maid Role

Within Dominant/submissive role-play, your guy might prefer being dressed up as a maid. In this context, you'd do many of the same things you would if he was your whore. The difference is he's more of a servant that a sexual slut. You can have him massage you, pamper you and draw you a bath. Again, he's in a place of servicing you from an alter-ego state. Dressing as a maid gives him the go-ahead to act in ways he wouldn't act when he's dressed as a guy.

Being Punished As A Naughty Girl

Many cross-dressers have a dual fetish. They like to be spanked or tied up when dressed. They feel the need to be punished or bound as a "mischievous girl". Perhaps that helps alleviate the guilt since it's clearly another person of the opposite gender who is being disciplined. Perhaps that helps alleviate the guilt or maybe he's just a reserved guy who wants to try on the role of a spirited girl. It's enjoyable to role-play these "disciplinary" scenes. Dressing provides another context and adds an additional layer to bondage or spanking fetish.

Reenact or play out an occurrence which may have happened years ago. Start in the bedroom and have him rummage through your panty drawer or closet. You can actually "catch him in the act" as he's trying on your clothes. Punish him by forcing him to wear your clothes, telling him, "If you're going to sniff my panties, then you'll have to get spanked in them." You would then order him to don your panties and get over your knee. Spank him heartily as punishment for rifling through your panty drawer.

Or if he's more of a bondage enthusiast, his punishment would be to be tied up and be left alone wearing female clothing and ropes.

If your guy enjoys both bondage and spanking, you can dress, tie and spank him, as he likes.

You get the idea. That's why you need to ask the questions from the previous section so you can communicate better and learn the details of his "dream scene."

A Word About Transgenderism

If at any point you sense that cross-dressing is more than play and your man says he has strong, ingrained feelings about being a woman trapped inside a man's body, then this is much more than a fetish. He may in fact be transgender and this is a serious, very real issue that needs to be dealt with in a proactive way.

Transgender people feel that they were born into the wrong sex. Transgender men identify with being female. It's not about who they are attracted to or what turns them on sexually but rather, it's a predisposition towards *feeling* like a woman in terms of their emotional make up and way of being in the world. Though anatomically they sport a penis, they do not inwardly identify with their masculinity.

If your guy opens up and admits that he feels uncomfortable or at odds with his male persona, you need to stop reading this book and seek out professional help immediately. There are a myriad of physicians and mental health workers who are knowledgeable about and supportive of individuals who identify as transgender.

Gender Identity Disorder is widely studied and currently being addressed more as a way of being rather than a disorder or aberration. There is growing evidence that supports the fact that one's chemical and genetic make-up are the actual factors which cause an individual to inwardly feel they should have been born the opposite sex. You both need to help in understanding the complexities of this way of being.

As his woman, you absolutely must address this issue. Transgender people are often inwardly torn apart because they feel like true outcasts. Education and acceptance are the first order of business. The reason transgender is beyond the scope of this book is because it is not a fetish; it's a way of being. You both need to seek out help so he can have a real outlet to express what he's been feeling inside all of his life.

Transgenderism is not to be confused with the fetish "transvestism" which is what we are addressing in this chapter. Transvestism merely has to do with a man who likes to dress up in women's clothing. Your job is to identify the extent, purpose and way your guy enjoys dressing up. The questions in the previous section will help you to pinpoint exactly where the fetish lies in his internal sexual being.

In Summary

Cross-dressing is a complex and expressive fetish. Since it starts early in life, it is a very prominent aspect of your man's sexuality. It needs to be embraced in order for your guy to feel like a free, whole, worthwhile human being.

Your man might like to dress completely or just wear lingerie. He may imagine having a female alter ego or dressing could just be a way to feel punished or humiliated.

Find out what cross-dressing means to him. Make friends with the "woman" in his (and your) life. But most of all, remember to have fun and make sure to get your own needs met while fulfilling his.

Chapter 13
Enemas

Of course, you know what enemas are. You may have even experienced one yourself. An enema is the procedure of introducing liquid into the anus for the purposes of cleansing. It's generally used as a decisive cure for constipation or when preparing for a medical procedure. But the idea of getting an enema for pleasure is a concept that is probably completely alien to you.

Now you've discovered that your guy wants to incorporate enemas into your bedroom play. You may find this abhorrent, completely distasteful and way beyond what you signed up for. I'll take a wild guess and venture to say that enemas are something that is not even remotely romantic or exciting for you. You think of them as medicinal at best and at worst, repugnant.

After all, who wants to induce a state of diarrhea and then make mad, passionate love? Who in the world? Your guy does, that's who. Simply put, he enjoys receiving and possibly even giving enemas. Maybe not right before sex but definitely as part of his personal bag of sexual turn-ons.

But before you flush this book into the toilet with despair, I'd like to propose that you learn a little more about this easy-to-understand, straightforward fetish.

How in the World Does This Desire Come about?

Some children are exposed to enemas as youngsters. Chances are these enemas were administered for medicinal benefits, but they may also have been given for the purpose of punishment. Think of an enema as an internal mouth-soaping. Some parents consider it a retributive type of discipline to "clean out" naughty thoughts, actions or unacceptable intentions.

Enemas are clearly a very frightening, traumatic form of punishment for a child. They are evasive, uncomfortable and embarrassing. Yet, the result can be cathartic and relieving.

To a child, physical trauma is often so shocking that the feelings they experience during the trauma are stored and remembered differently later on in life. This is the way we humans cope with and defend against evasive events. However, a horrible experience can actually be sexualized later on in life. It's a way of turning things around and remembering a bad circumstance as something positive or arousing. A twist on turning a negative into a positive. And as a result of these powerful memories, a fetish is born.

So, you've discovered that your guy enjoys receiving enemas. Though enemas can be pleasurable for both sexes, males find enemas particularly arousing because they stimulate the prostate gland. Because of this, an enema is a guaranteed erection.

Enemas can easily be incorporated into D/s, Fem/Dom or medical play. They can also be enjoyed as a self-contained experience. Your job is to explore and find out your man's psychological mindset about enemas. Start out by asking the following...

Q&A:

How did you figure out that enemas are a turn-on for you?

As a true fetishist, he'll probably remember exactly when and tell you about early thoughts or actual experiences. It's always helpful to get as much background material from him as possible.

What experience have you had with receiving enemas?

It's important to know whether he's actually been given an enema as an adult. If so, who did it and under what circumstances? Here's where you need to listen for other possible components of his fetish. For example, if a nurse administered the enema, you might find yourself donning a crisp, white medical uniform when you give his.

Do you enjoy giving yourself enemas?

Obviously, this is something that can easily be done alone. Most people elect to do this to/for themselves. Except someone who has an enema fetish. For them, the excitement is in the interaction.

If you could have your enema fantasy come to life, tell me where, when and who would be administering the enema? His answer to this question is key. Now he can elaborate and tell you his own enema ideal. Listen for attitude, setting and role. You might be required to administer the enema within the context of sexual arousal, discipline or as a challenge for your submissive/slave. He'll be able to describe the actual context for the scene, probably in exquisite detail.

Do you see enemas as a form of discipline?

This would relate back to the premise of early childhood fear or trauma. He may have actually experienced, been threatened with or heard about a friend being punished in this fashion. Now he's excited by the concept of receiving an enema within the context of a disciplinary scene. Many guys who crave enemas also like to be spanked. Both are disciplinary acts done with the spirit of correcting and improving behavior, a natural combination.

Unearth what your guy envisions in terms of an enema with disciplinary overtones.

- Is he spanked first?
- Is he given the enema over you knee?
- Is he made to stand in the corner and hold it in for a certain amount of time?
- Is he allowed privacy when expelling or is part of the punishment having you witness him sitting on the toilet?

Is receiving an enema an expression of your submissive nature?

Enemas can be incorporated into D/s scenes quite naturally. It's another way of being tested and proving that he'll take any form of degradation for your pleasure, as proof of his love and devotion to you. Enemas enhance his feeling of true submission. The very act of an enema renders a person helpless and out of control.

Psychologically, a special bond develops during the course of the act. That's why enema administration, works so well in the D/s fantasy. Enemas are a powerful tool for the submissive who wants to be pushed beyond his limits.

Do you enjoy getting an enema in conjunction with cross-dressing?

If your man likes to cross-dress, he may also enjoy getting an enema concurrent with that mindset. Substitute the word "enema" for "douche" and it will drive him crazy with passion. The enema is given for purposes of cleaning before being invaded by your "penis/dildo."

What feelings do you have when you think about getting an enema?

Some people interpret enema activity with punishment and discipline. Others remember enema administration as loving and nurturing:

- Mommy cared enough to give me an enema so my tummy would feel better.
- Mommy had so much power over me that she could even make my bowels move if she wanted to.

Thus, some develop the fantasy of discipline enemas while others acquire a passion for erotic enemas.

Is anal stimulation part of your passion for enemas?

Obviously there's a great deal of focus on the anus when giving an enema. You already may know that your guy is butt-oriented because he may also have a spanking or ass fetish.

In this light, his additional desire for an enema is natural. It's another way to receive attention to his bottom.

Do you also fantasize about giving an enema?

Don't run out the door! Remember, fantasies are just fantasies. If you are not inclined to have your guy give you an enema, that's understandable. However, you can still talk about it with him as a means of stimulation while you masturbate him. Remember that talking about a fantasy while stimulating your man's penis is often as arousing as participating in the act.

For the record, some couples do find the act of giving each other enemas pleasurable. They report that administering an enema prior to sexual intercourse increases the intensity of the experience. Some even wait to expel after orgasm. Sounds messy but don't forget about rubber sheets.

Giving and receiving enemas is obviously an extremely intimate act and therefore brings you and your partner closer together.

Would you prefer that I am present or absent during expulsion?

No matter what his preference, ultimately you make the choice. If the enema is being given under the guise of humiliation, you ought to be present. A good alternative is to order him to leave the door open. You can always walk away if watching is not your cup of tea; he'll be too busy to notice.

Some Tips on Administering an Enema

You've done all your research and are ready to go. You may be donning a nurse's uniform or your favorite fetish gear to do the job. You have a clear understanding of the mindset you'll be displaying during the administration—Dom or stern Mom or something else entirely.

One word of advice: read the instructions on the enema box beforehand (even a few times) so you're familiar with what you're going to do.

It's also okay to ask your guy for some enema instructions beforehand. Chances are excellent that he's already experimented, so he knows what kind of bags work best for him. There are a wide variety of gadgets designed for the enema fetishist. Some prefer the disposable type (think disposable douches) while others like old-fashioned rubber enema bags.

Experiment only after you're comfortable and familiar with enema basics. This has to be a good, positive experience for you, too.

Remember to:

- Use warm water.
- Squeeze the nozzle to let out excess air.
- Lubricate his anus.
- Let the water flow gently.
- Allow for lots of communication, especially the first few times.
- If he needs you to stop, listen to him.
- Make sure he's close enough to make a run for the toilet.

Enemas and Anal Play

Enemas are a good idea if your guy likes anal play. This means you might want to give him an enema or have him use a disposable enema on himself before you begin experimenting with backdoor toys. Enemas are essential for cleanliness.

There's no way of knowing if fecal matter is lurking in the anal region. Nothing is more off-putting than taking out a dildo and seeing brown streaks. Administering an enema before dildo or anal play ensures a cleaner, more enjoyable experience for both of you.

In Summary

Enemas are a surprising form of erotic interaction. The idea of giving an enema may feel initially repugnant but with proper education, it's a relatively easy way to satisfy your man.

Enemas are linked to many other alternative sexual interactions. They go hand in hand with Fem/Dom spanking, cross-dressing and infantilistic fetishes.

Enemas can create a special kind of intimacy. Your partner is giving you the gift of trust. Embrace this fetish and you'll forge a close, lasting bond.

Chapter 14
Erotic Hypnosis and Hypnofetishism

Let me guess, you're probably surprised to hear that your guy is stimulated by the act of being hypnotized. Hypnosis is generally associated with psychiatry or cheesy Las Vegas lounge acts. The concept of using hypnotism to turn him on is probably very startling. Yet, many guys, especially those inclined to enjoy Dominant/submissive exchanges, find the idea of mind-control highly arousing and stimulating. For them, it's the ultimate form of submitting to your wishes and desires.

Hypnosis is a technique used to foster a deep sense of relaxation and focus. Therapists use it to help their clients "be present" in the room and get totally involved in their session. It's a good a way to clear the mind of extraneous, busy chatter that is distracting and unhelpful to their treatment. Learning how to relax every muscle allows someone to get in touch with their own feelings and desires.

As a fetish, hypnosis is used within the context of Dominant/submissive interaction. The submissive literally gives up control of both his mind and his body. It allows for a deeper connection between "Mistress and slave."

Control is the basis for this desire. A submissive man likes the idea that the Dominant female "gets inside" his subconscious mind in order to wield her power over him. He entertain thoughts that his "Hypno-Dom" will implant suggestions into his subconscious mind that will enable him to be in a constant state of arousal. Hypnosis is a way to allow somebody to relax, focus and have a heightened sensual experience.

What Hypnosis Is and What It Isn't

Many people equate hypnosis with being the flashy performance that we see with stage hypnotism. This is not real hypnosis and oftentimes it's more about illusion that reality. Stage hypnosis is very much like magic; it's not what it appears to be.

Real hypnosis is about getting the subject to relax so that his subconscious mind takes over. The subconscious mind is experienced when one is in a trance-like state.

We've all experienced a trance-like state at one time or another. For example, when we're driving on the freeway for long stretches, sometimes we go into "auto pilot" and lose our sense of time and place. Yet we still drive carefully. The subconscious mind has simply taken over while you might have been thinking of something completely different than driving. The subconscious mind is the state we're in just before we drop off to sleep.

The goal of hypnosis is to get a person to retreat into their subconscious mind. In this place, we're all susceptible to suggestion. We're in a keen place to remember what we conceive as being helpful to us.

- The subconscious mind retains only what it perceives to be important.
- The subconscious mind has morals; no one can be programmed to do something wrong that would be hurtful to himself or others.
- The subconscious mind is there to help and ultimately wants to aid us in living more productive, healthy lives.

This is why hypnosis works well in developing good, positive habits and life-changes.

How To Induce A State of Trance or Hypnosis

Inducing a state of trance or hypnosis is very easy to learn. There are many books, CDs and DVDs that can give you detailed how-to techniques.

But for now, I'll give you this simple technique:

- Sit your guy in a comfortable chair, recliner or lay down on the sofa or bed.
- Place his arms by his sides, shoes off, legs flat.
- Have him take several deep breaths and close his eyes.
- Guide him to relax every single part of his body, starting with the tip of his toes to the hairs on his head.
- Be detailed and speak in a soothing voice. Your voice alone should get him to relax and focus.
- Remind him to keep breathing deeply.
- Tell him to imagine a white screen with neon numbers and have him count backwards from 10 to zero, focused just on your voice and breathing deeply.

Once he's in this state, you can talk about whatever it is that he would like to hear in his hypnofetish fantasies. Most likely, you will now be discussing various aspects of his sexual fantasies, which may include transformations such as cross-dressing or situations such as forced bi, threesomes or seductions.

Hypnosis is used a great deal within the context of Dominant/ submissive relationships. The Dominant offers suggestions that strengthen the image of power, control and obedience over the submissive.

Various verbal images can be painted in a hypnotic state such as Goddess worship, a longing to pleasure certain parts of your body such as your feet or legs, and a general desire to please. D/s hypnosis is also used to change mindsets. The subject can be given suggestions that will enable him to rethink various experiences such as learning that "pain is pleasure."

Before you can give suggestions to your spellbound subject, you need to know the focus and goals of hypnosis. To do this, you must pick his brain and figure out the underlying triggers of his hypnotic fetish. Does he fantasize about hypnosis for the sake of being put under your spell? Will hypnosis be used in conjunction with your Dominant/submissive relationship or a specific fetish?

Note: With this particular fetish, you can actually ask the questions *after* you've gotten him into a relaxed state. You know he already likes to be in trance. This is the perfect way to "pick his brain."

Q&A:

How is hypnosis arousing to you?

He may describe this as a feeling of being overpowered or seduced. If he's under hypnosis, tell him to breathe deeply while he describes his fantasy "seductress." What is she wearing? What is her demeanor? How does she speak and enunciate her words?

Submissives will tell you that they want you to gain further control over them when they are in hypnosis. They see it as the ultimate form of surrender. They are allowing you to actually enter their subconscious mind, the most deeply personal part of them.

Find out what suggestions would be helpful for him when he's in this state. Does he need you to feed him statements about being more emotionally compliant? Or is his desire more about being able to endure physical "suffering" from you as a proof of his love?

Submissive men tend to have difficulties expressing what they really want. Hypnosis allows you to find out their unexpressed desires. Consciously, they are saying that their own "will" does not allow them to visit the "dark, secretive sexual places" where they really want to go. Hypnotic suggestions give them permission to do what they truly desire. Ultimately, this makes them a more active participant in the Dominant/submissive interaction.

What benefits do you hope to achieve from hypnosis?

Hypnosis can take away negative thoughts. People who feel

guilt about their fetishes can experience relief by having some of their thoughts reprogrammed to include more positive feelings about fantasy and fetish.

Have you ever been hypnotized before? What was it like?

This is always a good question for your own personal information. Find out about what did or didn't work. Any techniques employed that were particularly useful? Anything that wasn't helpful or took him away from the experience?

Do you want the hypnosis to strengthen the bond between us?

Of course, he does! When you get him into a trance-like state, have some prepared suggestions. These "orders" will allow him to mentally think of you when you're not present. Here are a few ideas:

- Demand that he silently says your name at a designated time each day.
- Order him to imagine your face each time he pours a cup of coffee, stops at a traffic light or puts on his pants.
- Suggest that he spontaneously has an urge to do your dishes, buy you flowers or write you a love letter.

See? The possibilities are endless. Just make sure you have him think of you at appropriate times. After all, you wouldn't want to program him to think of you while he's in the middle of an important staff meeting!

Is hypnosis about being a 'money slave'?

Some men have a fetish about being controlled through money. They want to be ordered to give gifts as tribute. This is not necessarily noble and many men get taken advantage of while partaking in this fetish. If this is your guy's bag, you can always demand that he buys you gifts that will be useful to you both such as a fancy coffee maker (and make you the coffee!), lovely lingerie, a trip to an exotic locale.

Would hypnosis be helpful to facilitate your other fetishes?

Hypnosis can be a wonderful tool to relieve guilt. You'd be "commanding" him to enjoy worshipping your feet, receiving a whipping, dress like a girl, etc. In other words, you're giving him the gift of programming him to enjoy his own fetish without remorse.

Do you want to be touched while in trance?

Some guys find having a sexual release to be very powerful while in a trance-like state. This may be the whole reason he enjoys erotic hypnosis in the first place. Hypnosis heightens the sexual experience. It can also give you the opportunity to talk to him about sexual details he might be reluctant to discuss when he's not hypnotized. He may be more apt to disclose "sexual secrets" when he's feeling relaxed and safe.

In Summary

Hypnosis is something often used to strengthen D/s relationships and alter fetish behavior. It's also a means to relax and focus on heightened sexual feelings and states of arousal.

Chapter 15
Foot Fetish

Okay, so you're with a guy who gets turned on by your feet. It may seem unusual since we're so accustomed to sexualizing our more "feminine" body parts like our breasts, bottoms or vaginas. But who in the world would imagine he'd get turned on by tootsies? Yet, many guys get extremely aroused by other, "non-erotic" parts of us, including our feet. When someone objectifies and focuses on a specific body part, it's then considered a sexual fetish. In your man's case, he's the proud owner of a foot fetish.

Foot fetishes are very common, but common or not, your guy might harbor feelings of shame because of the connotations associated with feet. Most people consider them smelly, dirty and even unattractive. While society is very accepting of the "tit man" or "ass man", no one brags about being a "foot man." Yet, feet are a very common sexual stimulant. Many a boy experienced his first feelings of arousal when coming face-to-face with the female foot.

Origin

Imagine a toddler crawling on the floor. His penis accidentally brushes up against an unsuspecting woman's foot and he feels good. The stimulation isn't perceived as sexual, yet it produced pleasurable sensations. These feelings are stored up in his subconscious mind and reemerge at puberty. A connection is then made between sexual arousal and the foot.

The type of encasement which held the foot during that initial contact might also be a source of fetish as well. Boots or bare toes. Pumps or sneakers. His preference is grounded in that very first sexual revelation when his foot fetish originally occurred.

It will be your job to pinpoint the very specific way your tootsies can "float his boat". How he emotionally feels about his fetish will determine how he allows himself to participate. That's why it's imperative for you to understand the fetish's psychological makeup so you can interpret the correct way to bring it to life.

Men who attach shame to the fetish might view foot worship within the context of a D/s relationship where he's being forced or 'commanded to worship your lower extremities. Others prefer to simply give you the pleasure they themselves feel while honoring the beauty of your feet. Your job is to ask the questions that will reveal the core aspects of his unique obsession with feet. Here are some to get you started:

Q&A:

Describe or show me a picture that captures what you envision.

He probably has a number of favorite foot photos marked either on his computer or in magazines. Notice the patterns that prevail (types of shoes or nail polish) and probe further. Foot fetishists are very specific in their likes and dislikes. His pictures will also reveal the exact body part he prefers. Some foot fetishists limit themselves to the feet while others like feet and legs. Still others focus on a specific area of the foot such as heels, instep or toes.

Do you like bare feet?

Some foot fetishes like the feet they worship to be bare while others prefer shoes. Some are even very specific about heel height and shoe type. Bare feet may not be enough for your guy or it might be his total bag. Explore his answer further to understand the finer details of his fetish.

Bare feet that are clean or bare feet that are unwashed?

Believe it or not, some guys prefer the bare feet they worship to be pretty smelly! When it comes time for him to make contact with your feet, don't be squeamish if he prefers your natural scent. Work out or jog in tennis shoes and socks. Save the dirty socks and put them on your feet before you see him. He'll go wild if funky feet are his fetish. (The rest of you can be freshly bathed, however.)

Long or short toenails?

This is a valid consideration. Some guys actually like the toenails to be fairly long while others go for a short, neat look. Shape is also something to mention. Round or squared? Ask him just like your manicurist asks you.

Pedicured?

Lucky you, if his response is yes, because then you get to be pampered with a pedicure before you enact his foot fetish with him. To most "foot men," the color really matters. Ask his preference. Some are wild about slutty red polish while others prefer demure clear, elegant French tip or even a dirty-girl, punk rocker black.

Do you prefer feet that are encased in shoes? If so, what kind of shoes do you like?

This is a very key question. Detail is as important to a fetishist as precise data is to a scientist. Don't assume that he wants you to don classic stiletto pumps. He may like prim and proper flats, hippie scandals or even spotless white sneakers. The color is also very important. It's not enough for him just to say sneakers. Ask him to be specific about color.

What kind of a heel?

Inquire about whether the heel should be skinny or thick,

wedge or stiletto, flat or high - and if he likes his heels high, ask how high.

What about the toe of the shoe?

He may prefer pointy toes, open toes, partially open or closed pumps. Find out his preference.

What about material?

He might like leather, snakeskin, fabric or patent leather. Remember again, color counts.

Do you prefer boots?

Some foot fetishists are actually boot fetishists in disguise. A common assumption is that boot boys enjoy long, tall crotch-high boots. Not so. Boots come in many varieties. Inquire about his particular preference. He might mention ankle boots, ones that reach the knee or thigh-high boots. The heel may be stiletto, medium height or flat. Again, it's all about personal taste.

Are you a "leg man" in addition to being a "foot man?"

You might think legs are a whole separate fetish but feet and legs generally go together. No pun intended! Some foot fetishists like to concentrate on your feet. Others prefer to venture up the leg. It's important to establish this distinction in your thorough investigation.

If you like legs, should my legs be bare or should I wear pantyhose or stockings?

Bare legs vs. stockings are a very important determination to make. Equally important is the kind of hose. Some leg guys love the neatness of pantyhose (and tearing through it!) while others abhor the one-piece look. If he's into pantyhose, remember to inquire about the color and texture. Control top? Sandal foot? Some guys prefer a tight, glossy type of hose. Others might mention opaque tights.

Do you prefer traditional stockings?

Stockings too have many subtle variations. Distinguish

between seamed or seamless. Garters, garter belts or elastic tops. Don't forget about color: black, beige, tan or another hue?

Anything else I should know about dress?

Remember, every fetishist has his own specific turn-on. Believe it or not, your guy might actually like socks or knee-hi's. He might also have some specifications about the rest of your outfit. Girdles, mini-skirts or tight clothes could complete his dream ensemble.

Enacting The Fetish

Your initial foot fetish query had more to do with your man's internal visual. Now it's important for you to understand that there are many ways to enact a foot fetish.

Some fetishists simply enjoy the look of and "making love" to your feet and legs. Others prefer to be dominated and/or "forced" to get down on their knees. Still others want to be trampled.

Your job: find out the sort of interactions that go hand in hand with his foot fetish. Here's how:

Q&A, Part 2:

Do you simply like the look of my feet?

This is the easiest scenario for you if his answer is yes. To comply, simply present him with your feet exactly the way he likes to look at them. All you need to do next is dress in the proper attire. For him, the visual is the foreplay. It's so much more than the way you dress; you are now acknowledging his fetish. You're allowing him to express feelings he's kept buried inside for so long. He can finally be truthful with you and admire what he's secretly been sneaking peeks at all along. Honesty makes all the difference. A very real part of his sexuality is being validated and accepted. Let him look...and more.

Do you want to do more than look?

If this is the case, you need to find out the kind of interaction he wants with your feet. He might simply want to get down on his knees and do basic foot worship; which generally entails kissing, licking, massaging and smelling your feet, or any combination of the above. If this is the case, let him get down on all fours and show you what he wants. Or he might want to "make love" to your feet by rubbing his penis against them and climax.

Your man could also harbor more elaborate foot fantasies, which will be covered in the next few questions.

Are you happy just to play with my feet?

This kind of foot fetishist is happy to kiss, lick, worship and adore your feet and legs. He'll instinctually know exactly how he wants to do this. After all, he's been fantasizing about it for some time. Many men like to use their tongue and lap every inch of your feet and legs, giving you a real tongue-bath. Other guys are more into toe-sucking and will perform the equivalent of oral sex on your toes.

Do you imagine foot worship to be a part of an overall Dominant/submissive scenario?

"Get on your knees!" That's a common way to begin any kind of D/s action. Foot worship is a way to create the feeling of submission. He might prefer this kind of mindset in conjunction with his established foot fetish. In it, he wants to think of you as his "Queen" or "Goddess" while he performs foot worship.

Many guys like a dose of mild domination along with their foot fetish. This requires you to take the lead and tell him what to do. Be specific and tell him what you'd like. At a loss? Tell him to suck your toes, hard, soft, and for how long. Next, have him lap the soles of your feet, etc. You get the idea.

Now you're ensured a good night of pampering and massage if that's what you so desire. Dry kisses or toe-heavy sucking? That's now your call. Taking charge gives you more control. This role might be unfamiliar to you up until now, but I'm sure you'll find it extremely empowering and a boost to your self-esteem.

Do you fantasize about being forced?

While it's true that all submissives are in a subservient role, there are two kinds of submissive mindsets:

- Some subs choose the role in order to
  please a superior.
- Others imagine being in the submissive role
  because they feel deserving of punishment
  and degradation.

Sometimes it's difficult for someone to express a desire that feels shameful. It's hard to admit and allow yourself to openly participate in an act that you intellectually conceive of as being "wrong." In this case, our brains cleverly find a solution by erotizing humiliation. Foot worship is deemed as a punishment that your man is made to do at your command. It isn't something he *wants* to do, but rather it's something he's *ordered* to do. He has no choice in the matter.

This is very healing for him. Your commands relinquish him of responsibility. You're granting him permission that ultimately morphs into a feeling of freedom. He's performing "dirty acts" that both challenge and test his limits.

When you assume the role of his Dominatrix, you'll need to tap into your authoritative persona:

- Give him specific commands.
- Ask him to describe himself as he's performing.
- Listen carefully to the words you elicit from him.
  Those are his verbally humiliating buzzwords.
  Remember these buzzwords and repeat them
  back to him when you're in domination mode.

Your man might describe himself as lowly, undeserving or dirty. Please don't be upset by hearing him describe himself in this manner. Remember, the degradations are translated as eroticism by his brain. You aren't insulting him when you use his buzzwords but rather you are reaching inside of him and helping him pull out his deeply-held secrets. In a sense, you're freeing him from himself. Saying these words desensitize and normalize his inner conflicts. You're instrumental in facilitating and validating the secret acts he's secretly erotized for years.

Do you like trampling?

Some would say that trampling is entirely different than a common foot fetish. I'm including it in this chapter because it is foot related and can sometimes be combined with common foot fetish play.

Trampling is much more active than the standard foot fetish. It requires you to get up and dominate him with your feet. Trampling commands that he's told to strip naked and lie flat on his tummy on the floor. You will then literally take a walk on his back. Your attitude can be dominating or playful depending on how he views the interaction.

But tread lightly before you trample. First, you'll need to find out:

- Is trampling his only fetish or does he like it combined with foot worship and/or domination?
- Does he like to be trampled with bare feet?
- Does he like to be trampled with high-heeled boots or shoes?
- If it's high-heels, find out his pain tolerance level as heels can cause a certain amount of pain and leave marks.
- Does he like to be trampled with the heel or just the sole of the shoe or boot?
- What are some of the buzzwords he likes to hear when being trampled?

Trampling For Pure Foot Fetishists

Hardcore foot fetishists like trampling because they're having direct contact with the part of the body they love best. To that end, you can walk from their buttocks to the upper part of their back. You can then raise your leg and dangle it over his face. You can even have him kiss or suck the heel of your foot and leg. This type of trampling is teasing and sensual, not violent.

Trampling For The Purpose of Humiliation

Some guys who like trampling view it as a humiliating act. It's then appropriate to call him your carpet or rug and tell him that he deserves to be stepped on. He imagines himself as someone who is lowly and beneath you, and these seemingly harsh words feed into his desires. This guy will be most likely to welcome your walking heavily upon his back or digging your heels into his skin.

Remember that not every foot fetishist likes trampling. Not every trampling fetishist wants to suck your toes. However, some like the two combined. It's up to you to ask the appropriate questions to provide a scene that is satisfying for you both.

A Sample Scene

While all of this foot worship and/or trampling is going on, it's important for you to be interactive. I've outlined a sample scene here:

- Dress according to his tastes but also in a way that makes you feel sexy.
- Remove his clothes slowly and sensuously.
- Sit in a comfortable chair and have him kneel or sit at your feet.
- Command him to worship your feet.
- Tell him what feels good to you. Part of his pleasure is giving you pleasure. For example, you might want him to bathe the soles of your feet with his tongue or suck each of your toes.
- Ask for a foot massage, light kisses or sensual caressing.
- Experiment with this often ignored part of your body and enjoy!

You'll find that your feet and legs have a sensuality all their own. Enjoy extending your sexual feelings to a region that is generally overlooked. Both of you have an opportunity to derive intense pleasure from his fetish.

Always keep in mind that if he does something that is really unpleasurable for you, it's your duty to speak up. Some people have extremely ticklish feet. If you find he's causing you any kind of discomfort, please communicate so that you can make the necessary modifications.

How To Incorporate Foot Fetishism Into Traditional Sex

Foot worship can be part of your overall foreplay. You can also get him off by allowing him to have "intercourse" with your feet or legs. How?

- Apply baby oil to your legs; or better yet, have him do this.
- Hold your legs tightly together.
- Have him slip his penis between your legs.
- Or...get him erect by letting him masturbate himself between your legs or feet. In other words he's "fucking" your feet or legs before you permit him to enter into your vagina.

In Summary

Foot fetish is one of the most common fetishes. Its origins are easy to understand but can be complex to execute mainly because of the many variations. A foot fetish is not necessarily about bare feet. Foot attire can be a large part of it and each foot fetish is extremely individualistic and varies greatly from person to person. Think of yourself as a cub reporter out to discover the specifics of your guy's foot fetish.

There are also emotional elements that need to be explored and addressed. Many foot fetishes are subject to extreme embarrassment, which adds another dimension to the play. Degradation and being "forced" to worship feet are often elements that need to be incorporated in order to assuage a foot fetishist's sense of guilt. Remember to ask open-ended questions and to keep an open mind.

Rest assured that a foot fetish is simple to satisfy. The most complex aspect is unearthing the specific details of your guy's fetish. There are as many varieties as foot fetishes as there are types of shoes.

The proper execution of your man's foot fetish can be key to boosting his self-esteem and achieving ultimate peace of mind. And isn't that a gift you'd like to give? And best of all, it doesn't cost a cent.

Chapter 16
Female Sexual Dominance

Imagine having it your way, every day, all the time. You get to decide when, where, how (and if) to have sex. A confident you has the ability to take charge and direct the scene. The bedroom is your boardroom. You and you alone hold the reins.

Be honest, you're probably shocked that your guy expressed a desire for you to take the lead when it comes to sex. Since learning of his desires, you've frantically gone online and searched for answers about what this actually entails. Still no help. You wonder what in the world he's talking about. You may feel intimidated or even intrigued.

Sexual dominance is not as mysterious as it might initially seem. Men have naturally taken on the role of sexual initiators practically since the Stone Age. But the times they are a changing.

Today, women are getting more in touch with their own innate leadership capabilities. That "take charge" aura can also be extended to the bedroom. Trust me, you'll enjoy that feeling of empowerment. Especially when you see how sexy your guy finds it to relinquish control.

So, what do you say? Are you ready to take the driver's seat and steer the sexual energy in your own bedroom?

What Do You Mean By Sexual Dominance?

Sexual dominance is all about attitude. You are the initiator and the director of the sexual interaction. You call the shots and you allow yourself to be the recipient of ultimate pleasure. You are the producer and the director of each "act" of your lovemaking session.

You'll note that this is the exact opposite of the sex education our mothers and grandmothers received. They were taught that women were supposed to wait for direction and suppress their own needs. They were even taught to deny that they had any sexual needs at all. They were instructed to do whatever their mate said. Female enjoyment was supposed to take second place to male satisfaction. If you believed the old adage that men were "kings of the castle", they were also emperors, dictators or presidents of the bedroom. Women ranked down at the bottom of the totem pole as cooks, scullery maids and wenches. Not so true anymore.

Isn't it wonderful that your man wants to give you your say in bed? Guess what? He's giving you a precious gift. Now all you have to do is learn how to take this offering and use it to the best of both your advantages.

You may already feel this power, or you may still feel more comfortable taking on a more subservient role. Either one is okay. Being sexually aggressive is something that might not come naturally to you because of the way you were brought up. But this isn't to say you can't take on a new, more evolved mindset.

There's no one way to be sexually dominant. It's all about giving yourself permission to open your horizons, be creative and allow yourself the bliss of ultimate sexual pleasure. The answers lie within. I'm going to help you dig inside so that you can explore your own sexual needs. I'll also teach you how to communicate them.

Today's society is encouraging men and women to explore all facets of our personalities. Every human being possesses qualities that are considered to be "masculine" and "feminine."

Finally it's all right for men to get in touch with their sensitive side and for women to assert themselves.

The Conflict About Being The Initiator

Many of us were brought up with the notion that sexuality is a male-dominated playground. They are the "leaders" and we are the "followers." Men are supposed to make the first move, be knowledgeable about female genitalia and instinctively know how to place their penises perfectly into our vaginas.

These are old ideas. Open up the window and let them go. The simple truth is that leadership is not gender specific. Both men and women possess sexual aggression. The problem is that most females suppress that energy. We've been raised to feel that communicating our sensual needs or being verbally specific is not "ladylike" and a turn-off to men. Actually, it's quite the opposite. Men are appreciative when women are directive. They want to please us and give us orgasms; they just need to be led to our "hot spots" and be given specific instructions on how to please.

No one's a mind reader, and no one knows your body quite like you. We don't have external genitalia like men do so we didn't touch ourselves as naturally as they did as youngsters. They, after all, have to hold their penises when they urinate while we were taught how to do a quick, ladylike dab with toilet paper. Plus, most of us were discouraged from touching ourselves "down there" if our hands happened to stray that way.

We were also treated to early, non-verbal, negative messages about our vaginas. We weren't even encouraged to say the word "vagina" but instead were given silly "pet" names to call our privates.

The implication was clear that our sexual organ was hidden, secretive and something that we just don't discuss. Most of us had no idea that we had a clitoris or that it had the ability to bring us to orgasm. In fact until fairly recently, the female orgasm was barely discussed. No wonder women have traditionally felt sexually repressed and confused.

A healthy sexual relationship is balanced. No one should have to take on one specific role all the time. The bedroom can be a freeing place that allows you to exercise all aspects of your being. Sexual dominance is one of many tools to add to your erotic toolbox. Having the ability to direct a sexual encounter adds variety to your sexual repertoire.

Sexual dominance can be used in conjunction with D/s or S/M interactions. But it can also have a life of its own. It can be employed simply as an enjoyable bedroom activity.

Sexual dominance, like any act of eroticism, is something that needs to be discussed up front with your partner. However, in this case, you run the show. Before you talk to him, you need to get in touch with exactly what you yourself want to gain from the experience.

Many Men Crave Women Who Take Charge In The Bedroom

Today's male also feels conflict. He's been taught to see women as equals. He's used to working side by side with women at the office. He knows that men and women now compete equally for top-level managerial positions and hold other high offices, like in the government, for example. It follows suit that men would expect women to be more assertive in the bedroom. Unfortunately, they are often confused and puzzled by their women's reticence to communicate her sexual needs.

Claiming the Pleasure We Deserve

The climate of the new millennium actually supports female sexuality. We are now way more comfortable taking pleasure for ourselves. However, an overall change in societal attitude takes time. Most women are still shy about self-exploration. They may allow themselves the freedom of experimenting with an electronic massage device but there's still a certain degree of taboo around touching themselves and exploring the vaginal area with their own two hands. And sadly, we're still very shy about communicating specific sexual needs to partners.

Men and women are miles apart when it comes to self-body knowledge. Guys are much more comfortable with touching their own bodies. They really and truly like their penis and testicles. Men strongly crave receiving pleasure from this part of their body that they cherish. Conversely, most women aren't comfortable with the way their vaginas look, feel and the earthy scent they emit. Is their vulva too big, too small, too puffy or too thin? They haven't got a clue that vaginas come in all shapes and sizes and that they're all beautiful.

Well, it's high time for you to get acquainted with your own vagina. Only then will you possess true sexual command in the bedroom.

Let's Masturbate

Self-love comes in all shapes and sizes too. You can use your fingers or you can buy any number of sex toys online or in upscale sex shops, many of which cater specifically to women like Come Again, in the heart of a posh Manhattan neighborhood. These days, sex toy parties are replacing Tupperware parties. Women are feeling freer to purchase and talk about vibrators, easily discussing the pros and cons of each model.

Women are also stepping up and purchasing pornography, both online and at newsstands. Many prefer online purchases because they feel they're more safe, discrete and confidential. Porn definitely expands your sexual repertoire. Everything you see in a dirty mag might not be a turn-on, but at least you can pick and choose like you do at a salad bar. With online porn, you can freely allow yourself to view stories, pictures and video clips in order to see what really gets your juices flowing. Pun intended!

Knowing your body is essential for taking charge in bed. You really need to do your research in order to be able to clearly state your own sexual needs. Masturbation is normal, natural and very relaxing. When you masturbate, take special note of where your mind goes. What images, verbiage and fantasies do you conjure up? Do you concentrate more on your clitoris or on vaginal stimulation? These are essentials when you give your man direction. If you don't know how to pleasure yourself, then how can you tell him how to do it?

Now, I'm not going to tell you *how* to do it. I'm just giving you license to do it. So, have fun and...

Share Your Research

Again, communication is the key here. Be direct in stating what you want and what you need from your man. The best way to be sexually dominant is to savor and enjoy the experience. A good rule of thumb about being sexually dominant is to gauge it with your own level of pleasure. If you're having fun, I'm willing to bet that he's having fun too. You take center stage. You're the star of your own sexual experience.

There are no rules or regulations about how to be a dominant diva in the bedroom. You're the one who knows your body. Your only mission is to be confident enough to communicate clearly and concisely so you get all your needs met.

I know that sometimes sex is difficult to discuss. If you're shy, take it slowly, step by step. Experiment with non-verbal communication. Take his hand and lead him to the place you want to be touched. Take his head and guide it to your pleasure zone. You can even guide the stroking by taking his hand in yours.

If you have a specific fantasy, go online or dig out your porn stash. Show him the pictures or stories that really turn you on. That way he gets a visual understanding of your specific turn-ons. Who knows, you might even have your own fantasies or fetishes that you'd enjoy having him enact with you. It's perfectly okay to state your needs by sharing your own adult material with him. He'll be excited to know that you have your own private sexual life too.

As women, we need to give ourselves permission to masturbate, think sexual thoughts and communicate them to our lovers. It's difficult to let go of the small-minded mores of society, however we've done it in the workplace and now it's time to take it to the bedroom.

Q&A – For Yourself:

What does sexual dominance mean to me?

Is it about taking control or is it about just allowing yourself to be indulgent. Pinpoint what you think you'd like about being in control.

How did I first become curious about this?

The concept of sexual dominance may have come from your man. He could have made the request and you want to find out what he means by "female dominance." It may even seem a little paradoxical to you that you're being dominant because he wants you to be. But even if you're doing this to please him, chances are that it will ultimately expand your horizons and serve you in a positive way. Being sexually dominant will build your self-esteem and confidence.

Sexual dominance might be a natural extension of your personality. You may be a take-charge kind of gal in your home or at the office. It would make perfect sense that you be the initiator in the bedroom. Perhaps you read an article and something in it resonated for you. But whatever the reason you're exploring this further, go with it.

Am I doing this because I truly want to or because my man made the suggestion?

Again, I know it may feel contradictory to be sexually dominant as a request from your partner. But don't fret. It's fine. This is a book to help you understand the male sexual psyche. In the process, you're getting closer to your partner—and to yourself. Even if the initial idea came from him, you still have the ability to get into the role. Think of assertive bedroom behavior as something new to "try on," like an intriguing pair of shoes. If you do your own personal research, figure out what you really enjoy. Then when you actually step into the outfit, chances are good you'll have a perfect fit.

Do I want to establish myself as the sexual dominator in the relationship or is this something I'd like when I'm in the mood?

In reality, our moods fluctuate. I think it's good to be versatile and allow for all kinds of interactions with your mate. This is something for you not only to think about but to also talk about with your partner. Even if he has expressed interest in having you take a more active role in the bedroom, he may only want that part of the time.

What can I do to make myself feel as sexy as possible?

One word: clothes. Another excuse to go shopping! Wear
bedroom ensembles that make you feel powerful yet sensual.
Again, there are no rules. It's all up to you. You might choose
to wear a bust-enhancing corset or retro girdle, a garter belt
and stockings. Or maybe you prefer something more causal
and comfortable like slinky panties and a form fitting t-shirt.
Clothing, especially lingerie, reflects you and your own
personal style.

Setting is important, too. You can play music or light a
candle. You might want the lights up high so he can see every
sensuous inch of you or keep them mysteriously dim. It's your
time and you can create whatever atmosphere feels right for you.

*If I imagine lying back and being serviced, what would I enjoy
having done to me?*

You might imagine being massaged, having your feet rubbed
or being gently kissed all over. For other women, it would be an
oral sex extravaganza. Imagine that you were paying for a sexual
experience. How would you enjoy being serviced?

*As part of being sexually dominant, would I like to add some
bondage, spanking or other S/M activities into the mix?*

This again is entirely up to you and your partner. Bondage,
spanking and other S/M activity can definitely be a part of your
sexual foreplay. Partaking in these activities would certainly
mark you as dominant. Do them if they would make you feel
sexy and if they would be enjoyable for you and your man.

Some Ideas To Help Get The Ball Rolling

Have Sex With You On Top

This may seem obvious, but many women shy away from this
position. They say they don't like being "in the spotlight" or else
they don't know what to do once they get there. This time, you
won't be relying on him to get the ball rolling, so to speak.
You're going to fuck him. You're going to control the thrusting
– the pace, rhythm and length of time.

Close your eyes and let your body take over. Move your hips in a circle and slow-dance on his penis. Grind into his pubic hair. The rule could be that he can't come until you do. And the good news is that many women climax easier in this position. If you sense he's getting close before you're ready, stop and slow it down.

Experience Your Power

Allow yourself to feel the power of your position. When you're on top, you have the ability to control the action. Rub your clitoris on his groin so you get optimal stimulation. Use his penis like it's your own private sex toy—which it is. If you get tired of thrusting and moving take a break and rub his shaft up and down along your vulva and clitoris. Do whatever you need to do to get ultimate gratification.

Tease and Please

Now is your chance to do some light bondage with soft rope, silk scarves or ties. Or you can simply order him to put his hands under his head, behind the pillow and lay still while you have your way with him. Tease him with your fingertips, tongue or a feather. Notice his reactions and find his personal hot spots. Don't forget his nipples, earlobes, the back of his neck and beneath his testicles.

Proceed with the teasing for a good long while and remember not to touch his penis. This will really drive him wild and add a new dimension to your sexuality. Remember that men are goal-oriented and are used to having their genitals touched as soon as they want, the way they want. The tease lies in making him wait and letting him get aroused by touching other non-sexual areas of his body.

Rubbing or Frottage

As part of the tease, you can rub your naked or semi-nude body against his body while he lies helplessly beneath you. It's particularly stimulating to allow your own nipples to graze his.

If you're so inclined, use his body to stimulate yourself. Rub your own genitals against his leg, chest or belly. This is commonly known as frottage.

Take a vibrator and pleasure yourself while making him even more aroused. Have some orgasms of your own while he gets hotter and hotter just watching.

Icy Hot

For an element of surprise and delight, drip candle wax onto his skin and then mix the heat with the cold shock of ice cubes. Experiment with "edge-play," which is erotically running the blade of a knife lightly over his body. His reaction will give you pleasure and power.

Smothering or Face-Sitting

Squat over his face wearing your panties. Let him smell your gorgeous perfume. You can get as sexual as you wish; or not. Order him to kiss, lick or touch you.

Smothering entails you to actually sit on his face and let him inhale your aromas. The only air he breathes comes from you. Sitting on his face is symbolic of your female supremacy. He is literally lying beneath you and is subject to your personal whims. Remember, you run the show.

Forced Cunnilingus

This is usually done within the context of an intimate D/s relationship. It's a great climax to any bondage, spanking or general Mistress/slave type of scene.

The key word here is "force". You order him to get between your legs and instruct him on how to kiss, lick and make love to your clitoris and vagina. It's really a blatant role reversal. Imagine that you've grown a penis and now he has to get on his knees and service you.

Act More Like A Man

Your guy is never reluctant to let you know that he's aroused or horny, right? Now's your chance to do the same. Women are traditionally advised to gently hint when they're in the mood for sex. We might wear something sexy, dim the lights or bring him a glass of wine. The signs are perfectly clear to us but not always to them! These indirect signals are often confusing to the male species. Men are very direct creatures. They like to be told exactly what you want and when. It's fine to say, "I'm in the mood. Wanna have sex?" It doesn't sound crude; it sounds honest. Your man should find this a welcome change and will gladly comply.

Tell Him What You Want

Maybe you want intercourse but you could also want something else. It's all right to say, "I'd like to have you eat my pussy." No guesswork involved, no beating around the bush. Now you're speaking his language. Don't tell me you've never heard him say, "Suck my dick." Politely demanding oral sex from him is the same thing. And don't stop there. If he isn't a proficient pussy eater, teach him how.

Since you've hopefully begun masturbating, you have a clear idea of what feels good. Tell him specifically what you do and don't like. Believe me, he'll feel comfortable with that. Men always complain that women expect them to be mind-readers. Unless he's particularly gifted, your guy isn't psychic and don't expect him to be. Tell him what you like and how you like it - then demand it from him!

What's In It For You?

Everything! No more second-guessing makes for a happier relationship. Direct communication gives each of you the ability to really know how to please each other. This is a sure-fire guarantee for real, honest-to-goodness bedroom satisfaction.

In Summary

Sexual dominance is an inside job. It's about feeling confident and claiming your own power. It's about feeling deserving of pleasure and learning how to communicate your needs.

Women are no longer sexually inferior. We have equal footing with men in the bedroom and in the boardroom. And once in a while, it's nice to take on the role of being superior or even a Goddess.

Chapter 17
FemDom Domestic Disciplinary Relationships

Yes, I know, this fetish is quite a mouthful. It's very complex and multifaceted besides. We can refer to them as DDRs, for short.

I'd like to begin by saying that there are some discrepancies surrounding the terminology FemDom. Some use it to describe women who spank men. Others contend that it describes a whole myriad of fetishes where women are "topping" or dominating men in a variety of ways. Still others use FemDom interchangeably with the terms S/M or B/D.

For the purposes of this book, when I refer to FemDom, I mean the relationship where women spank men and otherwise dominate them.

A FemDom Domestic Disciplinary Relationship is very much like Dominant/submissive power exchanges but with three subtle and very important differences:

Difference One
The female is always in charge. She is often referred to as the "Top".

Difference Two

Activities take place in a domestic rather than in a dungeon-type setting. Many men dream of this kind of relationship as a way of life. In this context, it's all encompassing and not for the purposes of sexual foreplay.

Difference Three

Domestic Disciplinary females do not wear leather or latex. They assert their dominance through attitude and a strict demeanor.

The Allure of DDR's

Men seek out a Domestic Disciplinary woman to set up and enforce rules and well-defined boundaries. Infractions are met with swift, ritualistic or humiliating punishments. The foundation of a Dominant/submissive (D/s) relationship is about pleasing the dominant while DDRs are based on disciplined harmony.

I'm sure you have many questions. I'll proceed by addressing some of the most common queries people have about DDRs.

What does a Domestic Disciplinary Relationship entail?

Think of a DDR not so much as a fetish but as a lifestyle. It actually incorporates one or more fetishes when partners interact.

Sometimes people use Domestic Disciplinary Relationships and D/s interchangeably. It's important to establish exactly what your man means by a DDR. Purely speaking, DDR scenarios are not Mistress/slave-oriented. Your guy is seeking out a Disciplinarian; not a fictitious Mistress or Goddess. He wants a real, flesh and blood, 24/7 Disciplinarian; you.

DDRs are commonly associated with the spanking fetish. Guys who like spanking often dream of being in what they'd refer to as a Disciplinary Relationship. They literally want to live a lifestyle where they relinquish domestic control to their partner. They want to live their lives within a well-defined set of rules and regulations.

In a DDR, when rules are broken or boundaries crossed, the punishment would be a spanking or some other spanking-related activity such as corner time, mouth-soaping or humiliation. It's important for you to establish if your man wants to be controlled or if he merely wants to engage in spanking activity on a regular basis. I'll help you discern which category he falls into with a Q&A later on in this chapter.

Domestic Disciplinary Relationship activities require you to be a maternal figure. If your guy craves a DDR, chances are good that he missed out on having a nurturing, consistent "mom" during his formative years. He may feel as though he lacked discipline and got away with too much when he was growing up. He may also feel like he didn't get the kind of care and attention all human beings require.

Subconsciously, this deficit turned into a core fantasy with sexual undertones. He's not looking for a mom per se, but he is seeking out someone to keep him in line. He feels comfortable, safe and loved with an authoritative woman who is agreeable with running the household and all other aspects of his life. It doesn't mean your partner is a sissy or that he's "less than a man." But it does mean he needs some special attention that you as his woman can provide.

Pros and Cons of the DDR

The idea of taking charge may not come easy to you. You may have been brought up to believe in traditional male/female roles. Now you learn that your guy is actually driven by the concept of having you take the reins. This can feel pretty overwhelming and confusing. It might also feel like it's too much for you to undertake. If this is the case, you need to be heard and your guy must understand that he's asking too much of you.

However, I do suggest you try the role on for size so to speak. Test-drive it for short periods of time, like you would a car you're not sure you want to buy. Play the role for an hour, then look back and reexamine your feelings.

Perhaps you don't relate to feelings of power because you haven't acknowledged that part of yourself. Often these feelings lay dormant like muscles that need to be exercised in order to develop. You might actually find being the Top (or Dominant) a refreshing change of pace.

To get yourself psyched to play this role:

- Ask your man a slew of questions.
- Let him guide you in the role at first.
- Follow a script.
- Do your best to act the part even if you don't necessarily relate.
- Try it several times and don't give up.

With practice, there's a good chance you'll start to feel - and "own" - your inner power.

On the other hand, you just might be a woman who's always felt like she's in charge. Then this is the opportunity you've been waiting for. To you, it feels wonderful to have your inner feelings of power acknowledged. Some women take to the "top" role like a duck to water. Your guy might have subconsciously chosen you because you exhibited the traits of a take-charge woman. Now you just need to educate yourself and see what will and won't work in your relationship.

The education process is something you both have to be dedicated to fulfilling. You can't just start a DDR and make a total change overnight. It's a gradual transformation. Boundaries need to be introduced slowly but surely. Ultimately you both need to be aware that you're adults and should recognize human adult equality even if you have set up some unconventional rules you choose to live by.

Healthy Disciplinary Relationships

A true Domestic Disciplinary Relationship is unique to every couple. In reality few people truly live this kind of lifestyle all the time. Many have tried but in the end it's too demanding for one person. I've found that the healthiest relationships are ones where couples have the ability to express their sexuality and play out different roles.

If you're with a man who enjoys the idea of DDRs:

- Enjoy it in the way that it feels right for you.
- Take this as an opportunity to learn to express your own needs, wants and opinions.

- Revel in the feeling of empowerment.
- Work on your own ability to communicate.
- Don't feel obligated to be in role all the time.
- Set aside definitive times to play out the roles.

Some couples find that they naturally fall into a specific role. Other couples find that moods, needs and desires change over time and thus, dictate their roles. A successful DDR requires that you and your partner constantly monitor your relationship. Talk about things that are working well in addition to aspects that need improvement. It's important for you both to be gentle with yourselves and allow for mishaps. After all, you're trying out a revolutionary, non-traditional lifestyle. Not only is one person in charge but that same person also has to come up with creative consequences for misbehavior. This is not an easy task but can be a fun and challenging one.

I've found that the most successful, fresh and enjoyable DDRs are those that are done on a part-time basis. Designate one day each month to be Domestic Disciplinary Relationships Day. See how it fits into your own personality and try enacting some of the fantasies he's been secretly storing up for years.

Here are some important questions to ask before you begin:

Q&A:

What does the term Domestic Disciplinary Relationship mean to you?

Have him describe how he envisions you as the Top. Listen for key phrases such as, "Living a Disciplinary Relationship lifestyle" versus "Playing every now and again." Also note the kinds of boundaries he's looking to establish.

- Does he want you to order him to do household chores?
- Does he want you to force him to get organized?
- Does he want you to help him focus more on work?

Also take note of the kind of punishment he's seeking. Some guys who identify with Domestic Disciplinary Relationships are spanking oriented only. Others like different kinds of punishment including smothering, forced feminization and corner time.

When you fantasize about DDRs what images come to mind? Listen carefully to determine where he imagines the activities taking place. Is this strictly bedroom foreplay or does he see this more as a consistent way of life? Does he talk about taking this outside the bedroom and the two of you being in your roles for long periods of time? What aspects of his life does he want to turn over to you?

What kind of attitude does he have in the DDR?

Some guys like to be age regressive and tap into the bratty, sullen kid part of their personality. They want to challenge you and see what it takes to rile you up. Others enjoy taking on a more laid-back approach. They're the guys who often have high-pressure positions at work and find it relaxing and healing to come home to a take-charge woman. As one client so aptly phrased it, "Sometimes you just want someone else to do the driving."

Are you looking for a Disciplinary Relationships "lifestyle"? This needs to be well defined. Some men fantasize about having a DDR all the time, but as I mentioned earlier, this is very unrealistic. Your guy may fantasize about having to obey you— until the time he actually has to acquiesce to something that goes against his own desires. At that moment he may realize that he's not so agreeable or subservient after all. In time, he'll realize that a masturbatory fantasy is not something he wants put into practice 24/7.

If you do want to live a DDR lifestyle, what responsibilities are you willing to give up and let me handle?

Don't let him get away with talking in generalities! Have him be painstakingly specific so you can decide if you'd be comfortable with this kind of role. Sometimes a DDR might be as simple as having the female establish certain guidelines such as bed time, computer time or deciding social activities. Other DDRs encompass total female control including financial, household and long-term planning.

If this DDR exchange is only partial, tell me how you envision it working within our present living situation?

This allows for both of you to figure out where and if you're really going to have non-debatable decision-making. When the subject is discussed rationally, most couples realize it's never practical for one person to relinquish power in a long-term relationship. As your discussion unfolds, you'll probably agree that this, like any fetish, comes under the realm of an erotic turn-on. From that vantage point, you can discuss the specifics of incorporating some DDR play into your existing sexual repertoire.

What kind of punishment is exciting for you?

To most, the idea of punishment is what makes the lifestyle exciting. You set the rules and he's held accountable for his actions. Some fantasize about spankings, corner time, forced enemas, etc.

To illustrate this point, permit me to share with you the story of one fellow I know. "Jake" admits that he's terribly disorganized and messy. Left to his own devices, he procrastinates and creates internal stress because his chores pile up. When Jake and his wife entered into a DDR agreement, she took charge of his "To Do" list. Immediately, Jake felt better knowing he'd be held accountable for his actions. Cleaning the garage, paying the bills and doing paperwork became more fun under the threat of a spanking. His wife obliged his spanking proclivities either way but the intensity and type of spanking was commensurate with his performance.

What are some punishments you fantasize getting from me?

Common DDR-type punishments include corporal punishment, mouth-soaping, corner timer and enemas. Other disciplinary tactics take a more sexually-humiliating stance such as face-sitting and smothering, him naked and you clothed (or CFNM, an acronym for Clothed Female/Naked Male), dildo training, panty wearing, infantilism and forced bi.

Are you willing to do this on a part-time basis?

Explain that you feel this is the most practical, healthy way to approach a DDR. This is also your chance to express your own reservations and doubts if you have them.

How can we implement this DDR a little at a time?
Brainstorm about the way it can fit into your own unique relationship

If you had your way, how much or how little would we be playing?
By listening closely to his response, you'll get a good idea of how important the DDR way of life is to him. You can also express what you feel will work for you. Remember that everything is negotiable in a good, loving, healthy relationship.

Please get more detailed about the punishment aspect and how you imagine me carrying them out.
Here's a brief description of some of the most commonly-requested DDR punishments to help you understand them and ask him more questions about them.

Clothed Female/Naked Male – CFNM
This dichotomy expresses the fundamental makeup of a DDR. Some couples do this as a matter of course when they're in DDR mode. Another twist on this concept is to have him be completely naked but don a pair of your panties. Both ways represent your influence and control.

Corner Time
Some men find corner time to be very healing and meditative. Ordering lengthy corner time is a practical solution for a stressed-out guy on the go. You're doing him a service by giving him an opportunity to slow down and think about his life.

Corner Time is a good way to foster some reflection and can be as effective as meditation. Remember to provide him with positive rather than negative affirmations for reflection while he's standing in the corner.

Corporal Punishment

This is the core of DDRs. Women spank their men in order to punish or teach a real or imaginary lesson he'll never forget.

Spankings are generally administered over your knee while you sit in a straight-backed chair, on the couch or at the edge of your bed. Allow your hand to be relaxed and mold around the lower part of the buttocks region that connects to his thigh. Your arm should also be relaxed as you swing and allow your wrist to provide the force of each well placed smack.

Begin over his clothing and work your way down to his underpants then to his bare-bottom. Spank so that you get a clapping sound with your slightly cupped hand. Go back and forth from cheek to cheek. Vary the speed and intensity of the smacks. The very act of lying over your knee is demeaning and effective for changing an "uppity" attitude.

When your hand gets tired or if you want to intensify the punishment, use a wooden spoon or hairbrush that has a smooth underside. Small paddles fashioned from wood or leather are also good implements.

Bent-over paddlings or canings are synonymous with school-style discipline. You can easily capture these scenes in the comfort of your own home. Have him bend over the couch, chair or crouch on the bed, and proceed as described above.

Strappings also conjure up domestic discipline-type memories. Use a leather belt and administer these in the bedroom. Have him lie on his tummy and prop up his bottom with three or four pillows. Double the belt and use your wrist to make the belt snap. Have him keep his legs together so you don't accidentally hit his testicles, which can cause serious damage.

For more on corporal punishment, refer to the "Spanking" chapter.

Dildo Training

DDRs often use strap-on dildos as a way to demonstrate your power and belittle a tough guy. I predict that you'll enjoy the role reversal and feel wonderfully assertive as you literally take on the masculine role. Talk this punishment over with him extensively before you engage in it to determine how much he can take physically.

Purchasing the correct size dildo is important. You can make it part of the punishment to have him buy a dildo that he feels he can handle. Insist that he buy a small, medium and larger size dildo. Assist with the shopping either online or at your local adult bookstore. Again, having to go to the store is another way to assert your power. Don't forget to purchase a tube of water-solvent lubricant with your array of dildos.

Strap it on and proceed to punish.

Enemas

This is a time-honored punishment with the intent of providing the transgressor with a purge of intense wrongdoings. Some people have an enema fetish and love the feel of being cleaned out. Enemas can also be incorporated into a DDR scene. Enemas as a means of punishment are very embarrassing, but they can also be very nurturing. Find out what kind of feelings the idea of receiving an enema evokes in him before you begin.

I encourage you to research before actually administering an enema. Start with something simple like a disposable Fleet-type enema before moving on to more hardcore bags.

Sometimes enemas are administered over the knee in conjunction with a spanking. Tell him to hold the water in place until he's allowed to expel.

For more, consult this book's corresponding chapter, "Enemas."

Face-Sitting or Smothering

This is a punishment that asserts your own physical dominance. As you sit on his face, he is literally beneath your bottom and can only breathe the air you permit him to. It's a very humbling position, which may mentally fit into his picture of DDR living. I discuss face-sitting and smothering in greater detail in the chapter which discusses *Ass and Anal Play*.

Forced-Bi

As you and your man get into the DDR lifestyle, you might connect with other like-minded couples. At these events, many of the punishments described will be carried out in public. Again, it's very humbling for your guy to be punished publicly. You may have been using a dildo on him in private. Presumably, you've taught him how to lick it and service "your cock", and have inserted it anally. Imagine his mortification by having the "real thing". Forced Bi is a strong sexual fetish that has DDR origins. This is something he may communicate wanting to explore during your investigation. If so, it's your choice as the Top whether or not you want to "force" him to partake in a bisexual encounter. For more, refer to the Forced-Bi section in the Humiliation chapter.

Infantilism

Diaper-wearing is another way to humiliate and punish. It's particularly effective for men who are argumentative or irrational. If he acts like a baby, treat him like one. Make him wear diapers for a designated period of time. If you're in a particularly wicked mood, feed him baby bottles filled with the liquid of your choice. Force him to drink until he has no choice but to wet his diaper. Then punish him for wetting it.

Mouth-Soaping

This is a good solution for the foul mouthed "bad boy." Use plain soaps with no added fragrance. Ivory is a good one to choose. Have him bite the soap and keep it in his mouth for a certain length of time. Equally effective is brushing his teeth with the bar of soap.

Public Humiliation

This is about taking your DDR roles outside the house. Public humiliation involves making him do subtle things that only the two of you know about. For example, you can have him buy his own punishment devices such as butt plugs, hairbrushes, straps, etc. Make him wear girly clothing underneath jeans when he goes shopping. These are all symbolic ways to remind him who's boss. It gives him pleasure to know that you're exerting control even if you're not physically with him. Those frilly panties are ever-present whether or not you are!

Ongoing Communication About Disciplinary Relationships

He may have told you about the activities described above when you did your initial investigation. If so, this is when you would have discovered that he has a true fetish for spanking, infantilism, cross-dressing, forced bi, etc. DDRs are ongoing and progress as you become more confident in your role. The interactions may start and end with spanking if this is his major fetish. However, as time goes on and more trust is established, you may add other activities into the mix. Remember to always keep the lines of communication open and do what is enjoyable for the two of you.

Also remember to have non-verbal signals when trying out new behaviors. A scene or encounter must stop immediately if either of you feel uncomfortable or wants to back down. True, the fantasy is about being pushed, but the reality is that as adult human beings we are allowed to change our minds.

In Summary

Domestic Disciplinary Relationships encompasses a wide variety of activities. Many of these are specific fetishes that are enjoyed in a singular fashion. The DDR guy is generally open to a range of disciplines initiated by you, his proclaimed Disciplinarian.

In order to keep things fresh and safe, the lines of communication must remain open and active. Dig into his imagination and bring his DDR fantasy to life in a way that feels enjoyable and liberating for you as well as for him. Investigate the myriad of Web sites that offer tips and easy-to-use gadgets to enhance your play. And by all means, flip around to different sections of this book to learn more about other fetishes which might overlap in the DDR, including Spanking and Humiliation.

In fact, most of the punishments mentioned here have a separate chapter that deals with the particular fetish exclusively. For further information, read the chapters that pertain to your relationship. For starters, read the corresponding chapters on *Spanking, Adult Babies and Infantilism, Humiliation, Forced Bi* and *Enemas*.

Happy Playing!

Chapter 18
Humiliation

Imagine getting turned on by the thought of being verbally or physically ridiculed. Can you visualize anyone getting aroused by degradation? Believe it or not, the idea of being forced into embarrassing and compromising situations stimulates many guys, including yours. It's really not so difficult to understand, though. Similar to extreme sports, people who have this fetish view humiliation as a challenge and a way to push limits.

Submissive males like yours interpret humiliation as an expression of their devotion. They'll do anything, even abhorrent acts, to please their dominant partner. They see humiliation as a sacrificial gesture.

Even though your guy mentioned humiliation as a sexual trigger, be aware that humiliation varies greatly from individual to individual. Everybody has their own personal preference. You'll need to ask many questions in order to discover his unique triggers. When your man says he wants to be humiliated, he might be talking about verbal phrases or physical acts; like being forced to do something he would never do in real life. The idea of being humiliated happens when he's feeling sexual.

Most women are extremely puzzled by this particular fetish but when you consider the etiology, or the study of causation, of fetishes, you'll see that this one is easy to grasp. You've got to remember that sexual fetishism is strongly linked to anxiety or emotional trauma. This fetish develops almost accidentally because it's coupled with early experiences of feeling helpless. Humiliation is very much about giving up control to the point that performing questionable acts or hearing derogatory phrases is arousing.

As a quick example I'll tell you a story about a client of mine who liked verbal humiliation:

Kevin distinctly remembers his first nocturnal emission during a powerful dream at age eight. In this dream, there were many little boys going down a factory conveyor belt. They were all stark naked. There were a number of women along the belt watching, pointing and laughing at these nude boys who were obviously objectified and seen as commodities.

Upon further exploration, 50-year-old Kevin also recalls being taunted and teased by neighborhood girls about the same time he had the dream. Thus, little boy Kevin used this dream as a way of soothing himself from the teasing. He saw himself more as a dissociated product. So, in effect, he wasn't the subject of ridicule. Instead, the women found the "object" to be so amusing, not him. For Kevin, this calming dream and the resultant subconscious emission became forever linked to a feeling of sexual arousal.

You're probably wondering what my client did about his feelings of being aroused by humiliation. In real life, he's a highly-successful businessman. His inner sexuality doesn't match his lifestyle or even the way he feels about himself. Kevin's self-esteem is actually at a very healthy level. The way he deals with these "less than" feelings is by acknowledging them and accepting them. He feels fine indulging his thoughts during masturbation and even during sex. (Remember, what a person thinks about during sexual encounters is their own private business.) On occasion, "Kevin" visits a trained Dominatrix who is understanding and knowledgeable about sexual humiliation. He finds these encounters extremely healing because they reinforce the idea that sexual humiliation is a fantasy and not the reality of his day-to-day life.

Finding Out More About Your Man and Humiliation

Humiliation is a broad term. Learning more about your man's specific interest requires that you ask a series of open-ended questions and allow yourself to gather all the facts so you can help facilitate his fantasy. Remember to listen with an open mind and empathetic ears.

Also remind yourself that this is only a fantasy. You can participate as much or as little as you feel comfortable. With knowledge comes power. Even if you find his fantasy difficult to carry out in real life, often just talking about the fetish is all it takes to drive him over the edge erotically speaking.

Q&A:

What does humiliation mean to you?

This is the most important question of all. Everyone has a different definition of this word because it expresses such an intense feeling.

By humiliation does he mean that;

- He likes to be embarrassed?
- Taunted?
- Teased?
- Made to perform degrading acts?
- Dressed?
- Have you do specific things to him?

These are all part of his humiliation mindset. You need to understand exactly what humiliation means to him in order to deliver and master the details.

Is the humiliation physical or verbal?

Often verbal humiliation is done within the context of fetishes like cross-dressing and foot worship. When he's in fetish mode, he enjoys being called certain names while forced to do other acts.

Sometimes the humiliation is physical. For example, your man might like the concept of being forced to strip naked. When he's nude he might want you to comment on the inadequate size of his penis. He might also like to be spanked or whipped. The point of the nudity is the connection between being out of control and the feeling of powerlessness. To him, nudity is viewed as vulnerability.

What are some of your buzzwords connected to humiliation?

Everyone has their own words that stimulate arousal. Some common humiliation buzzwords are:

>pantywaist
>slut
>whore
>pansy
>human garbage
>tiny dick
>inadequate penis
>cum receptacle

Again, a buzzword is a highly personal preference and something you'll have to ask him about directly.

Is humiliation connected with another fetish?

Generally speaking, it is. Many men who like to worship feet, the buttocks, cross-dress, perform homosexual acts, drink urine or eat excrement, also like to be forced to do these acts. When they're commanded to do these acts, they propose to dislike it or find it abhorrent. It then becomes humiliation. See the connection?

I've addressed forced foot worship and forced cross-dressing in the "Feet" and "Cross-Dressing" chapters respectively, so you can cross-reference them there. Other humiliating acts will be covered here.

Do you enjoy being mocked for having a small penis?

It's not surprising to hear that men are very "size conscious". It's equivalent to the way we compare ourselves to other women or the way guys might sneak peeks at the urinal. What may be surprising to you is the fact that your guy gets turned on by hearing that his penis doesn't "measure up". This fetish is one that has to do with demasculinization. It's generally a verbal kind of fantasy.

Find out what he wants to hear. Usually, it has to do with your telling him that his size is inadequate and you'd prefer his having a bigger organ. You can point to it, laugh at its size and talk about how you like large penises. This fantasy calls upon your ability to verbalize and capture the buzzwords he wants to hear, even negative ones.

Do you fantasize about cuckolding?

Remember that word "cuckolding" from Shakespeare and Chaucer? The cuckold fantasy is closely related to the small penis fantasy. It has to do with a man getting turned on by the idea of his woman being with another man. At the core of the fantasy is the concept that he is unworthy and not well-endowed enough for his woman; that's why she's cheating on him. Again, this fantasy is something that would be fulfilled verbally. Most guys with cuckold fantasies don't really want their woman to be with another man. It's all about the idea of being put down and devalued. It's a way of dealing with inner psychic pain, insecurity or inferiority.

Verbalizing and exaggerating negative feelings are actually a healthy way to cope. It's like putting these unhelpful ideas in a box and storing them away. The humiliation is his way of acknowledging the feelings but not letting them interfere with his present day self-esteem. It's actually a brilliant way to deal with ingrained but unrealistic feelings of inadequacy!

Ever thought about having to suck on a tampon?

Yes, that's a humiliation some guys think about. Tampons can also be used as a butt plug or as part of a forced feminization session. He is now a girl so he has to insert a tampon to symbolize his femininity.

Do you imagine the humiliation happening privately or in public?

As we've discussed, many men find the idea of public humiliation to be extremely exciting. They see being told to strip naked in front of one or more women as being highly stimulating. They view being told to dress up in a maid's outfit and serve food to an all female dinner party to be very embarrassing but thrilling. You're on a quest to discover what turns your man on, so pointed questions like this one are the best way to get the answers that will help the two of you realize his fantasies.

Is your desire something you truly want to act upon or is it a fantasy that you'd just like to hear about?

The idea of storytelling and talking about an act is something you need to fully understand and integrate into his fantasy realization. Sometimes a fantasy is really just that: a fantasy. It's highly arousing to think about, read about or hear about a fantasy. However, it might not be something he actually wants to happen.

For example, many people fantasize about getting an extremely hard whipping. But when they finally get a chance to receive one, they feel one stroke of the whip and it's done. Their fantasy outweighed the reality of their distaste for pain.

Sometimes acknowledging and hearing about a strong turn-on is all it takes for a person to get gratification. Accepting your man's fantasy means that you accept him. Once you find out about it, bring it up in the bedroom while you're masturbating him or making love to him. This kind of verbal expression will bring you closer than you could ever imagine. It's the real key to ensuring that he never strays.

If his humiliation fantasy ever includes another woman (and the two of you agree about this aspect of it), you'll be the one to make the arrangements because you and only you will understand what he really needs.

Humiliation within the Context of a D/s Scene

The common depiction of a Mistress/slave relationship usually shows a male being degraded with name-calling, wearing a dog collar and being treated like an animal. This is an incorrect depiction usually derived from someone who doesn't understand the complexities of true Dominant/submissive interaction.

While it is indeed a fact that humiliation can be a part of a D/s scene, it's not always a necessity. It should only be incorporated into the scene if your guy likes humiliation. Never assume that he wants to be degraded. Only use humiliation if this is a part of his own sexual arousal. Submissives who are not into verbal or physical humiliation will take great offense if you naturally employ this technique without checking it out first. Humiliation is appropriate only if it's something he wants to experience.

You'll know if, when and how to use embarrassment by asking the correct questions in your investigation. Simply discovering that he likes to be humiliated is not enough. By asking the above open-ended questions, you'll know if he fantasizes about being humiliated verbally or physically.

Verbal humiliation involves name-calling, criticism about small penis size and cuckolding. A woman that I know, a real sweetheart, once told me that all she ever learned about verbal humiliation, she learned from her mother, a very domineering, critical woman. Though she had a difficult time at first saying the kinds of hurtful things that her man found arousing, all she had to do was summon the spirit of her verbally-abusive mother and she became a bitch on wheels.

Physical humiliation requires that you "force" him into his fetish by, for example:

- making him wear female garments
- worshiping parts of your body
- making him perform with another guy
- or he might have a few ideas of his own

Next, I'll discuss some of the more common fetishes which often go hand in hand with humiliation. Many of these sub-categories are all discussed in their respective chapters but I also wanted to provide a small bit of information here.

<u>Noteworthy Fetishes Directly Connected to Humiliation</u>

Forced Ass Worship, Cross-Dressing and Foot Fetishes
The idea is that you're initiating the very act he probably wants to do anyway. But the trick is that when he's commanded, he loses control and ultimately this gives him more freedom to participate. Conversely, sometimes the "forcing" is about pushing limits. There's a thrill connected to being tested and seeing how far one can go. It's very similar to TV shows which make contestants eat live bugs or perform daredevil stunts to test their limits.

Forced-Bi
Many mistake this fantasy as an excuse for the person to do something they really want to do: engage in same-sex acts. The owner of this fantasy is usually seen as someone who wants to experiment but doesn't have the guts. Not true.

For many men, the idea of a forced bisexual act is directly connected to extreme embarrassment and is considered the ultimate display of humbleness and subjugation. The fantasy revolves around being made to do something that is highly distasteful and thus, an extreme punishment. It's often coupled with some form of Fem/Dom role-play and domestic discipline. It's viewed as real, hardcore degradation.

Many guys find the concept of forced bisexual much more arousing than the actuality of it. This is something you might want to use as a verbal fantasy story, especially in the beginning. There are many DVDs that cater to this fetish. I suggest you watch them together and see what he likes. Then see what happens.

One easy way to engage in this fantasy is to buy a strap-on dildo:

- Take it for a test-drive.
- Pretend it's your penis.
- School him in the intricacies of how to lick and suck it.
- Use the buzzwords that turn him on.
- Make him perform the acts he imagines in his fantasies.
- This includes licking, sucking and possibly even deep-throating.

Your guy may even imagine being penetrated. If so, you'll need to go slow and give yourself time to learn how to do it forcefully without hurting him. The two of you will have to figure out the logistics if this is indeed something you both want to pursue.

If his bisexual desires continue over time, you might consider doing it for real. You'll have to do extensive research to find the proper venue and partner. Large cities generally have a number of gay clubs and adult-oriented newspapers even have ads placed by professionals who feed into this particular fantasy.

However, this is one of those fantasies that might not ever turn into a reality. It is, however, something you should be aware of and at least acknowledge. Again, it doesn't mean your guy is gay or even bisexual. An act he finds repugnant might be the way he chooses to express his humiliation fantasies.

Cuckolding

This is another of those fetishes many women find difficult to grasp. We generally think of our men as being pretty possessive. Why in the world would he want to imagine us being with another guy?

Think about it. This intricate fantasy enables him to both have control and lose control. He has the ability to "give away" his prized possession and at the same time, watch her with another guy. It ties into feelings of power and inadequacy all at once.

It's definitely a humiliating idea to imagine that one isn't good enough for their partner. The stimulation he feels ties into the emotion of embarrassment and being helpless. There's also a voyeuristic quality of watching you with another man, of being able to stand back and appreciate the depth of your pleasure.

Excrement

Brown showers are again something that can be done as a sign of real commitment between a Mistress and slave. It can also be done or talked about as a highly demoralizing experience. You never have to actually do this if you don't want to but since it's his fantasy, it's important that you acknowledge it and talk about it.

If you ever do want to try, proceed slowly. Again, remember that the actuality may not be as exciting as the fantasy.

One good tip: clean yourself out first with a Fleet enema before indulging in an excrement fantasy. You can then have him lay in the bathtub naked wearing a surgical mask. Give yourself a second enema and expel. Mostly water will come out this time so it won't be too messy, but it should be enough to satisfy his fantasy. Coupled with the buzzwords he likes and the attitude he finds stimulating, your guy will be a happy camper.

Farting

Sitting on his face and passing gas is discussed in the *Ass and Anal Play* chapter. It's included here because sometimes farts are seen within the context of humiliation. If this is your man's "thing", he probably wants to hear that he's "not good enough" to breathe oxygen and he just "deserves" to breathe the gas that you emit.

Public Humiliation

Some people have a bit of an exhibitionist in them and like the idea of being humiliated in public. That's why so many attend S/M "play parties". Here, the couple does their private thing in a room in front of others. The bondage and whipping activities generally performed in private are done in front of other people. Usually, both the male and the female are the exhibitionists in this case.

What if a little bit of danger or the fear of getting caught turns him on? Again, you'll have to figure out what's going on in his head and what works for you, but sometimes a bit of subtle outside play is fun. If he's into dressing, have him wear girlie panties under his clothing and take him out to a fancy restaurant. He'll enjoy the feeling of silk against his bottom while sitting there. Then imagine his despair/delight if he eventually has to use the men's room!

Wearing some kind of jewelry or symbol is often used in D/s play. You can have him wear a piece of jewelry like a gold chain which resembles a collar but only the two of you will know it's true significance; which is that he's yours, that you own him.

Or you can command him to rub your feet at a party or at an S/M event. In a sense, he's doing something that turns him on but only the two of you will get the meaning.

Water Sports

No, it doesn't imply swimming or diving; it involves urine. Plain and simple, some guys fantasize about being urinated on. One term you may have heard for this is "golden showers".

Find out exactly what your man's fantasy is and then do as much (or as little!) as you feel comfortable. You might find this incredibly liberating or incredibly embarrassing. It depends on your POV.

Before doing anything, though, you need to know if your man sees being urinated on as a sign of degradation or if this is something he wants to do as a symbol of his love and devotion. Many submissive/slaves want to drink urine in order to have the Mistress "inside" them. In this case, the urine is not humiliating, but a gift.

Water sports are considered an act of humiliation when they're done as punishment or done as a forced act. For example:

Your man does something that you find distasteful like leaving the toilet seat up. As punishment, you can...

- Urinate on his face and turn him into your human toilet.
- Have him use his tongue and clean you like toilet tissue.

It's the attitude which makes this humiliating. Water sports is a fetish that can be considered humiliating depending on the context and how it is perceived by the person who's being urinated upon. Again, you'll have to find out if this is a humiliating or a rewarding activity for your guy, and then take it from there.

Here's another daring idea:

If he likes "golden showers", have him take you to a fancy restaurant and have him order steak. Next, go in the restroom and pee into a tiny cup you've concealed in your purse. Discretely pour your urine over his steak and make him eat it. I know this is a very bold thing to do but if your man is a guy who likes humiliation and urine, you'll be providing him with a profoundly exciting experience.

In Summary

Humiliation is a broad term that can encompass many fetishes. Your job: find out what "humiliation" means to him. It may be key words or phrases that he finds stimulating. It may also be acts he's "forced" into doing—worshipping your feet, armpits, ass or other body parts.

Humiliation can be used in conjunction with a general D/s scene, foot fetish, cross-dressing, bisexuality and toilet fetishes.

Despite the way it seems on the surface, humiliation is actually a healthy way to work through deeply ingrained, low self-esteem. The fantasies and the accompanying verbal humiliation are so extreme that it enables one to get in touch with the absurdity of the feeling. Finally, he connects to the fact that he's not such a "worm", "slut" or "garbage" after all. Hearing the words and doing the acts allow him to express, get in touch with and then release the feelings. It also desensitizes potentially painful and damaging thoughts. Humiliation is an extreme form of psychodrama. Ultimately, it can be very therapeutic and healing.

Chapter 19
Leather, Latex, Lingerie
and Other Articles of Clothing

You may have just learned that your guy has a fixation for women dressed in leather, latex, silk or fur. Those are the four materials most commonly connected with the "object" form of fetish behavior. Sometimes the fetish is about the *look* of the item and the woman who's adorned in the clothing. Other fetishists like to experience the feel of the clothing by touching you or by wearing the clothing themselves.

This is a relatively easy fetish for you to share; and enjoy. It may only require you to do something as simple and sexy as donning a pair of leather gloves and masturbating him to orgasm. However, the dress aspect of your guy's fetish may also be a part of a more intricate Dominant/submissive scenario. If this is the case, you'd need to dress up and take part in some kind of dungeon scene that incorporates flogging, bondage, nipple or cock torture, whichever his preference.

So, as you can see, material fetishes can be simple but they can also be intricate. When you do your homework, you can fully understand, accept and bring your man's fetish to life.

First, you need to find out if he prefers leather, latex or some other type of material like rubber, perhaps. Although these fetishes do overlap, I'm going to give you some specific questions to help you understand each fetish.

Q&A - Leather:

What do you like about leather?

He may tell you that he likes to see women dressed in leather. Plain and simple. Or he may also mention that he likes the way leather feels and/or smells. Likewise, the leather could only be part of an overall D/s or S/M scene. E.g. he imagines his "Top" (that would be you…the Top, the Dominant, the Mistress) exquisitely encased in leather clothing. She would then carry out specific acts related to a particular scenario he fantasizes about.

Is it leather in general or some specific leather article of clothing that turns you on?

Some leather fetishists love all things leather. Others are more precise in their preference for a particular type of clothing or object.

It could be thigh-high leather boots or stiletto heels. It might also be leather pants, a skirt, vest, panties, bra or gloves. Leather objects include floggers, restraints, cock and ball devices, belts, and so on.

Do you like to wear leather too?

Some fetishists get a thrill from wearing leather themselves with or without you thrown into the mix. If he enjoys the feel of leather against his skin, find out the article of clothing he likes wearing. It may be leather underwear, pants, jacket or a vest. Even if he already has the item of his desire, it would be a nice gesture of support and acceptance if you bought one for him.

What do you like about leather?

Many leather fetishists go wild for the aroma of leather, while others enjoy the tactile feel. Some have a special penchant for soft, supple or thick leather fabric. Discover his personal likes.

What does the leather ensemble represent to you?

Leather "themes" include the traditional Dominatrix, Biker Chick or sensuous, leather Goddess. While some guys like sexy leather lingerie, there are other leather fetishists who prefer a realistic, utilitarian touch to their leather. Those leather guys get excited when they see the kind of leather garb worn in cold climates. Meaning they prefer jackets as opposed to corsets. They want to see thick leather coats, motorcycle boots, gloves and hats. They enjoy seeing items women might wear in their day to day lives rather than leather for costuming purposes.

Is the sensation created by leather important to you?

Sometimes the fetish is really about the feel of the material against bare skin. If so, your man may request that you wear leather gloves and sexily stroke various parts of his body. Likewise, he may crave the feel of tight leather restraints or the sting of a leather flogger. Find out his preference.

Do you fancy being hooded or gagged?

This is another way he can have a relationship with leather. A tight leather hood pushes the scent of leather up his nose and the feel of leather against his face. The leather gag allows him to taste the leather. What is your guy's "thing"?

Do you enjoy leather body worship?

The leather fetish goes far beyond the visual. Lots of guys want you to wear leather so that they can, in essence, have sexual contact with their woman in leather. Ask which sense is strongest for him.

Are you turned on by the smell of leather?

Never forget that scent is an aphrodisiac. Leather has a distinctive, sensual aroma. If it's the smell of leather that sends him over the moon, you'll definitely want to have him worship you by rubbing his face against your leather-clad body...and more.

How about the taste of leather?

If he likes the smell, chances are good he'll also like the taste of leather. Include smelling and licking when you order him to worship your leather-encased feet or buttocks.

What kind of leather?

Leather comes in many varieties and colors, from creamy smooth to thick and non-pliable, from black to purple to snow white. Find out his favorite brands or places to shop. If he's a real leather fetishist, he'll be able to supply you with very specific details.

What do you want to do to me while I'm dressed in leather?

Body worship is only one activity associated with wearing leather. Your leather outfit may also be paired with other dungeon activities.

Q&A - Latex and Rubber:

Latex is actually a thin type of rubber, so it technically falls under the category of "rubber fetish". The questions for leather can also be applied to your investigation of latex. However, I've added a few here which are specific to latex and rubber.

Is your preference for latex or rubber?

He'll be able to tell you exactly what kind of material he likes. Rubber can actually encompass old-fashioned, everyday, non-sexy items like rubber bathing caps or rain boots. But they're sexy to him!

Latex is generally thinner, tighter and more associated with fetishistic activity than rubber is. Common latex items for gals include skintight boots, gloves, skirts, pants, dresses, cat suits, bras, stockings and panties. For men, latex garments are generally pants, vests, socks and underwear.

Are we both going to wear latex? If so, what will we do when we're wearing it?

Many latex/rubber fetishists like to don their outfits and

actually engage in some kind of sexual activity. They find it exciting to oil up the latex and rub against each other.

Sometimes couples like to hit the town wearing their outfits. Leather and Latex are currently tres fashionable. It's fun to be seen at trendy restaurants or nightclubs dressed in your finest fetish gear. For many, going out dressed is like extended foreplay. Your man will be so turned on that he'll be dying to ravish you the moment you get some privacy. Or else you might enjoy having contact in semi-private, semi-dangerous locales such as alleyways, the car or a restaurant restroom. For him, the uncertainty of getting caught adds another dimension of thrill to the experience of being dressed.

Do you enjoy being mummified?

Many latex fetishists like the idea of being in some kind of bondage bag so that they are actually immersed in the feel and smell of latex. I go a bit deeper into straitjacket bondage and mummification in the chapter on Bondage.

What about fantasy costumes?

Believe it or not, there are leather/latex outfits fashioned into various types of uniforms. These would include maid, nurse or Super Hero type outfits. If he likes these uniforms, find out more about the fantasy that goes along with the costume. From there, ask about any props needed to bring his fantasy to life. This should involve a discussion of any medical, D/s or S/M play he'd like to enact.

Other Kinds of Material or Outfits

Leather and latex are probably the most common fetish materials but your guy might also like other fabrics. Material fetish can vary greatly from person to person. I've known guys who love angora sweaters, silk or fur. Some have a fetish for "retro" lingerie like binding girdles, garters, stockings or tight corsets.

Uniforms would also be included in on the list of material fetishes. Some fellows get turned on by schoolgirl clothing, French maid outfits, naughty nurse's garb, cheerleaders, and military-type uniforms. Even tight blue jeans have fetishistic meaning for some.

If your man has a penchant for any of these types of materials, you're encouraged to probe deeper with more detailed Q&A. The questions I've outlined for leather and latex can be used interchangeably with any material your guy might prefer.

What To Do Once You're Dressed

"Okay," you might be thinking, "I'm wearing a rubber Super Woman outfit, now what?"

Sometimes all you have to do is get dressed. My guess is that some type of body worship will be extremely satisfying to him. By worship, I mean having him kiss, caresses or lick various parts of your material-encased body. Experiment and find out what feels good to you. You'll be surprised to discover that it's actually quite pleasurable to feel a wet tongue against a tight leather or latex outfit.

Attitude

Often the dress-up session requires a certain attitude or scenario. Certainly leather and latex is frequently coupled with D/s play. Wearing these outfits will help you get into the role. You'll immediately feel different, sexy and saucy once you're dressed. Order him to kiss your leather boots or tongue your latex-clad ass.

Your investigative Q&A will clue you in on the particulars of what to do once you're dressed. You can incorporate all kinds of fantasy play:

- Be the aggressive temptress and seduce him with your power.
- Be a leather Goddess who was meant to be admired and adored.
- Be the sexy sadist who enjoys inflicting painful-pleasurable sensations.

Together, the two of you can create a sensual scene that you'll both enjoy. Dressing up can be a transforming experience, for you and for him. If you enjoy it then so will he.

Fetish Balls

Leather and Latex Fetish Balls are currently very vogue and "in". Attendance ranges from young to old, blue collar to executives, well-toned to fabulously flabby. One fetish brings together all kinds of people from all walks of life. It's pretty amazing and pretty wonderful at the same time.

People who enjoy dressing are often a bit exhibitionist. They like to be seen. Fetish Balls are usually no different than any other dress-up affair such as weddings, bar mitzvahs and awards ceremonies. Think about it, tuxedoes and gowns are also costumes, aren't they? You'd be surprised to discover how benign and comfortable these fetish events usually are. Go if you enjoy getting dressed up and socializing.

I'm willing to wager that he'll happily hand you his credit card so you can treat yourself to something that makes you look extra gorgeous and sexy to wear to the event. Fetish Balls are great for the ego. All of the females present get boundless attention, admiration and are tastefully ogled. It's great for your self-esteem. And it's also pay-off for all your hard work of getting a handle on his fetish. Your man will feel proud that he's got a woman who pays attention to his needs. Not only will you experience deep appreciation from him but a sense of forbidden fun and admiration from others.

Play Parties

Don't confuse Play Parties with fetish events. Play Parties require you to dress AND participate in some way, shape or form. There is much more physical interaction at Play Parties than at Fetish Balls. Play Parties generally include some sort of D/s activities or on-stage demonstrations. Participants are embraced but observers are welcomed too.

Seasoned players like to go and demonstrate in public what they have practiced in private. Tops will tie up and flog their bottoms, or submissives. The amount of thrashing a bottom can take is a demonstration both of the Dominant's skill and of the submissive's love for them. It's quite interesting to see--big, strong men will grovel at their petite woman's feet. Sometimes couples do a bit of exchanging with other couples. It's like swinging for the S/M crowd. People switch partners and couples will either play together or drift off into separate areas.

Play Parties can be helpful in finding other like-minded people, and showing you that your man's fetish isn't so uncommon after all. Newcomers can also learn from more seasoned players.

Rules of Public Play

Before attending any sort of fetish event, set up ground rules in advance. Be prepared for anything, and try not to pass judgment. Decide ahead of time whether or not you'll be participating or just observing. If participating, will you play together as a couple or exchange partners? And how far will you go?

Overt sexual activities are usually not condoned at Play Parties. Scene people are respectful of boundaries. However, just like at any other type of party, there are always those who try and break the rules. You and your guy should establish some type of private signal so you can alert each other if things are not going smoothly or if they get out of hand.

Attend a Play Party only after you feel comfortable with your own partner's fetish. Though they are educational, the idea of exchange and playing with other couples may be something you're not quite ready for at the moment. But don't completely rule it out for the future. Right now your main goal is to please your one special guy.

In Summary

Materialistic fixation is considered the core and base of fetish behavior. Simply put, it's about getting turned on by exposure to certain kinds of material and posturing. It's the equivalent of going to your neighborhood lingerie store and purchasing an outfit to later set the mood in your bedroom.

Sometimes the outfit itself is the turn on. I know one man who says he can make passionate love for hours as long as his woman wears sexy, latex gloves. Unfortunately, many women ran for the hills when he produced these gloves. Finally, one adventuresome lady found the concept amusing and a little bit kinky. While wearing the gloves she reports that she was promptly rewarded with the best orgasm of her life. She also acquired an appreciative, loving, loyal husband in the deal because they eventually married and are still together, happily ever after.

Material fetish is often coupled with other kinds of fantasies associated with standard D/s interactions.

Dressing up can be a fun, pleasurable fetish that couples embrace in a variety of ways. And as a bonus, this fetish usually requires you to go shopping. How can you resist?

Chapter 20
Male Domination

Perhaps while conducting your investigation you found out that your man wants to be the person in charge. Some fetishes are not gender-biased. Either the male or the female can be the Top, or Dominant. During your Q&A, you discovered that your guy enjoys topping or being the dominant. He wants to be the one in control; at least some of the time.

Some guys also like to switch. This means that sometimes he's the Dominant and you're the submissive. Other times, you switch roles.

Being a sometimes submissive is an excellent way for you to learn his personal predilections firsthand. Generally, when he's in Dominant mode, he'll be demonstrating the very acts, attitude and verbiage that he personally enjoys. You trying on the submissive role for size is the best way for you to learn exactly what he likes. It's been said that the best Dominants are those who have experienced the submissive side first.

Which Fetishes Pair Up With Male Domination?
While many of the fetishes are exclusively male submissive,

there are a number that can be enacted both ways. These fetishes include but are not limited to: Dominant/submissive roles, spanking, tickling, bondage, nipple torture and infantilism. Consult the corresponding chapters to teach you about the nuances of each of these fetishes.

This chapter will focus on how you can personally embrace and participate in the submissive or "bottom" position. Before we address your feelings, it's important to get a basic understanding of the psychological components of the male dominant fantasy.

Origins

Male domination fantasies validate your man's primal male ego desires. Just like the submissive guy who has a desire to acknowledge his softer, more feminine side, male dominants want to experience power. The nice thing about Dominant/submissive exchanges is that it allows everyone to explore both their masculine and feminine traits. Since your man fantasizes about being dominant, he has a sexual predilection towards the idea of control. Perhaps he feels beaten down at his job, grew up with overbearing parents or struggles with feelings of powerlessness. Acting out or fantasizing about being dominant soothes and heals. It's like the boy who imagines being a superhero when forced to stand in the corner.

We live in a society that no longer glamorizes the traditional male. Just look at the change in our masculine icons. It used to be John Wayne. Now it's Johnny Depp, who isn't afraid of dressing in drag and playing the role of a transvestite, as he did (and convincingly so!) in *Before Night Falls* and *Ed Wood*.

The same goes for music. Back in the day, male rock stars wore leather, moved aggressively and sang tough, angry lyrics. Today, "rock stars" are more carefully choreographed in attire, lyrics and moves. Compare punk's Sid Vicious with Justin Timberlake and there's no comparison!

Fashion further backs up this theory. In the past, men were relegated to hues of black, brown, tans and grays. Now their clothing comes in a variety of shades including pink! While society still only sanctions men in pants, masculine clothing is loosening up in the concept of stringent dress codes. Just look at the guy who happily sports a BabyBjörn while carrying a tote bag full of diapers.

There's no doubt about it that in the new millennium, men sometimes feel sissified. Their genetic makeup calls for them to exercise their innate male qualities. Male domination fantasies reinforce the basic nature of the male being. Your guy simply has a need to express his masculinity and he has chosen the bedroom as his arena.

Playing the role of the Top gives permission for men to be men. It allows for the expression of repressed masculine feelings. As a male Top, he enjoys the image of seeing you helpless and reliant on his protection. Although he's the one who's rendering you defenseless, he's also the one to rescue his "damsel in distress." It's a win/win situation because he plays the role of villain and hero. The feeling of power surges his sexuality.

Conversely, women often like playing the submissive role because it gives them permission to get in touch with their own primal femininity. These D/s scenarios are very much like male/female roles in traditional fairy tales. The charming prince rescues his beloved but helpless princess and they all live happily ever after.

Your Feelings

While it's easier and requires less skill to allow him to take charge, it's much more difficult to master since it's not a part of your own inner sexual psyche. The submissive role requires that you agree to let go and experience sensations that may be unusual or unpleasant. People who are masochistic get pleasure from pain because the brain interprets the experience as sexually arousing. Since that's not the case for you, it's more difficult for you to in this "bottom" position. It will require some mental reprogramming for you to "swallow your pride" in order to take on the subservient or slave-like role.

This may very well go against your feminist ideals. However, you need to stay focused and remember the goal of this book: you want to learn, understand, join in and be your man's very best lover. Sometimes this requires you to perform acts, say words or take on roles that are foreign to you.

You can be submissive as long as you do two things:

- Change your thinking.
- Negotiate and communicate.

Change Your Thinking

It's been established in the chapter *Feelings vs. Taking Action* that your thoughts have everything to do with the way you feel about enacting your man's fantasies. You can either choose to be unconditionally accepting and view your sexual investigation as something that will ultimately be helpful to your relationship, or you can think his fantasies are perverted and ultimately feel bad that you made a wrong choice in picking your man. The way you think will directly affect your enjoyment of playing out the submissive role.

Some women have a negative automatic knee-jerk reaction to the very idea of being controlled or taking on the subservient slave-like role. They feel it doesn't coincide with being a modern woman in today's society. It doesn't acknowledge their education, job title or social status.

All of this is true. But remember that you are merely taking on a role, playing a game. This role doesn't define you. It simply reflects a sexual fantasy in which you have chosen to participate or a game you have agreed to play like Monopoly or Clue.

In order to be able to get into this role, you'll need to change your thinking. It's actually very simple to replace negative thoughts with newer, more forward-thinking ideas which will help you meet your goal of enacting his fantasy.

An Example

Here's an example to help illustrate this mode of thinking:

Your thought: Being submissive is degrading. How dare he think of me as someone lesser! He has a lot of nerve to want to control me.

When you think this way, you won't be able to go any further in enacting his fantasy. It's an emotional dead end. Those type of thoughts will bring up feelings of anger and you'll start to feel like he's just taking advantage of you. When you work yourself into an outraged state, the slightest sensation of being spanked will feel extremely painful to you. One nipple-tweak and chances are you'll scream, slap his face and storm out.

Now, try substituting and re-examining your first impulsive thoughts. Challenge yourself.

New thought: Does he really want to degrade me or does he just want me to be the star of his sexual fantasy? Is it really that awful to have him put me over his knee and sexily bare my bottom? Isn't pinching my nipple the way he expresses his attraction for me?

When you allow yourself to modify your thinking, your feelings will change as well. You'll remember the original goal you had for picking up this book and conducting a deep sexual investigation of your man. You'll recall that you're coming from a loving place and truly want to be the person who fulfills your guy's every sexual need and fantasy.

Instead of dwelling on the word "degradation", think of how you'll find the sensations to be stimulating. The brain often confuses pain with pleasure. Train yourself to perceive the sensations you feel as something pleasurable. Think about how sexy you look to your man when you're helpless and vulnerable. Channel the female of a different era when women were thought of as fragile flowers. In the submissive role, you get to be his pampered China doll. See? Your thoughts can greatly control how you respond to this role.

Conversely, you may be a woman who actually identifies with the submissive role. This could be a great opportunity for you to get in touch with your basic, often-repressed female desires. Today's woman is required to be adept at home, in the office as well as in the bedroom. You multi-task and are always on the go. Taking on the submissive role gives you a break. He's the one who has to create the scenario and do all the work for a change. Your job is to allow yourself to let go and enjoy the experience.

Negotiate and Communicate

Some Male Dominant fetishes do require the infliction of

some kind of pain or stimulation. You might take issue with acts that you may feel are violating or painful. That's absolutely understandable and by no means should you "grit your teeth and bear it". You should never allow anyone to hurt you under any circumstances.

At this point, I'm assuming (hoping!) that you have a changed attitude about being submissive. You're clear on the fact that you are merely playing a role and that role is not you. But now you're puzzled about how you'll handle sensations that you might really and truly find to be uncomfortable at best and downright painful at worst. Remember, the key words are negotiation and communication.

In fact, the major components of all fetishes are attitude and verbiage. Your guy doesn't have to tie you up completely immobile if the very thought of this freaks you out. Who says you have to be tied tightly to squiggle, squirm and act as if you couldn't possibly break free of his bonds? He doesn't have to whip or spank until you bruise purple. His major fetish is to see you act contrite, distressed and repentant while being punished. Act is the operative word here.

First, find out about his fantasy and then explore your own limits. You can even have a few "test runs" before you both get fully into your roles. Ask for one spank, one smack with the paddle and one pinch of the nipple. You can then communicate if the pain is too much, too little or just right. This will help prepare the two of you for your scene and won't detract from the action once it's rolling. Think of it as doing a test color swatch before painting the whole room to see if you like the shade.

During the actual scene you can continue to negotiate with the use of your safe words or phrases. As the submissive, you're ultimately the one who controls the amount of sensation and sets limits for the scenario you create together.

I've included some questions and suggestions on how to play safely. This will ensure greater probability that the scene will go according to your own needs and level of comfort while realizing his fantasies.

Q&A:

What do you like about being dominant?

Listen for clues about his motivation, attitude and issues involving control. This will reveal to you how he approaches the dominant role. You also want to hear him talk about respecting your limits. A trusted Dominant provides a pleasurable experience for his submissive and always has her safety in mind. He runs the show but the production is ultimately about performing enjoyable acts.

Of course in your case, you might think none of the activities involved are exactly what you want. I want you to promise to try to get negative attitudes like this out of your head. Upon discussion I'm sure you can find some common ground.

For example, if he likes bondage, you and he can agree that he tie you lightly with silk scarves, then treat you to a delicious orgasm with his tongue. If he likes to spank, the two of you compromise that he puts you over his knee and administers a very light hand spanking. If he wants to just dominate, then he orders you into a sexy outfit and you give him a massage. There's always room to play and be flexible within the context of the Dominant/submissive exchange.

The most important aspect of Dominant/submissive play is to establish a "safe word" or gesture beforehand. That's your free pass. Use it when you want him to stop or to modify anything he's doing. Insist upon communication before, during and after every single scene.

What actual experience, if any, do you have in dominating?

Every aspect of domination calls for experience and technique. He has to know how to use equipment, spank, whip properly and tie a knot without cutting off circulation or causing damage. If he has no prior experience, the two of you can practice on inanimate objects before you actually engage in the activity. Sometimes couples go to a professional Dominatrix or a bondage club to learn from the pros.

What kind of attitude do you want from your sub?

Some men want you to be very subservient and follow orders

without question. Other guys prefer someone feisty and bratty. Of course the best reactions are those which are genuine. The one thing every guy abhors universally is the sub who's "just going through the motions". If you really can't get into this, don't do it. But my strong suggestion is to give it a try with an open mind and heart.

What do you enjoy most about being a Top?

He might tell you that he enjoys the control. He feels powerful as the person who is rendering you helpless. He might mention that it's an opportunity for him to validate the manly part of his being, the part of him that wants to feel power and be the "captain of his ship". Listen closely to his response and try to figure out its significance.

Do you like to be the Top only or do you like to switch?

Many fellows claim to be Dominants only but the truth is they also enjoy being submissive. Some feel ashamed to admit their more docile side so it's important to ask this question in a gentle, manner. Fetishists are very particular about their proclivities but in general it's been my experience that most guys are curious about being Top and bottom. Each has a preference but visiting the "other side" lends itself to variety and a wider array of possibilities.

What do you want to do to me when I submit?

This is the question that gets down to the nitty-gritty of your man's own personal fetish preferences. In the next few pages (after the Q&A) I've listed the common ways that men top women. Reference each fetish to the corresponding chapter of the same name. In addition, I'll give a brief summary of how each fetish looks with the male as Dominant.

What kind of verbiage do you use during a scene?

Language is key to any kind of D/s exchange. Some dominants naturally use degrading words when on top. He may refer to use as "slut", "whore", "bitch", etc. Ask him about his buzzwords and the way he will refer to you during a scene.

Advanced knowledge will take away the power of hearing a word or phrase that might be negatively charged for you.

Some guys like the idea of verbal humiliation. It's all part of the turn on of being on top. If you have a grave objection and don't think you can handle this, speak up before the scene. But in time, you might find these words endearing. You're now "his slut", "his bitch", and "his whore", and no one else in the world is. I know of many women who actually find the dirty language stimulating. The words make them feel sexy in a naughty kind of way.

Some Doms are more positive. He'll praise, encourage and admire you. Compliance or taking a few extra whacks will elicit a "good girl" kind of comment. He'll admire you in bondage and compliment you on how beautiful you look in ropes.

Every Top has their own style. I personally prefer hearing a Top being encouraging to their bottom. But ultimately, this is not about my personal preference or recommendation. This all about what turns him on. And always remember the old adage "sticks and stones"...

What kind of safe word or gesture will we use if I need you to stop or lighten up?

The most common safe or safety word is "mercy". If you scream, cry, moan or groan, he'll just assume you're having a good time. But if you say "mercy", he must stop automatically. You then both get out of character and make the necessary adjustments so that you're comfortable. It's important that you agree ahead of time that "mercy" is the same as amnesty. You will communicate calmly without hurt feelings, anger or storming out the door.

Another easy way to establish safety is to use the colors of a traffic signal:

- Red means stop.
- Yellow means to lighten up.
- Green is the word to tell him you're doing fine.

How to Make Your Time on the Bottom Pleasant and Enjoyable

Dominant/submissive Role-Playing

In a Dominant/submissive or Master/slave relationship, he wants to be the one in control. Although some guys fantasize about playing roles as a lifestyle decision, I think that's impractical no matter who is the dominant. (See the chapter on *FemDom Domestic Disciplinary Relationships* for more.) I strongly advocate that all role-playing and sexual play needs to be reserved for special, sexy times. Real relationships cannot allow for 24/7 role-playing or fetish activity of any kind. That would be the same as having sexual relationships every day, all day long. Sometimes relationships start out that way. While that's nice for a while and a great aspiration, it's ultimately impractical. My suggestion is to set aside specific "playtimes" when you will submit to him.

Before you jump into the submissive role, find out what he enjoys doing when he's the Master. Sometimes it's merely about giving orders. If this is the case, he'll tell you to get on your knees and perform fellatio or some other type of sexual act. He also might want to see you dressed in a certain outfit. The "costume" might be as simple as a dog collar and stiletto heels.

During the scene he'll want to cause sensations that will feel sexy and erotic to the both of you. A variety of acts can be incorporated into a single D/s scene. For instance, he may want to tie, spank, whip or adorn your nipples with clothespins. Some male Dominants find it appealing to see their subs with a ball gag in their mouths or wearing a blindfold that renders them sightless—and helpless.

Experiment before you get into your roles. It will be a major turn-off if you whine or complain while he's in his Dominant mindset. Let him give you a few test spanks with the paddle or try on the nipple clamps in advance of playing. Do whatever it takes to let yourself enjoy the act of letting go. And allow him the freedom to surprise you in order to add sexiness into the scene. Remember, fear is an aphrodisiac.

He might blindfold you and cause surprise erotic sensations just as you do when you're in the Dominant mode. It's fun to be blindfolded and then be fed chocolate and strawberries.

A favorite Dom trick is to drip candle wax onto the sub's skin and then mix the heat with the freeze of ice cubes. He may even erotically run the blade of a knife lightly over your body; it's called "edge-play." The element of surprise is important in these cases. The key is to establish trust so you'll be able to relax and enjoy his sensual touch, be it hot, cold or chillingly sharp.

Bondage

There are a slew of men who absolutely love to see a woman trussed up in rope. This fetish dates back to the 1950s, to the days of Bettie Page. Almost 60 years later, she's the best-known and best-loved bondage model. Photographer Irving Klaus loved tying Bettie up in a variety of positions—and she always looked so wholesome, willing and cheerful. Klaus's Bettie Page photos are now classic in the bondage arena and beyond.

The act of tying and then admiring their handy-work arouses male devotees of bondage. Some guys enjoy see women "squirm and squiggle" while others prefer their victim to be still and hold position. You'll have to learn about your man's personal preference and taste.

Bondage can also be performed with chains, leather belts or even saran wrap. Some guys enjoy "mummifying" the woman so that she literally can't move. Mummifying is extreme and is not recommended for the claustrophobic person. Communicate beforehand and find out exactly what he wants to do before getting involved in the scene.

While you're in bondage he may want to perform sexual acts on you. That's something most women find very appealing. He may want to cuff your arms and legs to a four-poster bed, then slither his tongue all over your body and create intense orgasmic sensations. Lucky you if that's where his fetish takes you.

Bondage role-plays are focused on you being rendered helpless. Role-play gives a reason for the bondage to take place and adds a dramatic aspect to the fetish play. You might suggest role-playing as your own personal contribution to any fetish exchange. Again, the old "Cowboys and Indians" scenarios come to mind. Another popular scenario might be that he ties you up because he's playing the part of a thief and must render you immobile while he robs your house. There are a myriad of possibilities.

Infantilism

Generally speaking, he'd only want to see you in diapers if he has the fetish himself. It may just be the idea of switching in order to balance out his feelings of embarrassment or shame about the role. Go along with him. You'll learn more about his fetish and in the process, you'll also enjoy being pampered. Sure you might feel silly but so what? You're ultimately helping him feel okay about a strong need he himself has.

Nipple Play

It's often referred to as "nipple torture", but in reality it's more about him providing intense nipple stimulation on you. These sensations can actually be pleasurable as long as he stays within your comfort zone. He can lightly caress and tease your nipples until they become hard and aroused. He can use his tongue and lightly nip (but not bite!) them. Finally, if he really likes the visual aspect of nipple play, he can use rope to lightly (not tightly) bind them. If done correctly, the rope can actually look like a macramé bra. If he wants to see your nipples clamped he can stretch out the metal wires of clothespins so that they'll merely grab but not pinch your erect nipple.

Spanking

Many men with a fetish for spanking prefer to be the giver of the spanking. It goes hand-in-hand with the traditional mindset of the authoritative male taking his naughty female to task. He may find real or imaginary reasons to put you over his knee.

Spankings don't have to be administered hard for him to get satisfaction. It's more about your reaction as the mischievous imp getting punished than the idea of causing you real discomfort. Yes, he may want to redden your bottom a bit but it's purely visual. It doesn't mean he has to leave welts or bruises. Chances are, he just wants to see you squirm.

Spanking lends itself to a variety of role-play situations. He may want to be your pretend principal, teacher, boss or uncle. You can act the part of the bratty student, impulsive teen or sultry seductress. The one similarity in all these role-plays is the naughty female who needs to be put in her place. The spanking is being administered for "her own good" and the purpose is to provide "correction".

Pay attention to his attitude and you'll be able to pick up the tone of the kind of spankings he enjoys giving: disciplinary, playful, or motivational. Listen to his verbal cues and respond accordingly. As time goes on, you'll have ideas of your own and you'll get a sense of what kind of "naughty girl" you'd like to be.

To discover your guy's private spanking motivations and his underlying spanking desires, it's all about listening to the verbal signals he gives you and providing him with the proper response. To discover your guy's private stash of buzzwords, just reverse the questions that are given in the Spanking chapter.

Tickling

Tickling might seem harmless on the surface but there's a broad spectrum about how this fetish can be played out. It may be as simple and erotic as being tied with silk scarves while he uses a feather on your naked body. It can also be used as a form of torture and in this case, be extremely unpleasant to those who are ticklish.

Role-plays are often used in conjunction with tickling. Interrogation is commonly linked to tickling. You might be a spy and he tickles you to get some top-secret information from you. Another popular role-play scenario is one where he would sneak into your home and tickle you until he finds where your precious jewels are hidden.

Tickling doesn't have to be about torture. You can pretend to be in torment and that might very well suffice for him. It's important to find out what kind of attitude or reaction he wants from you. Some ticklers like to see their subject laugh, squirm and carry on while others want you to whimper with distress.

In Summary

Every Dominant is different. Your man may want to switch

roles in fetishes that were not mentioned in this chapter. Whatever the case, remember that switching roles is beneficial in teaching you more about what he personally enjoys. It also gives you the opportunity to take a break and let him be the one to orchestrate the scene.

Also remember that you're never required to endure any kind of real pain. It's all about your comfort level and not crossing a barrier. If he has a strong desire to cause some kind of pain or extreme sensation, you can always play-act the part. Are actresses really suffering in movies? Do they take real beatings, gunshot wounds or truly experience fright in horror movies? Of course not.

You possess the innate ability to pretend, so take advantage of it. Tap into your ability to take on the role of someone in discomfort or distress. The more you react, the more turned on he'll be. Submission calls for you to act out a part. Your convincing performance will make a huge difference in the way he experiences his masculinity and inborn desire to take the lead. So be your own Sarah Berhnardt and take on the submissive role of a lifetime.

Chapter 21
Sexual Role Playing: Characters and Uniforms

Believe it or not, role playing is recommended by leading sexologists. As the name implies, in sexual role-playing, couples don costumes and wigs, or plan "chance" encounters in public places as a way to spice up bedroom activity.

Ikea did a very funny television commercial for the French market called "Pig Hunt", which involves a middle-aged husband and wife, kinky clothes, a pitchfork, a pig's mask. The real kicker is when they're walked in on by their teenaged kids with the tagline: "Time to leave home?" I think this commercial is a healthy sign that role-playing has become almost mainstream.

Creating another character often fulfills the need for variety in a relationship. While sexual role-playing is an enjoyable diversion for many, your guy has a deeper connection to it. He has identified a costume or variant as a powerful aspect of his unique sexual make-up. When a craving like his is strong, specific and regularly repeated as masturbatory material, we classify it as a fetish.

Where It Comes From

Men usually very clearly remember the first female who produced a sexually-charged feeling in them. This could have been a neighbor, a friend's mom or even the maid. The role this woman played then became the basis of a sexual fantasy or trigger. It's very common for boys to daydream about women who shaped their lives such as teachers, nurses and babysitters.

Some of these characters may have also been viewed on television or in movies. It's not unusual for men to hold sit-com wives in a place of high esteem, anyone from June Cleaver to Lucy Ricardo. Fictional characters such as Princess Leia from Star Wars, Catwoman or Wonder Woman have also been known to get the male juices flowing. When I was growing up, a friend's dad had a thing for Emma Peel from the TV show The Avengers. At the time, I didn't know the significance of a strong, take-charge woman clad head to toe in black leather, but now I do!

The fact that your man has this preference doesn't mean he isn't attracted to you; his role-playing fetish began to crystallize long before you came into the picture. Instead of thinking of it as a rival, you can integrate his fantasy girl into your sex lives, starring you.

Always remember that fantasies and fetishes are imprinted in the subconscious early in life. Because of their longevity, they don't go away. In fact, they have shaped your man's own distinctive sexual chart. Choosing to participate allows you to join with him and become an integral part of his personal erotic library of images.

Sexual role-playing and costuming might be as simple as getting dressed up in a provocative costume or as complex as learning a whole library of key phrases and adapting a correct attitude.

From your initial investigation in the chapter called *Gathering the Information*, you've discovered that he's turned on by a particular character or uniform. Now it's time to tune in and get specific. Here are some questions you can ask in order to get some real answers.

Q&A:

Do you imagine a particular character or is it a general role?

Since this is an open-ended question, his answer will help guide the rest of your questions. Your guy will probably be very specific in his response since fetishistic behavior is unyielding. He may be fixated on a particular role, character or even a furry animal.

For many, role-playing is a combination of attitude and attaching the proper character to the role. Your guy might like the idea of authoritative women represented by teachers, doctors, nurses, nuns, police officers, military personnel, the strict babysitter or nanny. Other men are stimulated by subservient women depicted by secretaries, students, the girl next door, a waitress, virgin, Geisha girl or French maid. Still others like some kind of perceived "slutty" role such as a sorority girl, rich bitch, stripper, prostitute, punk rocker groupies or runaway.

Sometimes the roles are purely character-driven. For these men, it's more about the visual than the attitude. He may or may not have a specific fantasy that goes along with the role.

A number of guys fixate on having their partners dress up and have sex with them in costume. If this if the case, you'll need to find out if there are precise sexual requirements that go with the costume. Examples of costumed roles include vampires, Wild West girls, barmaids, Super Heroes and women from certain time periods like the past or future, including cave girls (remember Raquel Welch from One Million B.C.?) or amorous space aliens.

How do you imagine I get dressed for the role?

Ask specifics about clothing. I guarantee that this will be one shopping spree he'll be happy to finance! Remember to quiz him about undergarments, shoes, wigs, accessories, fabric and colors. If he has trouble describing what he likes, have him show you pictures. I'm willing to bet he's got quite a collection of visual materials.

When I get all dressed up, now what?

Some guys just want to see the outfit. Others might want you to get into character and interact with him. Find out if there's something in particular he imagines happening when you're all decked out. Ask about buzzwords, specific sexual acts and attitudes.

Are we having sex when I'm dressed?

This is a very important question. The role he envisions for you might involve intercourse or it might be more about enacting some other fetish behavior such as spanking, tickling, bondage, Dom/sub scene or medical scene. I'm sure he'll be more than willing to clue you in.

If we are going to have sex, what kind of sex do you envision?

Your man's fantasy scenario might lend itself to a brand of sex that's not in the realm of your usual repertoire. If this is the case, find out exactly what's required. A biker chick would perform oral sex differently than a Geisha girl, right? A Klingon from "Star Trek" would make love differently than a furry animal. The character, uniform or role he envisions will most likely dictate the type of sexual encounter.

Will sex be different while we're in role?

The beauty of role-playing is that it allows the two of you to be people other than yourselves. A shy person has permission to be more aggressive; a repressed person can transform into a sexual animal.

How can we communicate with each other during the role-playing if things aren't going well?

Once in role, people can get a bit confused if the scenario isn't orchestrated before you begin. Participants want to stay in character but they might need to adjust the scene or attitude while they're in the midst of it. Establishing some kind of non-verbal cue that you can give to each other if adjustments need to be made is important. This might be something as subtle as rubbing your nose or saying a key phrase to alert your partner that a break is needed.

Will we be working from a specific script or will we just let it flow?

This fetish in particular is all about communication. You both need to feel comfortable about being spontaneous. The first time might go more smoothly if you have a basic outline of how you want the scene to progress. Approach it the same as doing a scene from a play. You can actually write out dialogue or at the very least, jot down a prepared paragraph. You may or may not want to write an ending. Role-playing is often a catalyst for real spontaneity and creativity, so it's best to leave the ending open.

Do you get into character or am I the only one in character?

Some guys are purely focused on the other partner. This type of fellow just wants to see you dressed in the outfit and make love to "that girl." Find out his personal preference. Depending on the fantasy, he may want to get dressed too and play a different role other than himself.

What about ethnicity?

Lots of men have a thing for women who are culturally different than they are. African-American, Asian and Latino women in particular turn on many "white bread" men. Obviously, you can't change who you are but you can ask what he finds attractive about these particular ethnic groups. For example, many men perceive Latino women to be fiery lovers or Black women to be more experimental. Ask lots of questions and get to the bottom of his thinking. You can accommodate many of these types of fantasies by pretending to be a woman from another ethnic group by some creative role-playing.

Sample Characters That Can Inspire Fun Role-Playing

I've discovered that some men are a bit shy or unsure about what they envision their fantasy character doing. If your Q&A still leaves some question marks, here are some role-plays to match common characters I've heard about over the years:

Furries

This fetish role-play is a relatively new one. Perhaps something got into the younger generation when they were interacting with their plush dolls at home or engaging with a larger-than life-character at a pep rally. Furries consider themselves to be "anthropomorphized animals" that engage in Internet games, attend conventions and role-play sexual acts with each other. Think Barney with a boner.

Furries, or Plushies, connect their sexual feelings to an animalistic urge. They'll dress up as their identified animal while having sex with a chosen partner or they enjoy mutual group petting in a "fur pile."

If your guy tells you that he's a Furry, you'll need to ask the same open-ended questions that you would ask any fetishist. Find out who gets dressed as what. The chosen animals will then dictate the type of role-play in which you'll be engaging.

A very funny episode of the HBO series "Entourage" involved Furries. You might want to view it "On Demand" to get the goods on these frisky, fuzzy critters.

Military

Enacting this role can go either way—you're his drill sergeant or he's ranked above you and he calls the shots.

Next-Door Neighbor, French Maid, Babysitter

These roles all smack of seduction. In this role-play, you can be the leader and entice him into having sex *your* way. Perhaps it's his first time and you're the older woman "showing him the ropes". His own personal "Mrs. Robinson" from *The Graduate*, as it were. These roles put you in a position of playing the part of a knowledgeable, confident, sensual female. This type of play can also benefit you and your own self-esteem. You'll find that you'll get in touch with your own needs while identifying the ways for him to please you.

Nun and Priest

This would be an example of a dual role-play. Each of your roles is necessary for the scenario. The role playing can certainly go in many different directions. Let your imagination run wild here. Since religious reenactments are taboo to many, naughty behavior often inspires sexual stirrings.

Prostitute

This role puts you in a position of power as well as an open-minded listener. Men often tell hookers sexual secrets they'd never tell anyone else. Often they view hookers as objective observers, sexual psychiatrists of sorts who are being paid to satisfy them instead of listen to them. In this sense I've been asking you to be your guy's hooker all throughout this book. With a prostitute, your man doesn't have to censor his thoughts, but rather, he spells out what he wants. But remember that even hookers have boundaries and negotiate about what they will or won't do. Allow yourself that luxury too.

Sorority Girl or Rich Girl

Your man may fantasize about taming a spoiled, bratty woman. His fetish might revolve around some kind of mild spanking, bondage or sexually "taking" (i.e. sexy rape) to "teach them a lesson." Again, find out what he thinks and devise something fun for both of you to enact.

Teacher

A teacher can be seen both as an authoritative or a seductive character. The strict teacher can punish or spank a naughty boy. A sexy teacher might be the woman your guy wants to conquer. Remember the Van Halen song "Hot for Teacher"? How amazing to finally have sex with the fantasy schoolteacher! Find out which type of teacher is the instructor of his dreams.

Virgin, Student, Secretary

These roles call for you to be more innocent and wide-eyed than the others do. In them, he gets to take the lead and communicate the way he likes to orchestrate sex. Your job? To be pleasing and open to his suggestions.

Sexy, Consensual Rape

While having a role play that enacts an act of violence in real life is something that people may shy away from or initially feel repulsed by, rape fantasies are one of the most traditionally popular female sexual fantasies. It's been documented even before Nancy Friday's groundbreaking 1973 book *My Secret*

Garden. In female fantasyland, the woman is "taken" and "has to" comply sexually. Intercourse or other sexual acts must be performed "or else." But unlike an actual rape, which is a crime of violence and a traumatic experience, in rape fantasies, the female truly wants to be taken.

This fantasy was particularly popular in days past when women were taught to deny their own libidos. Back then, women weren't supposed to admit sexual desires. Today, society recognizes female sexuality. Still, a rape fantasy may be an exciting way for you to allow yourself to experience a raw kind of sexuality that is different that the kind of sex you enjoy with a steady partner. Your guy also might find it stimulating to pretend rape you in some of your fantasy role plays. It ties in strongly with male dominant/female submissive playing.

Planning A Role Play

The fun of role-playing is often in the planning. The two of you will need to figure out when, where and how the scene will get executed.

For example:

- Will you work from a script with real lines or will you improvise?
- How will you communicate when you're in role?
- What kind of advanced shopping will be required?
- How will the scene progress?
- What do you hope to accomplish within the scene?
- What is the ultimate goal of role-playing?

And perhaps most importantly, ensure that you have a safe place to enact the scene without being interrupted by your kids, neighbors or roommates. Just like in that Ikea ad, your children, especially, probably wouldn't understand or take well to seeing their mommy and daddy dressed up as hairy animals, vampires or Super Heroes.

Always remember to include "red" (safety) words so that the scene can flow safely and uninterrupted.

In Summary

Whether your man has a definitive fetish or if he just wants to play, character role-playing is an exciting way to spice up your bedroom activities. Role-playing allows you to dress up, try on and assume behaviors that are part of your alter ego.

The preparation period is also a time for bonding as you are, in effect, planning and executing a private, mini-play complete with costumes, props and several scenes.

Sexual role-playing is fun, enjoyable and lets you to step out of yourself for a few hours. Think of it like taking a mini-vacation, without having to pack.

Chapter 22
Smoking

These days, smoking might be considered politically
incorrect, but it's still a turn-on for many men. If your guy
reports having a smoking fetish it means that he gets aroused at
the thought or image of a female smoking a cigarette. Sometimes
the fetish is used as part of an S/M or D/s scene. Other times, it's
just the idea of seeing you or another woman smoking.

Where Does The Smoking Fetish Originate?
Perhaps more than any of the other fetishes discussed here,
it's easy to see how the smoking fetish originated. Until recently,
smoking was considered to be a very glamorous activity. Think
of the sexy movie sirens of the 1940s and 1950s. How many of
them were photographed holding a cigarette or with a ribbon of
smoke curling out from between their slightly-parted lips? Rich
ladies and Hollywood starlets alike were often depicted holding a
cigarette slipped into a long, slender holder. It isn't much of a
stretch to make a phallic connection!

Smoking is also strongly tied in with sexual activity. Movie
after movie depicts couples smoking after engaging in torrid sex

or as a substitute for sex itself. Remember that classic scene from Now, Voyager where Paul Henreid lights two cigarettes between his lips and hands one to Bette Davis? I imagine cigarette sales skyrocketed after that film.

Cigarette smoking was also played up for sexy laughs in that memorable scene from The Graduate where Benjamin kisses Mrs. Robinson for the first time. Trying to impress her with his sexual prowess, he plants a big one on her lips just as she takes a deep drag on her cigarette. Seemingly unimpressed, she lets out the smoke after he releases her and picks up the conversation where she left off. In fact, Mrs. Robinson smokes profusely, and quite erotically, throughout the entire movie.

By being exposed to images like this, a young mind is influenced to form an association between smoking and sexual activity. While the association is formed by many, smoking is only considered a fetish if it becomes a requirement for arousal. As you now know, fetishists are people who possess a genetic proclivity towards making sexual associations with non-sexual objects or acts. In your man's case, he made a definitive association between smoking and sexual activity and is therefore aroused by it.

How Do You Participate If You're a Non-Smoker?

No one is suggesting that you develop an unhealthy habit to satisfy your man's fetish. If you're a non-smoker you can participate in his fantasies as fully as a "pack-a-day" woman. With knowledge and props, you're already halfway there. How? You can always hold a cigarette in your hand, right? And you can also talk about smoking as part of your verbal repertoire, can't you? But whether you actually light up, inhale or simply talk about smoking, you'll need to find out what images, scenarios and buzzwords he associates with the act—and is aroused by.

Every smoking fetishist has specific needs so you'll want to ask the following questions to find out his.

Q&A:

What is it about smoking that turns you on?
Remember fetishes are complex and specific to each

individual. Your guy might simply like the aesthetic of seeing a woman inhaling and exhaling. He may not care about the type of woman doing the smoking, the brand of cigarette she smokes or even the way she smokes. He just likes the idea of smoking, plain and simple.

However, fetish is usually more specific than this. Your guy's particular smoking images may include a cigarette holder, glossy red lipstick or even long, red painted fingernails. Ask if he has photos of his "Smoking Queen" to show you. If he's a smoking fetishist, chances are he'll readily produce a mini scrapbook of pictures.

Do you want to watch me smoke?

Again, don't get caught up with the idea of smoking. Listen to the rest of his fantasy. He may want to see you with a cigarette in your hand. This means you can light up but you don't have to inhale. It's important for you to focus in on the details of his fantasy.

Find out specifics, like:

- Where you are sitting?
- How are you positioned?
- What you are wearing?

Smoking might also be his secondary fantasy for another fetish. For example, many leather and latex guys will love you to don some of their preferred fetish gear, then light up a cigarette.

Pure smoking fetishists might also envision a specific outfit that goes hand in hand with his fantasy. It may be garters and stockings, tight jeans or a frilly sundress. Who knows? Only he can tell you what, if any, particular clothing accompanies his own fantasy image of seeing you smoke.

Should I be wearing a certain kind of lipstick or make-up?

Remember, smoking is often depicted as a glamorous activity. It's common for smoking fetishists to enjoy watching you wrap your highly-glossed lips around the tip of the cigarette. Red is the preferred color but double check about his preference.

Many smoking fetishists also delight in seeing the butt of the cigarette after you smoke. Part of the thrill is seeing the mark you made on it with your lipstick. In their minds, it could be symbolic of the "mark" you might make on their penis with your lip imprint.

Heavy make-up, complete with eye shadow, false lashes and noticeably rouged cheeks often complete the picture for the smoking fetishist. It's your job to dig and find out as much as you can about your man's own particular requirements.

Do you prefer a special brand or type of cigarette?

I can't stress enough how important details are to the fetishist. For example, he may have a preference for a "feminine" brand of cigarette that features a long, thin shaft. Other cigarettes are rolled with dark paper. Does he like filtered or non-filtered? Would he like you to roll your own? Mini cigarillos or thick, manly cigars?

Do you like cigarette holders?

Never make assumptions. Some smoking fetishists have a preference for a cigarette holder; others do not. He may even have an aversion to a cigarette holder if he gets aroused by seeing your lip prints on the cigarette. You'll never know unless you ask.

If he does say he'd like to see you using a cigarette holder, find out more details. Inquire about length, color and shape. Ebony, ivory, plastic or polished wood? There are a host of possibilities.

Should my hands be gloved?

Gloved hands are often associated with vintage cigarette smoking. Just recall those images from the 1940s and 1950s. Many men think gloves provide an elegant look especially when coupled with the cigarette holder. And it's not just any glove. Chances are he'll have a preference for the gloves' fabric, length and color. Ask, ask, ask.

What about my hands?

If gloves aren't his thing, then manicured nails might be. Find out if he associates smoking with fingernails. He could prefer nails that are long, medium or short, rounded or pointy-edged, painted red, black or another color that triggers his passions.

Do you want me to blow smoke in your face?

Now we're getting into the interactive aspect of the smoking fetish. If your guy craves your participation, one common need is for you to blow smoke in his face. Find out the significance of his request. Blowing smoke might symbolize some kind of dominance. Or it might simply be that he enjoys the feel, smell or humiliation of the act. Be aware that you can realize this aspect of his fantasy without inhaling the smoke deeply into your lungs, just into your mouth.

Do you want to be my human ashtray?

If his answer is "yes", this requires you to make him kneel or lay by your side. Have him open his mouth, then flick your cigarette ashes onto his tongue. Many men even like the cigarette extinguished on their tongue. Believe it or not, the ash doesn't burn them.

Have you ever swallowed or imagined doing anything with the cigarette butt?

Some fetishists like to suck or even swallow the cigarette butt. Submissives in general like the concept of taking something inside them that has previously been in contact with you, their beautiful Mistress. In this case, the cigarette has been in your mouth, so all the better. Again, this is a good way to test his limits and expand upon your dungeon play when you're in the Dominant role.

Is smoking part of an overall D/s kind of fantasy?

At this point, you already know whether or not he's a submissive. Smoking is simply one thing among many you can do when you're leading a Dominant scene. You could tie him up and blow smoke in his face. You could also have him lick your boots while you enjoy smoking or playing with a cigarette. Or you might test him by threatening to make him your human ashtray. Remember, true submissives and slaves like have their limits stretched. Flicking an ash in his mouth might be a thrilling addition to D/s play.

In Summary

Smoking is an act that many men find to be sexy and arousing. As a fetish, it's both simple and intricate. Many details are required in order to bring the fantasy to life exactly as he imagines it.

Remember that he's asking you to join in and participate in his own private sexuality. It's you smoking the cigarette. Therefore, you and he are together engaging in intimate sex play. It's an interaction which brings you closer together in sharing his secret desires.

Chapter 23
Spanking

Imagine a grown man wanting you to put him over your knee and spank him like a naughty boy. Imagine getting excited by thoughts of people in positions of power such as school teachers, principals, bosses or strict aunties administering a bare-bottom spanking. That's exactly what I'm asking you to do. Imagine it and realize it, because your man is one of those men.

When you first heard about it, you might have believed that these kinds of thoughts don't mesh with your idea of erotica. Yet a very large number of adults (your guy included) get sexually aroused by certain words, phrases and story lines that depict one person spanking another in a traditional, ritualistic manner. If your man has inclinations toward the spanking fetish, you need to dig deeply to discover more about his individual, complex spanking needs.

Spanking and D/s are often used interchangeably, when in reality they're only distant cousins. (See the following chapter called *Spanking, S&M and D&s: The Different Mindsets Explained*). In truth, spanking is a self-contained fetish with specific rituals, verbiage and procedures.

Spanking fetishists, or spankos (as they refer to themselves in the spanking community), don't relate to those who enjoy dungeon activity. Spanking is a reality-based fetish strongly connected to the guidance we received from adults during our formative years. People who crave being spanked also crave nurturing, boundary-setting and parental care. Spanking often fulfills needs that were not met in childhood.

Some spanking fetishists were spanked or disciplined as children but others were not. However, all unconsciously use spanking as a vehicle to compensate for a human need that they lacked while growing up.

You might have a visceral knee-jerk aversion to the concept of spanking because of your own painful (literally!) childhood memories. You might also feel that adults who are aroused by spanking are abnormal and that this fetish should be discouraged because of its association with children. Let me assure you that you're not alone in your feelings. Most of society stands side-by-side with you here.

Many years ago, I submitted a proposal to lead a support group for spankos which would be held at a community-based adult education facility. Though this same school supported a class in S/M, my group was turned down. Why? Because spanking has its origins in childhood and was therefore deemed inappropriate.

That being said, adults who like spanking are *not* pedophiles in any way shape or form. They merely have sexual feelings about the *act* of spanking within the context of role-play or reenactments of real or imaginary happenings that may be related to childhood or present-day events.

Purist spankos all report that spanking as early as age five aroused them. They say they remember looking up the word "spanking" in the dictionary at least once during puberty. Ninety-nine percent admit that they think about some kind of spanking act or word at the moment of orgasm. So, like all fetishes, spanking is deeply rooted.

Spanking is a fetish that is particularly strong and will never leave. The fact that spanking is so misunderstood is particularly difficult for a spanking fetishist to accept and deal with. From their point of view, it's highly embarrassing to be turned on by something that is socially unacceptable and linked to childhood memories. Yet the charge that a spanko receives from thoughts of spanking is much stronger than their guilt. No matter how much they wish they didn't have this fetish, spanking is strong, pervasive and ever-present in their masturbatory thoughts and sexual feelings.

Most spanking fetishists don't understand why their thoughts go to spanking when they're engaging in sexual activities or masturbation. They aren't exactly sure where these thoughts come from or how they first got embedded into their brains. Most remember thinking about spanking from an early age. Usually the thoughts subsided until puberty when they came back full force and with a vengeance.

Some spanking fetishists are unconsciously working through childhood abuse or neglect. Others became stimulated at the thought of someone else getting spanked at home or at school when they witnessed the act as kids. And they remember the instance with exquisite details: what it was like...what it felt like...if tears were produced from pain or from the horrible embarrassment of having their buttocks exposed for all the world to see. They can recount all this and more to you when asked.

Spanking depicts a private, mysterious, scary event. Pants are pulled down, bottoms bared. Genitalia is exposed and sometimes, inadvertently stimulated. The young brain somehow made a connection between sexual arousal and spanking. This same connection is made whether the spankings actually happened to them or to a friend or relative.

With the advent of the Internet, it's much easier for spankos to connect with each other. There are literally hundreds of Web sites devoted to spanking erotica, video clips and chat rooms. And happily, spankos don't feel as isolated and alone as they once did.

Most spankos get aroused at the mere word "spanking". They imagine different spanking scenarios when masturbating and reliably orgasm to thoughts of spanking. Many spanking fetishists keep this a secret from their partners because they're terrified of rejection. When and if they finally do share it with an accepting person, they feel true elation and relief. This sense of relief happens whether or not they actually enact the fantasy with this person they've entrusted. It just feels good to unburden something they've kept inside for years.

I'm not exaggerating when I tell you that spanking fetishists require spanking in their lives. Your guy probably wishes he didn't have this desire, but it will never go away. In order to maintain a close relationship with him, you have to get involved with his spanking fetish on some level. Acceptance is the key. You don't necessarily have to physically spank him but you do have to acknowledge his genuine need. Participating with him in some way will ultimately bring you closer together. He will no longer have to keep his secrets tucked away. You possess the key that unlocks powerful feelings of arousal and best of all, you can enact his fantasies with items you probably already have in your kitchen drawer.

The following questions hold the secret to understanding the multifaceted fetish of spanking.

Q&A:

Do you like spanking as part of an overall D/s scene or do you like the idea of an entire scene built solely around spanking?

This is your first and most important question. If he says he likes spanking to be part of an overall D/s scene, you can skip most of this chapter and instead concentrate on the "Dominant/submissive Roles" chapter. If D/s is his true desire, he uses the word "spanking" interchangeably with whipping or smacking the buttocks. Spanking, for him, is something to do when you're in the dominant position. Spanking represents a form of control and power. You can incorporate spanking into an overall scene and combine it with aspects of bondage, tickling, CBT, NT, tickling, teasing, and so on.

If he answers that spanking is just a small part of his D/s fetish, spanking is not a passion for him and your guy is not a born spanking fetishist. If, however, he says that his fantasy life is built entirely around spanking, he is most definitely a spanking person. There is a reason behind the spanking and a definite way to carry out the punishment, so read on.

When did you first become "spanking aware?"

I use the term "spanking aware" because generally, spanking fetishists will report having strong feelings about spanking early in life. The reason? Children are often threatened with a spanking or witness somebody else getting spanked. The feeling of fear is eroticized and subconscious associations of spanking and sexual feelings get intermixed.

The same kind of erotic feelings for spanking may happen to someone who was abused as a child. When a child is treated with cruelty (verbally, physically or by just plain lack of attention), he sometimes splits off and mentally leaves the abusive situation. (There is a wonderfully poignant depiction of this phenomenon in the movie *The Savages* where a boy actually leaves his body and rises above the scene, watching sadly as his father delivers a thrashing.) In its place, the child often fantasizes about something humane, loving and caring. This subconscious wish might take the form of a spanking that is interpreted as something predictable, ritualistic and caring.

Spanking arousal usually lays dormant until a person becomes a sexual being. That's when he is attuned to the fact that thoughts about spanking are arousing thoughts. Mostly likely, your guy will tell you that his feelings associated with spanking have been with him forever. That's proof positive that he's a true, blue (or black-and-blue!) spanking fetishist.

Do you have any idea where your spanking thoughts came from?

He may or may not have a clue about the connection of spanking experiences to his past. He also may or may not have been spanked as a child.

Do you like to get spanked, give spankings or both?

Many people who like spanking enjoy the concept of playing both roles. This is called "switching". Switching is actually very healthy to do in a spanking relationship because unlike D/s, it's not necessarily about power exchanges. It's the idea of one person playing the role of concerned caretaker and dishing out correction. Relationships are fluid and both parties have the ability to do right and wrong. As humans, we still retain a childlike part of our personality. Being both spanker and spankee affords an opportunity for both people to exercise different facets of their personality. Sometimes one may be feeling parental. Other times, they might feel childlike.

Switching is actually a great learning opportunity for you, so great that I've devoted a chapter to it. Let him give the spanking and take note of his demeanor, attitude and way he carries the scene. This way, when it comes time for you to deliver the spanking, you'll know how he likes it dealt out.

As far as pain level is concerned, you will need to work this out with him before you subject yourself to a spanking. Some spanking people like to be on the receiving end of a pretty thorough spanking. Since you are not a born spanking enthusiast, he'll have to hold back on the actual impact of the spanking.

Are you a butt man?

Chances are pretty good that if he likes spanking, he also likes the female bottom. Even the guys who prefer just receiving get turned on by watching another female get spanked. Why? Because he likes to see a bare or partially-clad female behind jiggle, wriggle and grow red while it's getting spanked. To that end, he might enjoy spanking you so he gets an up close view of your bottom in action. I know one spanking "switch" (someone who enjoys both giving and getting spanked) that achieves great satisfaction from spanking his girlfriend "softer than soft", as he so aptly phrases it. He taps light rhythmic beats on her buttocks in time to music. She, in turn, enjoys the pleasant sensations and satisfying her man's joy of spanking.

Have you had any adult spanking experiences?

He may have played around with former girlfriends. Or he may have brought up the idea with someone else previously only to get rejected. It's important to tune in and find out what kind of spanking interactions he's had in the past and if they've been favorable. People who've been hurt in the past are often reluctant to divulge their spanking secrets for fear of being hurt again. Convey an open, accepting, positive attitude and he'll open up.

Tell me about your actual experiences, both good and bad.

Listen carefully as he shares with you his past experiences.

Note the positive aspects he describes and file them away. Also remember things that were unfavorable so you don't make the same mistakes. It's important to remember what a pivotal moment this is for him, and for your relationship. Just by listening to him and showing interest in his fetish, you're giving him a great gift.

What's your favorite spanking position?

Most true spanking fetishists will say that they prefer "over the knee spanking" or "OTK", which is fetish shorthand for that position. This is a classic spanking position that requires him to lay across your lap with his bottom upturned, waiting for punishment. OTK can be done on a straight-backed chair, on a sofa or on the edge of a bed. The image of you sitting in a straight-backed chair is the probably the one he has ingrained in his head; the one that's the star of his fantasies. True, it's classic, but in actuality, it's a little uncomfortable. Always be aware of blood rushing to his head when you're sitting on a chair and he's over your knee. My advice is to trade in the chair for the couch if you're giving a long spanking.

Do you fantasize about "corner time"?

Some spanking enthusiasts like to be positioned in the corner before or after the spanking. Corner time as a prelude to spanking allows for anticipation. Fear is a powerful aphrodisiac, so remember to tell him one or two luscious details about the punishment he's about to receive. That will get his juices flowing.

Corner time after the spanking gives him an opportunity to reflect upon his naughty behavior - and relish it. You can either leave him alone or stay in the room with him. He will also gain pleasure by displaying his well-spanked bottom to you, which he sees as a "badge of honor", the marks he bore as a declaration of his love for you. And you'll get satisfaction from seeing the fruits of your labor, as well as observing his pleasure.

Do you like getting spanked pink, red or sport some marks?

A good, sound spanking traditionally produces an even, apple-red bottom cheek. Other spankos relish seeing some kind of bruising or marks. He may view these markings as a "badge of honor", since he bore the marks, stripes or welts as a declaration of his love for you. Sometimes the welts are seen as a sign of endurance. Kind of like the way a sports enthusiast likes to test their limits. Hopefully, you will also enjoy seeing the results of the spanking and you'll get satisfaction from seeing the fruits of your labor, as well as observing his pleasure.

Ever think about getting your mouth washed out with soap?

Mouth-soaping often goes hand in hand with a hearty spanking, but you can't assume it's part of his personal spanking scenario. You need to determine if mouth soaping is something he also fantasizes about. Some spankos really like it. Others are indifferent but open to the possibility, and still others respond with, "Hell no!"

Are there other disciplinary activities you think about in conjunction with spanking?

At this point, we've established that the main focus of his fetish is spanking. However, some do like to combine their spanking fetish with other punishments. Possible punishments could include, but are not limited to: enemas, forced feminization, face-sitting and a consistent FemDom way of life. You'll find these other punishments discussed in their corresponding chapters.

Do you think about punishment or playful type spankings?

This is a very important question because you will need to adjust your attitude accordingly. Punishment spankings require you to have a real or imaginary reason for administering discipline, as punishment for not taking out the trash, for instance, or other bad behavior. It entails scolding and a reason for the spanking. Playful spankings are more interactive with back and forth banter. A good example of a playful spanking is one that would be given for losing a bet.

Are you looking for a disciplinary relationship?

This means that he wants you to set up rules and spank him for real reasons. This puts you in a position of power. Many women don't want to mix a maternal role like this in their marriage or sexual relationship.

Before you nix the concept, consider the possibilities. This role he'd like you to assume can be played on a part-time basis. It can also help you get some of the things you want from him. Use the threat of a spanking to get your dishes done, have the trash taken out or get household repairs accomplished.

Many men fantasize about a 24/7 disciplinary relationship where you would decide when, where and how the punishment takes place. This concept is usually better left in fantasy. See the chapter *FemDom Domestic Disciplinary Relationships* for more. In reality, spanking is an arousing activity which generally leads to sex. Just like we aren't always in the mood for sex, we aren't always in the mood to give or get a spanking.

Do the spankings have to be hard?

Some people really crave a pronounced sting to the point where they can take no more, while others enjoy the build up to a spanking as much or even more than the actual spanking. The anticipation of a spanking is the excitement of knowing that it's coming. Call him at the office and tell him that he has a spanking waiting for him when he gets home from work that night. This one simple telephone call might get his juices flowing as much as the promise of sex would for another guy. Thoughts of a spanking are sometimes way more arousing than the actual spanking itself.

Others are more into the sensation. They want to feel it as hard as you can give it. The more they feel it, the better. Find out what your man wants from the spanking experience and do your best to deliver it.

What are your favorite spanking buzzwords?

Spanking is an extremely verbal fetish. It's much more than just smacking someone on the behind.

To help yourself into his mindset, think: who, what, where, when, and why.

Before he gets spanked remind him of the reason for punishment. Tell him how it's going to happen and what the results will be.

Typical spanking verbiage would read something like this:

> *"You are going over my knee, naughty boy. You are going to be spanked and you are going to be spanked soundly. I'm going to use my hand and hairbrush. Once I get finished with your spanking you won't be able to sit down for a week."*

Find out his specific buzzwords and the spanking phrases he likes to hear. There are many standard spanking expressions but everyone has their favorites. Do your best to discover his.

How can we initiate spanking play?

Sometimes couples give each other verbal or non-verbal cues that they're in the mood. I know one couple who has a special spanking hairbrush. That brush is put in a specific part of the bureau when one is in the mood to play. If the other partner has a compatible mood, spanking is initiated. If the person puts the brush away, the spanking activity is saved for a later date. Discuss how the two of you might initiate your private spanking play.

Some couples initiate spanking when an unexpected "faux pas" (an accident, mishap or unforeseen event) happens. Perhaps someone forgets to pick up the dry cleaning or call before coming home late. Spanking can sometimes be used to alter moods or turn a dismal evening into something memorable and fun.

But remember to let go of anger or hurt before the spanking begins. Spanking should never be used to settle differences. There are many effective techniques designed for adults to negotiate and state their needs. Spanking is not one of them. Spanking is a pleasurable, sensual experience carried out by two consenting adults.

Do you like to role play?

Another way to launch spanking activity is through role playing. Role plays are short scenarios that give reason and build up to the spanking. Role-plays are a good way to get into a scene, use spanking verbiage and allow yourself to let go, feel emotions and immerse yourself into the part you're playing.

Many spanking fetishists find role playing helpful in that they can be someone else. This fosters some distance and the spanking is not taken personally. In other words, it's that other person who shoplifted and must be punished for it or that other person who didn't prepare for an exam. It also allows for age regressive play that is a natural byproduct of spanking interactions.

What are some of your favorite spanking stories or scenarios that you'd like to enact?

Classic spanking stories are based on real-life situations and events. For example, the person is punished for everyday occurrences such as being late, forgetting something important, not doing chores, etc. The role you play in this scenario depends on his inner fantasy life. Find out if he imagines being an adult or teen or even younger. Choose the role that coincides with his inner thoughts. If he likes age-regressive scenarios, you can play the strict auntie, harsh teacher or hot babysitter. Adult spanking mindsets require you to be an age-appropriate adult such as a stern boss, an upset next-door neighbor or spanking therapist.

Spanking scenarios always require that the sympathy be with the spanker. The spanker doesn't want to spank but has to do it for "your own good", i.e. he behaved inappropriately, carelessly or defiantly, lost his temper, forgot something important or willingly chose to disobey. The spankee clearly deserves the punishment he has coming. He grudgingly takes the spanking because he "has no choice". Within this broad framework, you can make up stories that support those conditions.

Here's another easy but effective example: You're a schoolteacher and catch him cheating on a test. His choice is to get spanked or be expelled. The spanking is administered to teach him a lesson.

Role playing is a helpful tool to get both of you in the mood. Role-plays allow for creativity, imagination and provide an enjoyable context for the "play". They allow you both to stretch your wings and be people other than yourselves, thus opening the doors for you to do things you wouldn't normally do. It often takes away the feelings of shame and embarrassment that many spanking people experience. It also puts you in a role of healthy nurturer. You get to take on the part of a maternal woman who is looking after and correcting someone you care about. This role can be very healing for those who never had this kind of care and attention when they were young.

What about spanking as a way to settle a disagreement?

Sometimes couples think they can settle disputes with the use of spanking, but I'm telling you to never, ever use spanking to push your own agenda or settle a disagreement. It's simply not healthy.

Spankos have an urban myth they refer to as the "Spencer Spanking Plan", which advocates the idea that spanking is a beneficial way for couples to settle differences and maintain order in the household. I think this idea is fine as long as it's kept within the context of fun and fantasy. In reality, spanking will never make an adult or even a child do something they aren't on board with. The paddle will not make your spouse take out the garbage if he isn't inclined. It won't make a woman iron if she'd rather go to the cleaners. However, "the threat of the paddle" can be an enjoyable tool in the context of play and certainly can make chores more fun for a spanking fetishist.

Were you ever spanked as a child?

This question in particular will help you dig into his past. Some spanking people were spanked as children; others were not. Those who were not spanked may have a subconscious desire to experience what they deem as a caring brand of discipline.

By his response to this question you may discover that your man has been beaten, abused or disrespected. I'm confident that you'll be an active, caring listener as he opens up to you about things he probably has never told another human being. The idea of a ritualistic, loving spanking is something that his inner child still craves. To him, a spanking connotes the feeling of care. A good, swift spanking takes away the pain of feeling rejected, unloved or worthless. The idea of a spanking is idealized and subsequently craved in adulthood.

Do you think of experiencing "subspace"?

Subspace is totally unrelated to the mathematical term of the same name! It's a state of mind where the spankee experiences a form of euphoria. The pain is no longer perceived as pain; it is now an integral part of the spanking experience. For many people into spanking, this is the ultimate goal. Subspace refers to the psychological state of the submissive partner.

In the context of subspace, the spanking fetish is a reaction to a secret desire to be punished "normally" or "with love". These elements of the spanking experience are at the core of achieving subspace. A person being spanked wants to know that the person spanking them is doing it because they care about them. They are spanking them to improve their behavior because they are genuinely concerned about their well being.

Thus, the spankee wants to be transported into that surreal place where these deep desires are satisfied. They want to exist in an entirely new realm. Oftentimes, this powerful experience of subspace leads to a cleansing release of emotions expressed with deep sobbing and tears. Which leads us to...

Do you imagine being spanked to tears?

The act of crying produces a true cathartic effect. It's also the natural response to a spanking. However, as adults we don't cry from pain. We might scream, complain or squirm when faced with pain, but real, pure tears are produced by honest feelings of sadness, self-reproach or regret.

If your guy wants to be spanked to tears he'll have to trust you enough to let go and allow himself to get in touch with some very powerful emotions. As the spanker, you can help him get there by your words, your relationship and your ability to provide a safe, caring environment.

It's not so easy for a grown man or even a grown woman to cry. Men especially have been taught to control that feeling. As a result, we all have emotions that are deeply buried. Spanking can be used therapeutically to allow us to release these withheld feelings. In order to produce tears, your guy has to connect emotionally to his inner pain. He has to truly feel like he's getting punished and the tears are about remorse.

The Ritual of Spanking

A great many spanking fetishists often grew up in households that were unstable, dysfunctional and chaotic. These people were raised in an environment based on uncertainty. Feelings of confusion or fear are a direct result of parents who fought loudly, were abusive or even neglectful. For them, spanking then becomes an unconscious longing to get something that wasn't attained in childhood: boundary setting with a clear-cut, well-defined sense of right or wrong. There's accountability for staying within the parameters and consequences for stepping over the line.

Spanking is a good way to compensate for a misguided childhood. As the spanker, you have the responsibility to re-parent in a positive, supportive, nurturing fashion.

Spankings are administered in a clearly-defined ceremonious fashion. Sit on a straight-backed chair, couch or at the edge of the bed. While the chair embodies the classic over-the-knee (aka OTK) spanking, as I've said previously, it's often uncomfortable for the spankee as the blood rushes to their head. A sofa or bed supports the head and allows for a longer spanking.

As the spanker, your posture should be straight and capture the look of someone in control. Place him over your knee with his bottom up. The ritual consists of spanking over his clothing, then over his underpants and finally, on his bare behind. This is one way to build up the intensity of the spanking, as well as the emotional anticipation of your hand against his bare buttocks.

The ABCs of Spanking

Although everyone has their personal preference, here are a few particulars about spanking:

- Scolding is proper before placing him over your knee. He should have a good sense of why he's being punished within the context of the role play or real life.
- You can take him by the ear or simply guide him over your lap.
- Mold your hand around the lower part of his buttocks and slap so that you can hear a good, clear smack.

- Repeat and repeat and...
- Hand spankings are the most intimate because they allow for skin-to-skin contact and control.
- Rubbing after a series of smacks provides the feeling of caring and it will give both of you a break.
- 50-100 smacks would be considered a good amount for one volley of hand spanks before rubbing and continuing.

The length and time of the spanking is something you both need to gage. It's a good idea to set parameters beforehand. Some people like to give and receive long spankings that last 10 to 20 minutes.

In many ways, a spanking is almost as tough on the spanker as it is on the spankee! If your hand tires, give him some corner time to give yourself a break. When he's standing there facing the corner, you have the opportunity to get some feedback about your spanking. Too hard? Too soft? Strict enough? Believable enough? The more you communicate, the better the spanking will be.

Seductive, Adult-Type Spanking

Initially, you might feel that spanking a grown man is simply beyond your own realm of sensibility. But now you've found that even after your Q&A session, you still can't wrap your head around the idea of punishing your man on any level; even in fantasy.

Here's another idea which might work better for you. Imagine this:

> He gets home from work earlier than you do. You walk into the house and find a beautifully set table complete with wine, candles and a brand new set of dishes. You smile and say, "Look at this. What have you done? You naughty boy you..." You proceed to take him by the ear and put him over your knee. Instead of saying his spanking buzzwords in a punitive way, you can say them seductively.

Any man who likes to be spanked would be fine with this revised scenario, using the spanking to reward him, not berate him. Be creative and adapt it to fit your needs. The spanking will be arousing and played out on a level that you might feel is more in tune with adult sexuality.

Attire For The Spanker

Go to the mall or to your closet. No, on second thought, go to the mall. You deserve a reward for fulfilling your man's spanking fantasies! Pick out any kind of outfit that makes you feel sexy but strict. The classic disciplinarian wears a tight black skirt with a crisp, white man-tailored shirt. You can complete the look with a business-type blazer. Wear stockings or hose to make your legs look more smooth and attractive. Remember, he'll be lying over your knee. Some men report feeling more aroused from contact with tight hose than with bare skin when they're receiving a rousing spanking.

Black pumps complete the look. You can also wear vintage or modern lingerie, nightgowns, garter and stockings, or even sexy tight jeans. If you're role-playing the part of a teacher, doctor or uniformed person, you can use special costuming. But always wear something that makes you feel sexy, in control and ready to spank. Comfort is important as well, especially in your upper body since you'll continuously be swinging your arm.

Before we get to how the spankee should dress, we'll discuss...

Switching

Spanking is a fetish where it's common for participants to go both ways. He might enjoy being the spanker as well as taking on the part of the spankee. If you don't have a personal predilection towards spanking, you might not enjoy being spanked too firmly. The reason a spanko can take such hard punishment is the fact that he's turned on, which make endorphins flow and cause pain to be masked with excitement and pleasure.

If spanking is not part of your sexual make-up, you probably won't be genuinely turned on. That's okay. Allow him to spank you lightly. Observe his attitude and listen to his verbiage. He is inadvertently demonstrating the way he likes to get spanked himself. If you position yourself the right way, your clitoris can come in contact with his knee, which will intensify your experience. Feeling his growing erection as he spanks you will also be a turn-on.

Spankings should feel like an intense massage. They should feel mostly pleasurable and have a light, stinging effect. Your comfort level and boundaries should be respected. Allowing him to spank you is a gift. He should honor your openness and make sure the spanking is a good, pleasant feeling for you. It doesn't have to be hard in order for it to be sexy.

Attire For The Spankee

Panties are a very important part of the spanking ritual. It's skirt up; panties down! You will be spanked on top of your clothes, then on your panties and finally, on your bare bottom. Take care to dress appropriately for your role. He might also indicate a preference, though. Some guys love to spank over tight jeans; others like to spank on a skirt or dress that sits below the knee. Panties should cover the behind completely. No thongs! This way he'll lead up to uncovering your bottom in much the same way a special gift is unwrapped. He'll also probably have a preference as to material, color and cut of your panties. Full-back, white cotton panties are a common request but everyone has their favorites.

Implements

You don't need to shop at a kinky store. You can find what you need at the mall, in your closet or junk drawer. Remember that spanking mirrors something that's supposed to happen within the context of a school or home. It's not about whips. It's more about using your hand (or perhaps some other tool) to drive the lesson home.

The hairbrush is the most common spanking tool. You can get a good spanking hairbrush at any beauty supply store. Make sure it's wooden and has a smooth back for spanking. You can also use men's leather belts. If you have the inclination or he has the desire, you can get fancy. Many Web sites sell paddles. The two of you can go online and pick out the ones that will work as realistic props for your role-plays. Then there are plain, old-fashioned Ping Pong paddles, which work just as well.

Spanking Tips For You

The human buttocks can take an amazing amount of punishment safely because of the thick layer of fatty padding. Nevertheless, it's important to do it right.

- First, imagine a line that cuts the buttock region in half. Always spank on the lower region, halfway above the thigh.
- Relax your hand and let it mold to his bottom.
- Use your wrist and slap. If your slap makes a sharp noise, you know you're doing a good job.
- Practice with him. Let him help you and allow him to tell you what feels good and right for him.
- Spank with caution because swats to the upper buttock region or lower back can cause serious spinal damage.

Spanking paddles range from leather or light balsa wood to heavy, dense wood or thick plastic. The general rule of thumb is the denser and heavier a paddle, the more it will hurt, mark or bruise. Again, you need to practice so that you strike in the correct place.

Belts folded in half are a good, domestic disciplinary tool. Be careful though, because belts aren't firm and you can easily miss your mark.

You can spank the back of his thighs to get his attention or to emphasize a point, but don't linger there because it can cause painful muscle bruising.

As spanker, you're responsible for monitoring the condition and reaction of his bottom. Talk about marking ahead of time. Some people like getting marked; others worry about the embarrassment of being seen in the locker room or at a doctor's appointment with florid bruises on their behind. One client tells the funny story of going on a "guys only" camping trip. He had some trouble explaining marks on his posterior given by his wife as a fun "farewell" spanking. Luckily he was able to tell his friends he had fallen a few hours before when walking through the woods to "do his business". He thought fast, kept a straight face and felt confident about his love of spanking because he had a supportive partner. Other spankos sometimes get embarrassed and flustered. That's why discretion is key.

If there are skin ruptures, it's time to stop no matter what he thinks or wants. At that moment he could be in subspace and will not be able to communicate clearly. It's your responsibility to make the call.

More About Subspace or Spanking Catharsis

Spankings can be highly emotional experiences. They can induce a state of mind which we discussed earlier, called subspace. In this state, you guy is totally immersed in the scene. He is focused, "in the zone", and not thinking about anything other than the way he's emotionally experiencing this spanking with you.

Sometimes spankings bring tears. The tears are not about pain. Be assured that they're not bad; they're just the opposite, cleansing and cathartic. Tears do not necessarily mean you should stop the spanking. Crying signifies a release and a letting out of pent-up emotions. This is one of the therapeutic values of delivering an emotionally-charged spanking. It's a catalyst for him to release deep feelings. The focused pain allows him to get in touch with something buried inside of him.

When he's in subspace, he loses ability to make decisions. He regresses to a childlike, dependent state. You have the opportunity (and the duty) to be focused and in touch with him emotionally. Allow him to have a cathartic release but also make sure you're clued in and know when he's physically had enough.

In Summary

Spanking is a highly-complex fetish, which requires a great deal of investigation and understanding from you. Do your homework and investigate thoroughly. The rewards are great in that you will be providing an experience that can have a positive psychological effect upon him. You can make a huge difference in his life by showing him acceptance for something that has been previously rejected. Your openness will create a strong, everlasting connection which will bring you even closer.

Chapter 24
Spanking, SM and Ds:
The Different Mindsets Explained

You man might say he wants to be spanked when in reality he wants you to dominate him. Conversely, he could say that he wants to be dominated when all he wants is a good, sound spanking. Many believe S/M, D/s and spanking are interchangeable, however this is not true.

In reality, the spanking fetish is vastly different from a true flogging, whipping or power exchanges delivered in the dungeon. Although both involve striking the bottom, the attitude, scenario and mindset are absolutely different. First, you need to find out what kind of role you'll be playing in order create the setting congruent with his fantasy.

The Difference between Spanking and Dungeon Activities

Here's the major difference: dungeon interactions are based in fantasy while spanking is more reality-based. A guy who envisions a leather or latex-clad woman administering his spanking is generally more interested in the concept of taking pain as an subordinate person, than he is in being punished as a naughty boy.

The terms S/M and D/s are interchangeable with slight variations. S/M or sadomasochism references a person who enjoys inflicting pain upon another person who equally enjoys being on the receiving end of that pain. D/s or Dominant/submissive is a newer, more accurate term for S/M which refers to the roles of the people interacting in this scenario. It's the Dominant who administers the sensation and the submissive who receives it.

Pain doesn't always need to be present within the context of a D/s relationship. It's often just about the concept of defining one person as superior over another. If he likes a dose of spanking with his D/s or S/M scenario, he's fantasizing about a "higher up" administering pain as a metaphor that validates your D/s roles. The degree of pain and the interactions between the players is the distinguishing feature between S/M or D/s. Strictly speaking, S/M is more about physical sensations and D/s is more about the couple's assigned roles.

Technically, there are subtle differences between S/M and D/s. However, the attitude and mindset are very similar. One person is the leader and the other the follower. Men who enjoy being dominated rarely do it for the mere sensation of pain. They submit because they want to explore a giving, subservient, softer side of their psyche. The purpose of being spanked, flogged or whipped is to demonstrate their ability to suffer as a sign of devotion. It's about relinquishing control, which in effect, offers a kind of freedom.

While practitioners of D/s and S/M would be considered siblings, spanking fetishists are distant cousins. Spanking fetishists psychologically relate to the concept of punishment. They feel an unconscious need to be corrected, admonished and endure discipline for a real or fabricated wrongdoing. A pure spanking fetishist never wants the spanking; he has no choice but to be punished in order to be forgiven, absolved or learn a lesson.

For them, the spanker is not a leather Goddess, Dominatrix or Latex Queen. Their ideal spanker is a nurturer who believes that the spanking is for the spankee's "own good". Spankings are administered with love; not anger. A proficient spanker never gets angry or out of control. She spanks with authority and an air of confidence. Ideally, she's a loving disciplinarian.

The word "spanking" is often used broadly. Since the terminology can often be very confusing, you need to find out exactly what he means when he says that he wants to be spanked. The questions below will help you distinguish whether he likes spanking within the context of dungeon play or if he's a true spanking fetishist.

Q&A:

What do you mean when you say you want to be spanked?

Take heed to clues about scenarios, positions and instruments to be used. Also be aware of the context of the kind of spanking he craves. He might mention the idea of submission or he might talk about being taken over your knee like a naughty boy.

What age do you imagine being when you're spanked?

True spankos will really relate to this question. Spanking fetishists often like to age regress while being spanked. They imagine themselves as little boys being spanked by a parent or a feisty teenager being disciplined by a sexy schoolteacher. Others just want to be spanked in real time as an adult in need of being kept "in line".

Guys who think of spanking as an act of submission relate to being spanked as an adult. Note that the concept of age regression does not come into play here. Therefore, the idea of age is a key question to discover exactly what kind of spanking your guy craves.

What implements do you envision getting spanked with?

His implement choice is crucial in making the distinction between spanking or D/s.

S/M or D/s spanking devices include leather-crafted paddles, deerskin floggers and riding crops. Take notice that none of these items are household devices. Most of these tools would have to be purchased in specialty shops or online stores.

The hand, hairbrush, wooden spoon, belt and paddle (think Ping Pong, not necessarily a specialty paddle) are the kinds of instruments a true spanking fetishist envisions. They are all related to domestic punishment and are devices found in homes or schoolrooms.

How are you positioned for the spanking?

Again, his answer will be very telling. A guy who has masochistic tendencies wants to be restrained because he envisions spanking as a painful activity. Getting tied down would mean he couldn't escape punishment. A man who likes dungeon activities would also probably want to be tied or restrained since to him a spanking is about bondage and discipline. The dungeon guys might bring up the idea of bending over a leather gym horse or being tied to a specially-designed bondage cross. They also may envision the "spanking" as a whipping on the back as well as the buttock region.

Quite to the contrary, spanking fetishists will describe one position and one main position only. Nine times out of ten, guys who want a spanking imagine the traditional "over the knee" position. He wants you to place him over your lap, bottom up and ritualistically spank him on his clothes, underpants and then on his bare bottom. He may also imagine classic paddling positions for more stringent discipline. These positions would include hands on knees, hands flat on a desk with his bottom upturned and ready for punishment. True blue spanking fetishists never equate bondage with the spanking; it doesn't tie into that domestic mindset where he envisions spanking administered by a nurturing parental figure.

How do you want me to dress?

S/M and D/s guys generally prefer leather, latex, or sexy lingerie. They'll talk about stiletto heels or thigh-high boots. Fetish ware like this can be found at specialty shops or online.

Spanking fetishists, or spankos, as they like to be called, relate more to real-life attire. He might request that you wear a business suit, jeans or lingerie. Spankers typically wear clothing that reflects confidence and authority with a touch of femininity. Think of a crisp white-collared, button-down shirt worn with a tight black skirt or slacks. Some spankos enjoy seeing their spanker in old-fashioned lingerie such as a tight girdle, full-back panties or old-style brassiere.

Is a spanking reward or punishment?

When a Dominant finds out something her submissive enjoys, she can use it as a reward; i.e. "If you're a good boy, I'll give you a spanking." So if your man speaks of spanking as a reward, he's definitely an S/M kind of a guy. Spanking fetishists would never admit that they want or enjoy a spanking. To them, a spanking is necessary; never enjoyable.

What are some phrases or buzzwords you'd like me to use?

D/s folk think in terms of power exchanges. To them, spanking is the vehicle used to produce a docile mind state. He'll want to address you as "Mistress" or "Goddess". He'll want you to express your own enjoyment when punishing him. He'll love hearing that you like using his bottom as your "play toy". You may even tell him that spanking is a way for you to relieve your frustrations. He'll feel excited to take a spanking in order to please you.

Spanking fetishists or spankos don't ever want the spanking, though their mindset is all about deserving the discipline. They agree to the spanking because they have "no choice" in the matter. A spanking is endured so that their "naughty slate" can be wiped clean. After a spanking, all is forgiven.

Common buzzwords include phrases like:

- "Get over my knee, young man."
- "I'm going to give you a spanking you'll never forget."
- "This spanking is long overdue."
- "I'm sorry to have to spank you, but it's for your own good."
- "This hurts me, more than it hurts you."

The last phrase is very similar to a phrase used in an old "Our Gang Comedy" episode called "Anniversary Trouble" from 1935. One of the characters, coincidentally named Spanky, gets to "spank" his father in a weird role-reversal. Many spankees have reported early feelings of arousal when watching this scene in reruns as children.

Do you want to be spanked for a real reason?

To this, D/s people would generally respond, "If it pleases you," whereas spanking people would have a more definite reason for wanting the spanking. Spankos generally have very clear reasons for wanting red bottoms. They might want to be spanked for a past indiscretion or for breaking a rule that you imposed. Others enjoy enacting imagined scenarios that didn't actually happen to them but could have happened to others in real life. This would include spankings given at home, school or the office.

Describe your ideal spanker.

D/s guys will talk about a strong, take-charge woman. He'll discuss the importance of obedience to a powerful female. He'll feel a certain reverence for the lady who delivers the spankings. It's more about the woman than the actual spanking.

On the other hand, spanking fetishists will talk more about the concept of discipline. Their ideal female is the one who makes rules and sets boundaries. Spankings are given for the sake of correction, to set limits and to teach a lesson. The spanker is a caring person who spanks out of love and the desire to improve behavior.

How hard a spanking do you think you can take?

S/M guys will acquiesce to you, proclaiming, "I'll take it as hard as you wish to give it." Their goal is often to be pushed to the limit in order to prove their love and devotion to you.

Spanking fetishists are much more specific. Some spankos want to be pushed past their threshold in order to attain a cathartic release. Others desire the spanking to sting enough to have the spanking experience, but for them it's not about feeling unbearable pain. Rather, the spanking is more focused on the scenario, buzzwords and the embarrassment of having their bottom bared.

What's the ritual that goes along with spanking?

S/M and D/s folks will bring up bondage and discipline. This is probably the ultimate, telltale sign that he's more an S/M guy than a spankee. He'll talk about being suspended, tied to a spanking block or restrained in order to take the spanking. Or he may tell you that he'll hold a position for as long as you say to prove he's obedient. These are all the signs of an S/M guy.

Pure spanking fetishists never pair bondage and spanking. It's not in tune with the original concept of a parent spanking a child. Spanking fetishists are very precise and ritualistic when they think about spanking. It's all about being lectured, positioned over the knee and then being spanked over the clothes, on underpants and finally their bare bottom. Their penchant for spanking is so ritualistic that you should never deviate from his precise description of spanking.

In Summary

It's essential to ascertain what he means by spanking. Once you do your investigation, you can then flip back to the correct chapter in this book to learn more about his specific interests.

In some ways, spanking has become almost mainstream. Way back in 1979, there was a popular song called *Slap and Tickle* by the group Squeeze. I was pleasantly surprised when, around Valentine's Day, I noticed that a local bargain shop had a spanking toy of the same name which consisted of a fake hand and a pink feather. Perhaps spanking's day has come.

Chapter 25
Threesomes and Multiple Partners

Announcer: Ladies, what is the most common male fantasy?

Audience: Ding...ding...ding!

Announcer: Now ladies, don't all answer at once. The number one answer on the board is...Having a threesome! (with or without you).

All kidding aside, threesomes or multiple partner fantasies are the most common male fantasies. Men may also fantasize about having sex with more than one woman in a wife swap situation or gang bang setting. These thoughts live in the male sexual psyche. They are not considered paraphilias unless they are thought about obsessively. Likewise you shouldn't consider these thoughts to be troublesome unless they are acted upon without your permission.

If He Thinks About It, It's Not Cheating
That's right. Your man is entitled to think about whatever he

wants - and so are you. Remember all of that unnecessary controversy around Jimmy Carter admitting in a 1976 "Playboy" interview that he'd lusted in his heart? How silly, especially after what Bill Clinton did in the Oval Office with Monica Lewinsky almost 20 years later.

It's high time for you to allow your man to give voice to his fantasies without censorship. You don't have to agree with them or like them. However, it is essential for you to acknowledge his private, personal thoughts.

It may be painful to think that your guy wants another woman besides you. You might be saying to yourself:

- "Aren't I enough for him?"
- "Don't I satisfy him?"
- "How could he possibly think about anyone but me?"

Unfortunately, no matter how much we wish it weren't true, it is. Men do think about and fantasize about other women. It's a tough, bitter little pill to swallow, but it's essential if you want to truly participate in his inner sexual world.

Women are by nature monogamous creatures as long as we're feeling content. We may recognize a male as being virile and handsome. We may even have a fleeting sexual fantasy of our own but that's as far as it goes. We usually don't think about other men the way men think about other women. Our thoughts don't immediately travel to hardcore sexual situations. Monogamous women rarely entertain thoughts of threesomes with another guy. It's simply not in our nature to share in that manner. For women, sexual intimacy is about one-on-one closeness, not fluttering about like a bee from flower to flower.

Men on the other hand, do entertain thoughts of being with other women more often than we want to know. In fact, it's been said that if we could climb inside a guy's head and be privy to his thoughts, we'd probably never stop slapping him! It doesn't matter how gorgeous, toned or brilliant you are. It's not about you; it's about him. This type of male fantasy is hinged on the idea of freedom and variety.

Men are more prone to having frequent, vivid sexual thoughts than women are. Sometimes these thoughts may be about you but often they're not. Think of it like this: men love their cars but every now and again they want to test drive something new. It's a fact. How you choose to deal with it can positively or negatively impact your relationship.

Consider It An Opportunity

Your guy is probably guilty about harboring his threesome or moresome fantasies. After all, these thoughts are not condoned by society. If you're married, he took a vow of "Till death do us part." But this unrealistic proclamation doesn't address the fact that a man's penis has a mind of its own.

If you acknowledge your man's feelings and give him the freedom of expression, you will open up a deeper level of trust. He won't have to sneak or hide his fantasies from you. If he feels your unconditional love and acceptance, chances are good that he won't lie or cheat on you. Why would he? You're his best friend and most intimate partner. He can share everything with you, even his confusing desires. He'll realize he doesn't have to censor his thoughts from you. This knowledge will alleviate the anxiety that ultimately causes him to act on his feelings.

What Is Cheating?

Cheating is going outside the marriage for sex or intimacy. Most women who have experienced infidelity will tell you that the most hurtful aspect of it wasn't the fact that he had intercourse with someone else. The most painful part is the intimacy he shared with that other woman. Cheating is about betraying trust. Once that faith is broken it's very, very difficult to rebuild.

Sex is not always synonymous with lovemaking. Men have a real knack for being able to detach. Fetish behavior is the extreme way that men sexualize objects and situations which have absolutely nothing to do with their partner. When your man looks at or fantasizes about other women, he's simply indulging in a hedonistic part of his sexual make up. Often, he fantasizes to relieve stress and tension. Masturbation affords a wonderful, healthy way to relieve pent-up anxiety. Sexual fantasy is a distraction. It's the equivalent of window shopping at the mall:

it's fun to look, to dream. It's meaningless, harmless, diversionary behavior.

First, you need to discard the myths about what a relationship *should* be and accept the universal differences between men and women. You can't control the way he thinks but you can control the way *you* think about his sexual thinking. If you believe that sexual fantasies are wrong and that they mean he doesn't love you, chances are good you'll feel bad about yourself and your marriage. And he'll pinpoint your feelings in a second by the way you interact with him.

Many women pretend to be oblivious to their guy's roving eye but it's obvious to everyone (including him) that you're seething inside. What if you thought differently? What if you chose to accept his male behavior as a fact of life? By accepting his thoughts you won't upset yourself or him. Or better yet, you can also decide to get on board and figure out a way to manage this misunderstood but very real fact about men—that they fantasize about other women, pure and simple.

The questions below will help you get a better understanding of his inner desires. A once-taboo subject no longer needs to be the "pink elephant in the room." You don't need to keep secrets from each other. Instead, you can accept and even participate in his very private sexual thoughts. I bet he'll even invite you along while he's "test driving" the car he doesn't really want to buy.

Q&A:

When you think about women other than me, what kind of fantasies do you have? Do you imagine threesomes? Group sex? Wife swapping?

Notice how you're not being accusatory when you phrase the question in this way. You're just assuming he's a guy and that he has these kinds of fantasies. Be open-minded and stay curious. Allow him to freely express his thoughts without censorship or punishment.

If you could enact any fantasy what would happen?

Again, this is an open-ended question. Encourage him to give you details. Have him describe exactly what happens and with whom.

Imagine you were stranded on a desert island with many women. What would you hope happened sexually?

Here's your chance to cull some important information. He might reply that he'd want to watch the women having sex together. Or he might say he'd want to nail them all. Remember to be accepting and listen. It's only a fantasy.

Which would you prefer: watching me having sex with another woman, having a threesome where all three of us are going at it, or having me and our fantasy girl doing things just to you?

His response to this question is a mirror into his sexual soul. Some guys like to lay back and get serviced while others want to be more participatory. You will get a great deal of insight by seeing how this fantasy would actually play out in his head.

Another point: if he's a fetishist, he might imagine a scene where you and another woman dominate, tie him up, or spank him together.

On a scale of 1-10, 10 being highest, how strong is your desire to have a threesome with me participating?

Obviously, his answer to this question is the key to going further.

What Do I Do Now?

Let's say you've unearthed a real inclination toward your guy wanting a threesome. Should you go ahead and make arrangements? If so, how can you safely do this, both emotionally and health-wise? If you are absolutely turned off by the thought, what options or alternatives are open to you?

Should You or Shouldn't You?

First and foremost, you and your man have to decide whether or not this is something you really want to do. You need to ask yourself:

- How high on the scale is his desire?
- Is this something he's wanted to do all his life?

265

- Would he feel "robbed" if he died tomorrow and never got to have this experience?
- How do you feel about going through with this in reality?

Of course, it helps if you yourself are bi-curious; that is, curious about exploring bisexuality but have never actually done it. Many women do have a curiosity about what it would be like to have sexual contact with another female. Most of us have been conditioned to dismiss these thoughts but if you allow yourself to honestly examine your feelings, you may be surprised at what you'll find.

Having sex with another woman will satisfy your curiosity of what your mate experiences when he's having sex with you. You'll be able to experience the softer, gentler caress of a woman. Finally, you'll know what it feels like to be with a human being who has the same parts, the same pleasures as you do. You might find the thoughts arousing and decide to go beyond just thinking about it.

On the other hand, you might not have any desire to be with another woman. Yet you do have the desire to please your man. What if the idea of another woman in your bed brings up feelings of anxiety based on jealousy? This is really an important issue to consider and share with him.

As women, we're conditioned to compare and contrast. It's an unfortunate way to be but nevertheless, it's a fact. Women are very competitive with each other, constantly comparing the way we look, the way we dress. This competitiveness also makes us very possessive about holding onto our men.

If you experience these types of competitive thoughts you need to be up front with him about them. Let him know about them before you initiate that threesome. This way he'll be prepared to pay special attention to you during the act. He needs to understand that he's required to be extra sensitive to your insecurities before, during and after the entire process.

You can help yourself by changing your thoughts. Rather than imagining he's going to "fall for" the other woman, think about the gift you're giving to him and the potential pleasure for yourself. This is the ultimate expression of your love. You are doing this because you want to make the person you adore the most, extremely happy.

Please communicate with your man deeply about all the emotions and fears you have before delving into this life-changing event.

How Do I Make A Threesome Happen?

Now that you've decided to enact your man's ultimate three-way fantasy, where in the world do you find the woman? It's not easy.

Here's why: women are predatory creatures. It's natural for them to want to "attach to" the man they bed. They have no interest in having sex with your guy in the context of him being yours; they will naturally want to make him theirs. It takes a very special breed of woman who's in it for the sexual adventure aspect and nothing else.

You'll need to be very careful in the selection process. My advice is not to pick someone up in an internet chat room. You might be picking up a huge mistake! You also don't want to invite one of your girlfriends into bed. A "real girlfriend" is the one you'll want to call the next day. Inviting her into your bed would inevitably change and taint the relationship. Definitely not worth the risk. Last but not least, don't pick up a drunken girl at the bar. She'll probably end up in your bathroom being sick rather than in your bedroom. And besides, intoxicated people don't make the best decisions, so she might be doing something she will regret later.

You might want to consider some kind of swingers club. There, you'll find other couples who are like-minded and in a similar situation to yours. If you go this route, be prepared for the possibility that you may be required to have some kind of sexual intimacy with another guy. Swinger organizations are usually designed for couples. As a rule, you won't find single women there. So, for this reason, a swingers club will open up other possibilities that you and your guy may or may not embrace. It's not necessarily the logical place to have your man's threesome desires met. Go only if you both want to experience sexual relations with other consenting couples.

My best recommendation is to hire a working girl. Yes, a prostitute. This will make the whole experience a clean, up front business transaction. A professional won't be interested in your guy and your own jealousy issues won't come into play. She won't want to stay and be friends with you or your man. You'll live out his fantasy and then she'll leave you and your man alone with the experience.

I understand that prostitution is still illegal in most states. You might want to consider taking a trip to somewhere like Las Vegas where prostitution is legal. There are several established brothels just a short taxicab ride from the Strip. Travel abroad to a place like Amsterdam or Thailand where prostitution is legal. The women at these establishments are clean, pleasant and tested weekly for STDs.

Most brothels are also amenable to couples. I suggest you make an appointment before you arrive and communicate your desires for a threesome to see if the establishment can accommodate you. If they can, the threesome should be a positive experience all around and safe, emotionally as well as physically. You won't be inviting any kind of trouble in the way of emotional ties or in the form of STDs.

I know this can be a costly venture but it will be worth every penny if you choose to explore your man's desires. Your relationship and bond as a couple is at stake. At brothels, boundaries are respected and happy three-way memories are virtually guaranteed.

Other Alternatives

There are many other ways for you to satisfy his longing for a threesome without the actual physical contact of one. Many times it's enough for a fantasy to be talked about and acknowledged.

Describe the threesome to your man in detail while you're in bed making love. Masturbate him and tell him a story about you and the fantasy girl. If you recall your Q&A, then you'll know what he wants to hear. Tailor the story to the answers he gave. Talk about you and the other woman doing him or describe what it would be like having him watch you with another woman.

Don't be squeamish. It's only a story. Use this as an opportunity to be free and wild.

You could also try phone sex. Call a phone sex line and talk to the operator, describing your man's desires. This is a very easy way to have your threesome needs met. The woman on the other end of the line is a pro and will know how to take control of the conversation and the situation. You still need to lead the fantasy based on the information your man gave you during your Q&A. Many guys find the phone sex alternative to be extremely arousing and totally satisfying.

Online web cams are another way to have the threesome experience. Here, the girl would perform for the two of you on camera while you watched in the privacy of your home. This same type of encounter could occur at your local strip club if you hired a woman to perform for you in a private room or booth.

These last few alternatives will give your man the visual experience without the tactile part. In other words, no touching or being touched but the fantasy can still be realized.

In Summary

Acceptance is a powerful tool. Allow your guy to express his thoughts about threesomes and moresomes. Change your own way of thinking in order to transform your ingrained jealousy into the concept of giving pleasurable gifts.

Revamping your own thoughts is cutting edge and allows for freedom of expression for both of you. Your guy will feel comfortable in being able to express his true feelings. He won't have to stifle or inhibit his desires. As a result, the chance of him cheating on you are substantially lowered because he won't feel a need to rebel or seek his desires elsewhere since you're both seeking them together. The lines of communication are open for the two of you to experience unconditional acceptance and validation as a couple.

Chapter 26
Tickling

Everybody knows what tickling is. How can you turn something as sweet and innocent as tickling into a fetish, you may be wondering. Believe it or not, tickling is a fetish in which participants derive sexual pleasure by receiving tickles or by tickling another person. Tickling can be perceived as erotic stimulation or it can be used as a catalyst to maintain control over another person. Sometimes tickling is used in conjunction with bondage or some type of D/s scene.

I'm sure you've heard the old phrase "tickled to death". Used in this context, tickling signifies extreme pleasure or it can describe someone who is so sensitive that tickling goes way beyond pleasure to become something that is excruciatingly uncomfortable. In childhood, many kids hear this expression and don't quite know what to make of it—is tickling a good thing, a bad thing, or both. Though it hasn't been clinically proven, I have a feeling that many tickling fetishists may have heard about being "tickled to death" when they very young. The words led to a charged feeling which then triggered the fetish later on in life.

You're reading this chapter because you have a sneaking suspicion that your guy has a tickling fetish that goes above and beyond the kind of playful exchange couples have in the privacy of their own bedrooms. The tickling may be a fetish in and of itself and that's as far as it goes. However, the tickling might also symbolize his own feelings of being submissive. In other words, tickling is part of an overall D/s scene: the act of you tickling him makes him want to be helpless and submit to your will.

Here are some questions you need to ask in order to discover if your guy has a tickling fetish.

Q&A:

What do you enjoy about tickling?
Your man might say that for him, tickling is about the pleasurable sensation that engulfs his body when he's tickled. Some people find this very stimulating. He might also say that he enjoys the idea that extreme tickling produces out-of-control feelings.

Do you enjoy being tickled or do you want to tickle me?
Tickling, like spanking, infantilism and bondage, can be enjoyed both ways. Sometimes he's the tickler and sometimes he's the ticklee. If you want to participate as the one getting tickled, by all means do, but for the purposes of this book, I'm writing from the vantage point that you are the initiator and leader in the tickling play.

If your man is only interested in being the tickler, then you'll have to figure out if this is something you personally want to pursue. You can very easily use the questions in this section as a guideline and alter them to pertain to his dominant tickling fetish.

Remember, this book is about helping him bring fantasies to life. At the very least, you can accept his fetish and participate within the context of your boundaries. You can continue to ask the key questions provided here in order to obtain more information.

What do you enjoy being tickled with?

He might say your long fingernails, fingertips or the flats of your hands. Discuss with him the different sensations he feels when being tickled by different types of things. What feels most erotic for him? Experiment with using peacock feathers, furs, rose petals, etc. Your imagination is the limit. This is a nice way to make the most of your creativity and find pleasurable type of objects to tickle his fancy.

Where are your tickling erogenous zones?

Some guys will share but others may want you to discover his ticklish spots on your own. Popular tickle spots include the feet, navel, chest, nipples, armpits, ribs, sides, stomach, behind the ears, neck, forehead, eyelids and genitals.

Do you like to incorporate bondage with the tickling?

Some find it exciting to be tied down in order to feel "captured". Tickle all you want - there's no escape! Bondage also offers maximum relaxation and forces focus. His hands are tied so there's nothing he can do but lay back and helplessly enjoy the sensations you create.

Do you like light or hard tickling?

This question provides the key to where he's at psychologically. People who like "light tickling" usually are in it for the sexy sensations it produces. After all, tickling is a tease. It's titillation. The tickling strokes are introduced in a delicate, erotic way. Ask him to show you what he likes and where he likes it.

Those who like hard tickling are focused more on "tickle torture" - which is exactly what it means. They enjoy a rougher brand of tickling where it is tormenting to the point of being excruciatingly uncomfortable. When tickled in this fashion the person often loses control and has to beg for mercy.

If his response to the above question is hard tickling, then you might ask: Why do you like tickle torture?

Pay close attention to his response but I will also give you an answer from a "professional" POV. People usually like tickle torture for the same reason people like extreme bondage, whipping or any kind of torturous sexual stimulation. Tickle torture increases endorphins and brings people to a bliss-like state. The tickling feels so intense that it drives a person to truly let out their emotions with abandon. It's hard to find a "stoic" ticklee. Extreme tickling gives someone permission to laugh, scream and beg loudly for mercy. The tickling very quickly brings the person to the awareness that they are totally in your hands. They are completely dependent upon you to administer or cease their "tickle punishment" in this helpless state.

Administering A Tickle Torture Scene

A real tickle torture scene would require some use of bondage or restraint. A four-poster bed is ideal for this kind of episode. You need to tie in a way that gives direct access to his armpits, thighs and the bottoms of his feet.

Extreme tickling is generally done with your hands. You wouldn't use your fingertips as much as you'd use your fingers to capture the sensitive, most ticklish parts of his body and dig in wholeheartedly. The tickling motions would be interspersed with lighter, more sensual strokes so that your "victim" might last longer. The element of surprise is also extremely effective, so use of a blindfold usually heightens the experience.

For someone with a tickling fetish, the goal of the tickling is to get to a point where he can't take it anymore and he has to beg for mercy. Since tickle torture in its most extreme form involves losing control, the person being tickled might actually wet his pants. Of course, at that point he'd have to be spanked!

Note how three fetishes are successfully combined with this scene:

- Tickling
- Bondage
- Spanking

Fetishes are often combined to create the perfect, erotic experience.

Administering A Sensual Tickle Session

Make sure that your fingernails are well groomed. (A perfect excuse for a pampering manicure!) Gather a group of items that produce tickling sensations like: feathers, fur, a bristly hairbrush, toothpicks, etc. You can even use ice to create another cooler, prickly sensation. Put on your thinking cap and get inventive.

Role Playing A Tickling Scene

This is something your guy may or may not have thought about. If he didn't bring it up during your Q&A session, you can initiate this for yourself. It makes tickling even more fun.

Tickling lends itself to some very enjoyable scenarios. First and foremost, tickling always connotes the "damsel in distress." In this case, the damsel would be your guy. You can pretend he's been captured and tied to railroad tracks. He has to submit to an intense tickling before you release him.

Imagine that you are the "Tickle Bandit". You break into his house with the idea of tickling until he can't take it anymore. This scenario gives you permission to get outside of yourself and have some real fun. As the Tickle Bandit, you can take on a new, liberating role. You can shed any feelings of shyness or introversion and go wild. The Tickle Bandit scenario involves feeding an insatiable need to tickle her victim in any way she chooses, and the victim's helpless submission to laughing himself to tears.

Tickling is also a good catalyst for "inquisition" type scenes. Imagine he's a traitor or secret agent and you are the person trying to obtain some knowledge from him. He has to "talk or be tickled". The idea of making him give you information, real or imaginary, is a fun way to get into some rousing and exciting tickling interaction.

In Summary

Tickling has a very broad range. For some, it's a mild kind of foreplay and for others, it might just be a proclivity or preference. Tickling as a fetish is, of course, more extreme. For fetishists, there is enjoyment in doing, watching or fantasizing about someone being tickled to the extreme or being "tickled to death" as the old saying goes. But at its core, the root of a tickling fetish is grounded in feeling free while feeling helpless. The act of laughing uncontrollably is actually very liberating and relaxing. Just think of that great, big sigh of relief when it's over. Helping your man reach that land of Tickling Nirvana is a great gift.

Chapter 27
Honorable Mentions: A Potpourri of Fetishes

By now, you already know that sexual fantasies and fetishes
are as varied as each person's fingerprint. Generally speaking,
there are some commonalities in fetishes but each person has
their own individual turn-ons and triggers. Sexual fantasies reflect a person's uniqueness, imagination and early sense
memories. No two are quite the same.

There's often no rhyme or reason, no concrete explanation
as to why your man finds a thing, an object, situation or even a
word sexually stimulating. It's more important for you to accept
that it's there and then move on. The challenge requires that you
figure out ways to incorporate the fetish into your relationship
in a way that's fun for you both. It's your job to continuously
explore, question and investigate the nuances of his own
personal proclivities once you hit his particular "brand".

The previous chapters discussed some of the more common
male fetishes. But even within this broad range, there are always
distinct variations. That's why I encouraged you to make your
own investigations and ask questions. Inquiring helps you get
to know more deeply and better understand the person you're

involved with. The Q&A sessions I describe there are necessary for you to correctly capture your man's private fantasy as he imagines it when he's feeling aroused.

Be assured that there are myriad of fetishes and fantasies that aren't common enough to call for an entire chapter but nonetheless deserve an "honorable mention". Even if your guy's desires don't fall into the "common" category, it's important for you to have an understanding of the wide variety of images he might find stimulating. I encourage you to ask him the sorts of questions I detailed in the previous chapters to get a better handle on his unique fetish.

This "potpourri" contains fetishes that are popular enough to warrant mentioning. It's by no means a complete listing but more closely, it's an attempt to cover as many of the more common uncommon fetishes I have personally worked with.

If your honey mentions a fetish that isn't covered in the other chapters, take a look at the list of the fetishes covered here. If you still don't find it, chances are good that you'll gather additional information by doing an online search.

The intent of this book is not to be a fetish encyclopedia. Its main purpose is to help you understand, investigate and become involved with your partner's own personal sexuality. Ultimately, he's the best resource because he and he alone has the capability of explaining his innermost thoughts to you.

But before we get into the fetishes themselves, here are the questions you should ask when he tells you that he has one of the fetishes contained in this chapter or even if he tells you about a fetish that's even more rare and atypical.

Q&A:

Can you educate me more about this fetish?
You'll know a little bit about the fetish by reading the various descriptions in the following pages. This question is very important so you can listen openly without feeling shocked or turned off. Hear what he has to say and try and remember the fetish's key components. Ask him to paint a picture with words or to show you some of his favorite photos online or in his porno book stash, which I'm willing to wager he has.

When you masturbate to thoughts of this fetish what pops into your head at the moment of orgasm?

This is another telling question because the orgasmic answer is the core of the fantasy. It's the one aspect of the fetish that causes him to let go, literally, and explode. Though there are many other components to his fetish its orgasmic aspect is crucial.

What are some buzzwords you like to hear?

Keywords or phrases are a very important aspect of fetish sexuality, especially if he is aurally inclined. The more you understand, the better you can join with him and speak his sexual language. Verbalization of his fantasy can be as fulfilling as the actuality of enacting it. Speaking about his fetish is a good alternative if you don't wish to actually enact it with him. For more, see the chapter on "Bedroom Talk."

His images and buzzwords are unique to your guy. Ask him questions and be prepared for anything. The two of you will decide what works best within the context of your own personal, unique relationship.

Buzzwords and imagery can actually be a fetish unto itself, so you'll see it detailed later on in this chapter.

What about the visual image?

Some people are more visually oriented than others. While they may not be able to verbally describe their fetish they can point to a picture to increase your learning curve. Have him go online and show you his favorite websites. Tell him to describe what he likes about the photos he shares with you. Elicit specifics about the images. For example:

- What is the attitude of the participants?
- Are they there for purposes of enjoyment or punishment?
- Is the fetish seen by him as something "forced" or voluntary?
- If he could jump into the photo, what character would he most want to be, and why?

What involvement has he had or does he want to have with this fetish?

Find out what kind of participation he'd ideally want from you. Is your involvement merely accepting his fetish or is it something he wants to enact with you? If he craves your participation, find out what's expected and what you'll need to do. Have him get as detailed as possible. Ask if he can show you a video clip or demonstrate it in some way.

Do I need any special props or implements?

Many fetishes require some kind of accouterment. If you're participating, ask him to purchase this for you. Or better yet, go shopping for it together.

Have you had any real-time experience with this?

If his answer is yes, it may be difficult to hear that he's already been enacting the fantasy without your knowledge. But I'm asking you to put your feelings aside because at this moment you're conducting an objective investigation. Emotions will get in the way of your fact-finding mission.

Find out specifically what he liked and didn't like about past experiences. Remember to ask about details like the attitude of the participant, participation and chemistry that are necessary to capture the fantasy the way he envisions it.

Remember it could be very difficult for him to discuss personal fantasies that he believes are fundamentally incorrect. Be mindful of the guilt and shame he already harbors. It's your job to make him feel heard and accepted.

A Potpourri of Previously Unmentioned But Nevertheless Acknowledged and Recognized Fetishes:

Now that we've gotten the Q&A out of the way, I'll describe some of the more common uncommon fetishes below. They're listed in alphabetical order so that you can find them easily. Here goes:

Auto-Erotic Asphyxiation

This sexual proclivity gained notoriety after actor, David Carradine died this way. Erotic asphyxiation describes intentionally cutting off oxygen to the brain for sexual arousal. The "auto" part is when the person does this themselves and not with a partner. As evidenced by Mr. Carradine's untimely death, it can be a dangerous and even fatal practice. This is why I do not recommend it.

This sexual proclivity is sometimes referred to as "breath control play." Those who engage in this practice usually partake in some kind of secretive self-bondage. They masturbate and attempt to be at the point of losing consciousness at the moment of orgasm. Some guys will share this with a partner and want you to participate. This is dangerous play and I don't condone it.

However, an alternative way to cut off your man's air supply for pleasure is to literally sit on his face. (I've mentioned this in more depth in the *Ass and Anal Fetish* chapter.) It's easy to do: simply sit on his face and use your bottom to hinder his breathing. This will not provide the same "rush" as erotic asphyxiation but it is a good, safe alternative.

Your man may try and push you to engage in erotic asphyxiation with him. While your participation would, of course, ensure some degree of safety, there are no guarantees. Even if you are present, accidents can happen. If he admits that he enjoys this kind of sexual stimulation, take this as an opportunity to help him. If necessary encourage him to get counseling so that he can explore a safe alternative and get this dangerous compulsion under control.

Buzzwords and Imagery

Some people become incredibly aroused by a particular buzzword or erotic image. Practically anything can fall into this category. This fetish is very individualized and connected to your guy's life experience. His own personal buzzwords can be anything that has meaning for him. For example, I know of a former Viet Nam POW who's sexually aroused by being called "a helpless victim". Since traumatic events are often sexualized as a way to cope, this is a clear case of trying to make sense out of an insane experience.

Some of these buzzwords and phrases might sound downright silly to us but be assured that they are key to some men's arousal. These phrases are unique and plentiful as there are males in the universe. Some unique buzz sentences I've heard include:

- "I'm going to gouge your eyeballs out."
- "I'm going to put you in a pot and cook you alive."
- "I'm going to spank you."
- "I'm going to turn you into human toilet paper."
- "You are nothing but a lowly cum receptacle"
- "Sissy pants – panty waste whore!"

Your guy will undoubtedly have some of his own personal favorites to be used alone or within the context of a role-play or fantasy scenario. These images and phrases are unique to your guy. Ask him questions and be prepared for anything in response. The two of you will decide what works best within the context of your own private, unique relationship.

Cannibalism

Believe it or not, Bugs Bunny was the inspiration for this one! Some guys report fantasizing about being put into a cauldron of hot water and being made into stew. This is something Bugs Bunny has faced countless times and the fetishists have come upon as children. Obviously you'd have to improvise on that one!

Castration Fantasy

Most men prize their male organs and cringe at the thought of anyone causing them harm. Castration, the fantasy of removing male testicles, is the exact opposite of this impulse. It's primarily a fantasy, although some transsexuals (men who prefer to be women) do it for real.

At the core of the castration fantasy is the desire to totally surrender. Giving up part of his genitalia is the ultimate sacrifice of the male submissive. This fantasy is extreme or rare but you may very well be with a guy who likes to entertain the idea of castration.

If your man harbors these fantasies, he probably holds a strong belief about female superiority. He may find his own phallus to be an obsolete, distasteful object. He might like to entertain thoughts that one day you will cut off his balls, preserve them in water and display them in a beautiful vessel as a memento of your power over him.

Obviously, this is one fantasy that will have to remain just that. However, you can uncover what he really thinks about castration and discuss it with him. Use the buzzwords he likes to hear. Tie it in with your dominance over him if he's a submissive male.

Men who harbor a castration fantasy may also be aroused at the idea of wearing a chastity belt. This is a device that puts his penis under lock and key, literally. A number of varieties are sold online but again, this concept is something that newcomers should explore verbally rather than physically.

A fantasy alternative to the idea of the chastity belt is to control his orgasm. A mental chastity belt, so to speak. Put him on a schedule and allow him to masturbate at a time determined strictly by you.

At any rate, I encourage you to talk to your partner and explore the aspects of castration or denial which turn him on. Then try to reach some sort of middle ground to help him realize, within the safe realm of fantasy, his desires.

Clothed Females Naked Men (CFNM)
This fetish is exactly what it sounds like. It is hinged upon the idea of one naked man in a situation where he is alone with one or more fully dressed women. This fetish appears to be a spin off of the original fantasy of having the woman in control. Most men fantasize about this as a form of humiliation or domination, although some like it for its exhibitionist quality.

Crushing
An offshoot of a foot or trampling fetish, a crush fetishist enjoys the idea of watching you or a fantasy female crush or step on a small animal or object. I've worked with people who liked the idea of seeing bugs, mice or small animals stomped out with bare feet. Other times, it's about squishing some kind of food

like an eclair, cream pie or a raw, bloody piece of meat. Since the female crusher is often viewed as an Amazonian creature, this allows your guy to "exchange places" with the crushee and experience the fantasy of being small and overpowered by a powerful female.

Again, the idea of squishing something live might be pretty unappealing, but on the other hand, jumping into a chocolate pudding cake might be a hoot. You call the shots so that you can both have fun and he sees you as the star of his "crush" fantasies.

Edgeplay

This is a fetish that implies some danger. It has to do with taking someone close to their limits. It's achieved by using some kind of physical or psychological fear that brings on sexual arousal. It is closely related to auto-erotic asphyxiation and is sometimes synonymous with that fetish. It most often incorporates the use of knives or blades. Hence the name edgeplay.

If your man says that he enjoys edgeplay you need to find out what meaning it has for him. Some people get aroused by having a sharp knife lightly graze their body. Others talk about edgeplay as a way to heighten and extend limits. Edgeplay has a personal and individual meaning for everyone. Some consider this as the ultimate way of relinquishing control. Safe words may be discarded if he's a fan of edgeplay. You'll need to do lots of questioning and fact-finding in order to get a better idea of exactly what edgeplay means to him.

Equestrian (also see "Horse")

This fetish entails "horse-play" - literally. It means that your guy likes to pretend to be your horse. This taps into a submissive, subservient need. He wants you to ride on his shoulders and carry you. He has the desire to take on the role of being the carrier to a supreme being; you. In this role, he has to follow your instructions implicitly: trot, gallop, prance, etc. Some clients have reported that they merely enjoy the sensation of feeling their woman's thighs pressing against their necks and shoulders.

Equestrian fetishes are sometimes incorporated into D/s play. It's a big part of the overall D/s sub-scene. As part of your playing, you'd have him get on all fours so you could "ride" him. You control his pace with gentle but firm instructions and a riding crop.

Equestrian fantasies are easy and fun to enact. Ask the appropriate questions outlined here to unlock more about his specific needs.

Flashing

Flashing refers to briefly exposing one's body in a socially-inappropriate way. The flashing fetish is a similar type of paraphilia to Exhibitionism (also discussed in this chapter), since the origin lies in nonconsensual deviant behavior, which is out of the scope of this book. However, flashing is included here in order to acknowledge a sexual act that can be played out consensually between two consenting adults within the scope of role playing.

Role playing is an excellent way to indulge a flashing fantasy. The fear of getting caught adds an element of excitement. Be creative and make sure that neither of you will put yourself in the way of the law. I imagine there's nothing worse than spending a potentially sexy night in a jail cell instead of your bedroom!

If flashing is your guy's fantasy, it can be role-played in a consensual manner similar to frotteruism or frottage (also covered in this chapter). The fantasy lies in the nonconsensuality aspect, which is not within the context of this book. However as fantasy you or your guy can engage in some consensual exposing of your privates and pretend it's nonconsensual. Let's see what a good actress you are!

Food

Lots of people find food sexy. We're bombarded with sensual images in television commercials and print advertising every day, selling anything from hamburgers (remember Paris Hilton gyrating for Six Dollar Burgers?) to milk. Think about the aphrodisiac potential of bananas, grapes and whipped cream. These are actually some pretty mainstream fantasies which have

already been incorporated into Hollywood movies like
91/2 Weeks.

A food fetishist often takes his love of food to the extreme. Some use food to express their desire for control. Maybe they had a Jewish or Italian mama who used to force them to eat, even when they weren't hungry. I know a man who likes vegetable oil poured forcibly down his throat. He'd choke and gag and struggle, then after his session, he'd go out to enjoy a full meal.

If your guy says he has a food fetish be prepared for anything! He might want you to prepare him a concoction of eggs, meat and Tabasco sauce combined with dog food and then force him to eat it. He may also request that you use specific foods like zucchini or cucumbers as a dildo—on him or on yourself.

I've heard that ginger root is one food that has a special added zing. Whittle it into an insertable device and watch him go mad from the sting. It's a great way to cause intense sensations that are safe and temporary.

I've also known couples and swingers who've had fun with a huge tub of chocolate pudding. What a sweet way to lavish each others cream laden bodies!

The possibilities with a food fetish are endless. So keep an open mind - as well as a stocked refrigerator.

Frottage

This is a fancy name for a paraphilia that involves the non-consensual rubbing of one person against another to achieve sexual arousal. The contact is usually with the hands or the genitals and may involve rubbing a clothed body against another for sexual pleasure without their knowledge. One place this commonly occurs is on a crowded bus or subway train. An unsuspecting woman has no idea this is going on because of the jostling of the vehicle and the press of bodies.

Though the origins of this fantasy lie in an act with a non-consenting partner, it's still a paraphilia that needs to be addressed. If the impulse is out of control, the fetishist needs psychotherapy in order to learn how to manage it. You can be helpful to your man by accepting his fantasy and perhaps indulging with him in a safe, sane way. Role play may give some semblance of satisfaction for the fellow who enjoys the act of rubbing against a clothed body. You can pretend to be the unsuspecting lady while he rubs away to his heart's content.

Lovers of latex also enjoy frottage-type behavior. Latex fetishists take great pleasure in rubbing up against others who have also donned the thin rubber material. This population, however, is engaging in consensual behavior so this brand of frottage is not to be classified as deviant or problematic behavior.

Furries

This is a relatively new fetish. To enact it, men and women get dressed in cute, furry animal outfits and engage in sexual intercourse. Imagine…adult-sized pandas and Teddy bears going at it like, well, bunnies. People who like to dress up as fuzzy critters obviously equate their sexuality as something animalistic. Inquire as to what kind of furry critter your guy finds attractive, who's doing the dressing, get the costumes and you're good to go.

I made reference to the Furries phenomenon in the chapter on Role Playing and mentioned a funny episode of the HBO series "Entourage" which dealt with furries. You can also see various clips starring furries on YouTube which might spark some furry fantasies of your own.

Hair

Your guy might get turned on by hair in general: long hair, short hair, a particular texture, etc. This is considered a fetish; meaning he's aroused or extremely fond of human hair.

Sometimes a hair fetish also means that he's turned on by the idea of shaving hair. Usually, he wants his own hair shaved. This may be in conjunction with a Domination/submissive (D/s) scene where he's shaved for purposes of discipline, punishment or humiliation. Some submissives find this extreme act a way to prove their devotion to you. Or it may just be the act of getting shaved in and of itself. Again, this is something for you to find out in your Q&A.

Another possibility is that his hair fetish involves shaving your hair. Chances are pretty good you wouldn't go for that. Even if you were personally okay with the idea, it might not be advisable for your career or your job image.

But this doesn't mean your man's hairless fantasy has to be denied entirely. A little fantasy goes a long way. You can *talk* to him about shaving your head. Have him "make believe" he's cutting your mane with his fingers. (Don't put a scissor in his hands! It might be too tempting and he could get caught up in the moment.) If you're agreeable, you can even allow him to cut some of your other body hair such as shave your legs, underarms, or pubes.

Hairy Armpits (or Hairy Anything!)

Plain and simple, some guys just like hairy armpits! This fetish may be linked to a woman from their childhood, say an aunt or a neighbor lady, who didn't shave her underarms. Other men see female armpit hair as something forbidden or wildly natural. Perhaps it reminds them of their first sneak peek at a female's pubic hair.

These men might also have a penchant for furry vaginas. Although most women like to keep their privates groomed like a well-tended garden or even waxed, some guys prefer just the opposite. To these fellows, an unkempt snatch might signify a woman of wild abandon. To us gals, a carefully-tended crotch is a sign of good personal hygiene, yet there are some guys who like a "hairy bush". Again, this preference has something to do with their idea of seeing the "real thing", an early erotic memory or a penchant for the natural look.

Make sure to ask your man what he wants to do with your hair. For some with a hirsute fantasy, puffy hair "down there" is merely a visual. Yet others want to kiss, lick or suck on the hairs. If your guy likes a Hairy Mary, this is a relatively easy fetish to fulfill. Just find out the key elements.

On the flipside, a shaved mound is a turn-on for other guys. This can often be traced back to the first "bare bird" he ever saw. Ask lots of questions to get to the root of his desires so you can fulfill them.

Hand and Nail

Hands are another part of your anatomy that he might be lusting after. Something is considered a fetish when a body part is eroticized above and beyond conventional erogenous zones.

As with all fetishes, an interest in hands can encompass many different parts of that anatomy along with many different aspects.

Ask him if he's interested in fingers, palms, or hand size. Most "hand men" are interested in fingernails. Ask him about his specific nail-type preferences - long, short, round or pointy tips. Believe it or not, some guys like the look of bitten-down nails. Some also love gloved hands. Again, it may just be the visual aesthetic or perhaps he likes you to rub your well-manicured hand gently over his body. Maybe he wants you to spread your fingers. The hand fetish proves that any part of your anatomy may be the trigger for his unique sexual target of arousal.

Horse (also see "Equestrian")

A variation of the equestrian fetish, the horse fetish is grounded in the association between horseback riding and sexual pleasure. This, as with all fetishes, relates back to early sexual stimulation stored in the subconscious mind. Rest assured it has nothing to do with bestiality!

It's commonly known that people (women especially) experience strong pelvic sensations while riding on a horse. Guys with a horse fetish either like the idea of recreating the experience for females or "get off" on the visual of a woman riding a horse. The fantasy may also involve some kind of mutual pleasure of making love with a woman who shares the horseback riding experience with them.

This is a fetish that can be somewhat satisfied if you live on a farm or a ranch. Chances are you don't so your guy's horse fetish will most probably lend itself to a verbal fantasy fulfillment session. Use the outline given in this chapter to ask pointed questions about his own personal horse fantasy.

Medical

This fetish revolves around having a penchant for anything that has to do with a medical practice, including objects, costuming or environment. Sometimes a medical fetish incorporates a D/s scene. Other times it does not.

Some medical procedures commonly associated with this fetish include enemas, rectal temperature-taking, prostate exams, injections, suppositories and/or catheters.

A medical fetish can be complex or extremely simple. The simple scenario would involve the fantasy of you being the doctor or nurse and giving him a make-believe exam. The more intense variety has to do with the insertion and the use of highly-technical equipment. I know a guy whose fetish was so strong that he purchased an antique, leather dentist's chair and put it in his bedroom.

Please note: I do not personally recommend or condone nonprofessionals performing medical procedures which require skill and training. Inserting catheters into the urethra can be health-threatening and cause permanent damage. Proceed with caution when enacting this particular fetish.

Role-playing is the best and safest way to enact the medical fetish. You can always pretend to be carrying out the acts he finds stimulating. Remember to use your verbal skills. They go a long, lusty way in the realm of fetish and fantasy.

Money/Financial Domination

This is yet another fetish that originates from control issues. A money fetish means that he wants to relinquish power to you financially. Usually there's some kind of tease element involved: if he wants you, he has to pay for it. Though this may be his fantasy, I think it might be the ultimate female fantasy too! By all means, indulge in his money fetish. Let him take you on a shopping spree, but be sure not to take advantage and have him buy you a Jaguar if he can't afford it.

A variation of the Dominant/submissive theme, remember to always be a responsible Top. Before you play, get a clear sense of his budget and agree not to exceed it. After all, this is just role-play. An unreasonable charge card bill isn't anyone's fantasy!

Sploshing

What comes to mind when you think of The Three Stooges? Most of us conjure up images of eye-poking and unbridled pie fights. Does the thought of a pie in the face get you aroused? Probably not. What effect does it have on your man? If he gets an erection at the thought of someone's face getting splattered with food, he likes sploshing.

An offshoot of the "wet and messy" fetish, sploshing involves the act of rubbing, pouring or having foods thrown at you. Some get off on the actuality of having cream pies thrown in their face. Others enjoy sitting on cakes, in bowls of pudding, gelatin or having messy foods such as spaghetti in sauce rubbed all over their bodies.

As bizarre as it may seem to you, this is a fetish that both men and women enjoy equally. The questions to ask of your mate are obvious. Your participation should be a snap, as long as you bring your sense of humor.

Voyeurism/Exhibitionism

Although these two arousals are opposite sides of the coin, they can be discussed together because they're also grounded in similarities.

If your guy is a voyeur it means he gets his kicks from seeing something he isn't supposed to see. A Peeping Tom is the common image that comes to mind. Looking into the window of an unsuspecting woman is illegal, but spying on a woman who's in on the game but pretends she's unaware, is something else entirely.

The same is true of an exhibitionist who gets a charge out of exposing himself or "flashing" his genitals at innocent women. You can feed into this fantasy by pretending to be shocked and appalled (or turned on, depending on his desire) but still keep within the limits of the law.

I want to again stress that voyeurism and flashing are both illegal acts. However, exhibition and voyeurism can also be consensual activities that are acknowledged in a safe, healthy way by playing out fantasy games. Understand that these acts should not be condoned or encouraged if they involve unsuspecting partners.

If your guy has problems with flashing or peeping in real life then he needs professional help. This book is intended to assist you in showing him how to manage and enjoy his "fringe" feelings without getting into trouble.

In their purest form, Voyeurism and Exhibitionism lend themselves to many enjoyable fantasy-filled games and role-playing scenarios. For example, you can pretend he's peeping into your window. The repercussions when he's caught can be more than he's bargained for—i.e. he receives a punishment like having to lick your toes or is forced to masturbate while you become his voyeur. This fantasy can also be easily incorporated into spanking or bondage type games.

A voyeuristic fantasy also lends itself to you performing a sexy strip tease for him. Voyeurism is something that can be easily controlled. When you accept his desires, his anxiety level will diminish and his fetish can be played out in a safe, healthy (and legal!) fashion rather than solely as a way to relieve stress.

Similarly, exhibitionism can also be incorporated into fantasy role-play. If he's the exhibitionist, he might want you to watch him masturbate. Many men love to hear your thoughts about their penises. Having you watch them stroke themselves and comment in great detail on his endowment sexually arouses them. Now, that's not so tough to do, is it?

Some fellows like to incorporate exhibitionism into D/s play. For example, many cross-dressers enjoy being taken out in public while they're all dressed up. Other submissives revel in the thought of being displayed by their Mistress at some kind of fetish event. Still others like to be punished in places where they might get caught flashing. Both of you will have to ascertain a certain comfort level and think seriously about risk factors involved with any play that takes place outside the bedroom. A fetish club is the obvious choice and the safest legally speaking.

There's also a brand of exhibitionist who enjoys being watched while they're having sex. Video cameras are a perfect way to satisfy this craving. You can even pretend there's an audience in your bedroom or in your car, if you want to get even riskier. Always remember to be cautious and carefully assess any risk factors involved.

Wedgies

It's easy to see the origins of this fetish. Wedgies are common horseplay during boyhood years. A friend reports that her son's wedgie fetish became obvious at age nine, when she caught him sneaking peeks at wedgie video clips on YouTube.

Giving a wedgie, as you probably know, entails grabbing the back waistband of someone's underpants and yanking them high into the butt crack. It's uncomfortable as well as embarrassing.

If your man is a wedgie enthusiast, he may fetishize the event as an act of humiliation or he might crave the intense pain inflicted on his privates. He could also just like the way a wedgie looks on an unsuspecting female. Think of it as a do-it-yourself thong.

Wedgies may be an activity that he likes giving and/or having done to him. He may enjoy it separately as a fetish unto itself or it may involve the aspect of control and then can be incorporated within the context of a D/s scene.

Wet and Messy (WAM)

WAM is exactly what its name proclaims - getting off by being wet and messy. Imagine rolling around in shaving cream, chocolate pudding or mud. Yes, it's hedonistic and dirty but it's ultimately harmless, good, clean/dirty fun.

Ask a lot of questions to find out what your man finds so arousing about WAM. This fetish clearly has its origins in child play and is hinged upon letting go with abandon. Perhaps he was never allowed to "make a mess" as a child. Perhaps he's rebelling against his "clean freak" mom. But whatever the reason, let your man explore his WAM desires, which will be very healing and liberating.

To help your man realize his WAM dreams, you'll have to find out his substance of choice and how he imagines playing. For some, it's vanilla pudding, for others it whipped cream. Some fetishists picture having sex during or after the mess-making. Others find the act in and of itself to be gratifying.

I know of a man who had what I refer to as "the combo platter" which is a combination of sploshing and WAM. This gentleman enjoyed seeing a specific type of woman (pretty, innocent-looking, in her 20s, no tattoos) having her face splattered with different types of food. After he photographed it (to enjoy later), he indulged in sploshing her messy face with his semen.

WAM can be a fun fetish to enact. Give yourselves permission to be spontaneous. Cover the floor with plastic sheeting to catch all of those nasty spills and go to town. For easy cleanup, make sure you're close to the shower.

In Summary

There's no limit to the imagination when it comes to sexuality and sexual turn-ons. Your job as a loving, interested partner is to allow your man to freely express whatever goes on in his head during masturbation or sex. (And vice versa. It's a two-way street!) The image that causes him to ejaculate is ultimately the foundation of his sexuality. Helping him acknowledge and embrace his fetish makes for a happier, healthier, hornier mate.

Epilogue

I hope by reading this book, you've discovered that your man is not the only one who has sexual fantasies or fetishes that are considered by "polite society" to be out of the norm. I hope you've learned that sexuality is an individual phenomenon and that everyone has their own particular acts or phrases that arouse them. Some are more detailed, complicated and uncommon than others but they're all valid and deserve to be embraced.

Your acceptance and participation in your man's fetish will allow you to be a proactive, contributing member of your union. He doesn't have to sneak around and you don't have to feel shut out of this big part of his life.

The last thing I'll ask of you is to take some time to evaluate what's gone on since you've picked up this book.

- Have you done your initial investigation?
- What was it like for you?

You may have felt awkward, frightened or excited by what you've discovered. Although it's not easy to discuss in depth a previously disregarded subject, it also probably feels extremely healing to get it out in the open.

Recall how you felt when you talked with your guy. Think about how you feel now. Ask yourself:

*Did I discover something about my partner
I didn't know before?*

Chances are good you did. I hope you learned a great deal. You might have found out that his fetish is relatively mild or that he's deeply entrenched in the behavior. No matter what you unearthed, you now have choices. The two of you can make these decisions together. You both can decide how to proceed and embrace his fetish in a way that both of you find comfortable.

Remember, knowledge is power and you've unlocked the door to erotic wisdom. You've taken the essential first step to positively changing your lives by reading this book.

What To Do Next

It's important to consider how he felt about discussing his fetish with you. Did he feel intruded upon, relieved or excited? These emotions are generally mixed. Acknowledge that it must feel a bit invasive to have a secret aspect of your sexuality exposed, but at the same time it's also a great relief not to be burdened by that secret any longer.

The two of you need to take time to talk just about the fetish itself. Figure out how much or how little you would like to participate in it as a couple. Ask the best way for you to ease into it. What props, costuming or mindsets are necessary before you begin?

Embarking On An Exciting Journey

You and your partner are about to embark on an exhilarating trip of self-discovery. He will finally experience what it's like to live out his fetish with an intimate partner. You will discover your untapped capabilities and your deep capacity to love unconditionally.

Participating in his fetish brings about the following positive changes:

- You are now bonded together in a very intimate journey.
- You share his "secret".
- You are his primary source of pleasure.
- You will "spice up" your relationship and deepen it.
- You will relieve him of guilt and stress.
- You will have fun together.

Take Care of Yourself

It may seem as though you're doing a great deal for him. You are. You're taking time out of your busy schedule to get inside his head and explore a part of his being that was previously foreign to you.

However, the task at hand could also create anxiety and stress for you. Although it feels good to give, you may also feel like you need to receive. Just as he's communicated his needs to you, it's important for you to communicate your needs. Tell him when you need more attention, a hug, a kind word. But my guess is you won't have to because he'll be so grateful for the gift you've given him.

It's also important to give yourself validation. You're about to enter foreign, unknown territory. It's okay to feel a little apprehensive, nervous and scared. And excited.

Yes, you are really doing this! Give yourself another pat on the back because you're truly an amazing woman. But before you embark on his fetish fantasy, be sure to give yourself a gift as well. Treat yourself to a shopping spree, a manicure, a pedicure or a day at the spa. You deserve it!

And finally, I'd like to thank you for placing your trust in me and seeking my advice in this book. I wish you and your lucky man the best, the deepest, most passionate voyage of self-discovery possible.

I'd also love to hear how you're doing. Please feel free to drop me a note at: **therapywithcare@roadrunner.com** or **therapywithcare@gmail.com**

You can also visit my website: **www.therapywithcare.com**.

Happy exploring!

Follow-Up Quiz: Your Sexual I.Q.

I thought it might be fun - and educational - for you to take this quiz again after you've read the book to see if your sexual values have changed. Chances are, they have. I hope you're pleased with the results, which can only strengthen your sexual bond with your partner.

Select a number below each question to indicate how strongly you agree or disagree with each statement. When you're done taking the quiz, tally up your score. And don't peek at the answer key at the end!

1) Do you feel there's something sexually "wrong" with your man?

> 3 - Not at all
> 2 - Somewhat
> 1 - A little
> 0 - A lot

2) Do you feel upset about the possibility that he enjoys sexual acts that are foreign to you?

      3 - Not at all
      2 - Somewhat
      1 - A little
      0 - A lot

3) Does the future of your sexual relationship feel hopeless?

      3 - Not at all
      2 - Somewhat
      1 - A little
      0 - Very

4) Do you feel *he's* the one who has the problem so *he's* the one who has to change?

      3 - Not at all
      2 - Somewhat
      1 - A little
      0 - Well he's the one with the fetish

5) Do you have a favorite sex position?

      3 - I enjoy them all
      2 - Most of them
      1 - Sometimes I'll get on top
      0 - Missionary only, thank you

6) Do you find sexual activities such as oral sex distasteful?

      3 - Not at all
      2 - Somewhat
      1 - A little
      0 - Very

7) Do you mind dressing up for your partner when you're having sex?

       3 - Love it, I have lot's of outfits
       2 - I have one or two costumes
       1 - Sometimes I'll wear lingerie
       0 - Is this really necessary, I have enough laundry

8) Have you and your partner ever experimented with sex toys or other props?

       3 - We have a closet full
       2 - We have a few toys we enjoy
       1 - Once or twice on special occasions
       0 - Are you nuts, get that thing away from me!

9) Do you have any objection to using certain phases or erotic buzzwords to help stimulate your partner?

       3 - Not at all
       2 - Sometimes
       1 - Potty talk belongs in the potty
       0 - A lady never uses such language

10) Do you believe that your partner should focus his attention only on you during sexual interaction?

       3 - Not at all, fantasy is healthy
       2 - What goes on in his head is his business
       1 - I'd prefer if he's focused on me
       0 - He'd better be focused on me

11) Do you wish he could take a pill and be "cured" of his unusual sexual proclivities?

       3 - Not at all
       2 - Sometimes
       1 - How much is this pill?
       0 - Call the pharmacy now

12) Do you believe that anyone who is turned on by sexuality out of the norm is perverted and needs to be cured?

    3 - Not at all
    2 - Somewhat
    1 - Maybe
    0 - Absolutely

13) Do you worry that his sexual predilections could be the demise of your relationship?

    3 - Not at all
    2 - Sometimes
    1 - I can't help but worry
    0 - I'm sure of it

14) Are you willing to be flexible and learn to participate to some degree in his fetish?

    3 - Bring it on
    2 - If it keeps us together
    1 - If its his birthday and I'm in a good mood
    0 - Hell no

15) Would you be willing to share something about your own sexuality with him?

    3 - I love to tell him my fantasies
    2 - I'll tell him some, but not all
    1 - A girl has to have some secrets
    0 - Mind your damn business

Your Sexual I.Q. Quiz Results

0-4
Established
You have rigid beliefs when it comes to sex. This came from the way you were brought up and reflects strong messages from your parents, schools and church. You ideally believe that sex should take place between married couples. Right now you are encountering a problem that you strongly wish would disappear.

5-10
Conventional
You are a slightly open-minded but prefer conventional, married, "vanilla" sex. Ideally it's your hope and belief that sex is all about the bond that brings you together as man and wife.

11-20
Borderline Traditional
You recognize that his fetish is something that affects you both. You would prefer to have a traditional sexual relationship but you are willing to entertain other ideas. You're curious and willing to explore other possibilities in order to help your relationship.

21-30
Getting There
You have opened your mind to the possibility of change. You're pretty certain that your man has something different and/or unusual about his sexual tastes but you're open-minded and want to explore the possibilities of getting involved with his fetish

31-45
Congratulations!
You're on your way to being your man's best lover. You're willing to find out what he likes and then "go for it" the best you can. You are inwardly confident and know your capabilities. You will do only what you honestly feel is right for you. You have the

inner strength to say no but will do what it takes to acknowledge his fetish and fulfill it to the best of your capabilities.

Dedication

This book is dedicated to you, the man who entrusted me with the sexual secret you swore you'd take to your grave. Prior to seeing me, you may or may not have tried opening up to your partner. Oftentimes you were rejected, dismissed or ridiculed. It was bad enough feeling sexually different from your friends but when your wife turned a deaf ear to your desires, your nagging thoughts were validated - "There's something wrong with me. I'd better keep these nasty thoughts to myself. Nobody must ever know that inside I'm just a perverted freak."

And so you hid, from others and most importantly, from yourself. Nobody would ever guess that you went to *those kind* of websites or entertained such bizarre, unconventional thoughts while masturbating or making love. But still the thoughts plagued you. You wished they'd go away but no matter how hard you tried, the same ritualistic images appeared in your head while your penis was erect and you were at the moment of orgasm. These thoughts, these feelings, these obsessions just wouldn't leave. They haunted you. Guilt and shame plagued you and became ever-present in your life.

Then you and I met. Finally, you found someone who "got you", who understood what made you tick sexually and didn't pass judgment upon you. I gave you relief, guidance and an outlet of self-expression. I helped you understand that your unique sexual "fingerprint" is merely an aspect of your whole erotic personality.

Now you know that your inner voice feels as powerful as its ability to freely exist and that deprivation only leads to craving. The more a fetish is squelched, the more it wants to emerge. Its like scratching an itch or eating after a period of starvation. You also know that acceptance quiets the compulsive aspect of a fetishist's longing and compulsion.

Yet, even with all of this healing knowledge, you still experienced sadness. No matter how satisfactory it was to see me, you still wished that you could share your fetish with the woman you loved. I heard you loud and clear when you confided in me:

- "I love my wife. Why can't she understand?"
- "How can I get her to participate in my fetish so we don't have secrets?"
- "How can I tell her about my fetish without feeling embarrassed, ashamed or humiliated?"
- "I'm engaged - Should I tell her or will she call off the wedding when she finds out?"

True, women are often reactive. They are also very in tuned with their feelings and are quick to label things as "good" or "bad". This "all or nothing" mode of thinking is reflective of their feelings about sexuality. Women have definite images of romance and the way it's *supposed* to be. We are products of our environment.

But the good news is that women are also, by nature, extremely giving and nurturing. We like being needed, praised and pleasing to the people we love.

A few years ago, it occurred to me that I could give voice to the thousands of men I've met and treated in the past three decades while educating women about fetish and appealing to their giving, nurturing side. It is you who inspired me to write

Sex, Fetish and Him and for this, I thank you. The experience of creating this book has been extremely cathartic and fulfilling for me, as I hope reading it will be for you.

I hope this book will hold the answer to your having a closer relationship with the one you love. I hope this book will teach your woman how to be the best lover possible for you. And in turn, I expect you to communicate, appreciate and cherish her desire to learn about your unique brand of sexuality. This book is dedicated to bringing the two of you together, abolishing secrets and living without apology.

Here's to openness, acceptance and harmony!

Acknowledgements

Thanks to Vinnie and Cathy for making this happen.

About The Author

Jackie A. Castro is a licensed Marriage Family Therapist (MFT) with a private practice in Los Angeles, California. She was born and raised in New York City but has lived most of her adult life in California. She studied education and received her BA in Elementary Education from Boston University. She received her Master's Degree in Clinical Psychology from Antioch University and then went on to do post-graduate work at the Institute for Advanced Study of Human Sexuality in San Francisco.

Jackie's gift is being open minded and accepting of all human beings. She is compassionate about their struggles and always maintains an attitude of respect and genuine empathy. She's been actively involved with alternative lifestyle communities for most of her life. Jackie is proud to give voice to a community that's often left unheard.

Jackie currently advocates for those in the fetish community. She also offers individual and couples counseling for all people in need, including, but not limited to, those in the LGBT community, and of course, those who struggle with sexual fetish.

She has written numerous articles, as well as the books
Sex, Fetish and Him (Volossal Publishing, 2011)
and
Fetish and You (Volossal Publishing, 2015).

Visit Jackie's website at:
www.therapywithcare.com

Contact her directly at:
therapywithcare@roadrunner.com
or
therapywithcare@gmail.com

Fetish Glossary

Adult Baby: a person who gets sexual gratification from pretending to be an infant. Interests may include dressing in baby clothes, being tightly swaddled, drinking from a bottle, etc. Refer to the *Adult Babies and Infantilism* chapter for more.

Auto-Erotic Asphyxiation: intentionally cutting off oxygen to the brain by self-strangulation for sexual arousal and a more intense climax. A dangerous and sometimes deadly practice, not recommended or condoned.

Bedroom Talk: the art of using key erotic words and sexually-explicit phrases for the purposes of arousal and ultimately, gratification. Sometimes referred to as "dirty talk".

Bi-Curious: inquisitive about experimenting with bisexuality.

Bondage & Discipline (or B/D): the act of one partner using physical restraint (i.e. ropes, handcuffs) or mental prowess to discipline the other.

Bottom: another word for a submissive (see below), usually paired with the word Top or Dominant.

Buzzword: a particular word or words which translate into instant arousal for a fetishist.

Caning: a spanking administered with a wooden switch or cane, popular in schoolboy fantasies. British pornography of the late 1800s and early 1900s is brimming with caning scenarios.

Corner Time: being "forced" to stand in a corner as punishment for a transgression, usually goes hand-in-hand with some type of domination fetish. Discussed at length in *FemDom Domestic Disciplinary Relationships*.

Crushing: deriving sexual pleasure from watching a beautiful woman crush something - food or even a small animal - with her bare feet.

Diaper Lover: an Adult Baby (see above) who also enjoys wearing and soiling diapers. Covered in *Adult Babies and Infantilism* chapter.

Dildo Training: using a dildo (strap-on or hand-held) to wield power over a misbehaving male. See *FemDom Domestic Disciplinary Relationships* chapter for more.

Dom: refers to either a Dominant or a Dominatrix (see below).

Dominant: a person who is aroused by dominating or controlling another. Many fetishes employ some aspect of domination.

Dominant/submissive (or D/s): refers to the person or the fetish relationship where one party dominates over the other, both physically and emotionally, each receiving sexual gratification from their respective roles. See *Dominant and Submissive Roles, FemDom Domestic Disciplinary Relationships* and *Female Sexual Dominance*.

Dominatrix: a woman who is paid to dominate men who enjoy being subservient to women. Generally speaking, the title Dominant (see above) implies that the woman isn't paid for the act, but rather is involved in a D/s relationship to fulfill her or her partner's fantasy. A Dominatrix usually refers to a paid professional. The capital "D" in the words Dom, Dominant and Dominatrix is symbolic of their power.

Edgeplay: lightly running the blade of a knife over someone's body to produce erotic sensations. Can also refer to a scene where someone is psychologically or physically taken to or beyond their own comfort level.

Enema: fetishly speaking, cleansing the bowels as punishment, administered to humiliate and/or "teach a lesson," representative of purging the transgressor of his wrongdoings.

Endorphins: chemicals which convert pain into pleasure.

Exhibitionism: becoming aroused by exposing one's genitals or participating in a sex act in public.

Face-Sitting: the act of a woman literally sitting on a man's face, common in males with an ass fetish. Discussed in the *Ass and Anal Play* chapter and in *Female Sexual Dominance*.

FemDom: describes the relationship where women spank men and otherwise dominate them; short for Female Domination. Others use it to describe women who spank men or the fetishes where women "Top" or dominate men in a variety of ways. See *Female Sexual Dominance, Fem/Dom Domestic Disciplinary Relationships, et al.*

Fetish: A fixation on an object or body part that is not primarily sexual in nature, and the compulsive need for its use in order to obtain sexual gratification. When the fetish is all-encompassing, non-consenting and the only way a person can be orgasmic, it is classified by the Diagnostic and Statistical Manual of Mental Disorders (DSM IV) as a paraphilia.

Flashing: exposing one's body in a socially inappropriate way, usually in a public place.

Foot Worship: quite literally, the act of worshipping the female foot, which generally entails kissing, licking, massaging and smelling, or any combination thereof.

Forced-Bi: "forcing" a man to partake in a bisexual encounter as a form of punishment. Discussed in *FemDom Domestic Disciplinary Relationships* chapter, among others.

Frottage: clinically defined as consensual rubbing between partners, but can also be non-consensual, as on the subway.

Furries: a relatively new fetish which involves people dressing up like large, furry animals and having sex with each other in costume. Also known as "Plushies".

Golden Showers: the act of being urinated upon, usually from above, hence the name.

Human Ashtray: a phrase which is a turn-on to smoking fetishists and certain submissives, it entails flicking a cigarette ash into a waiting mouth and perhaps even ducking it out on the tongue.

Humiliation: in fetish terms, the act of becoming aroused by being made to feel humiliated. Seen by submissive males as an expression of devotion, can be accomplished by being forced to cross-dress, being spanked, etc. Covered in several chapters including *Humiliation* and *Female Dominant Domestic Disciplinary Relationships*.

Master/Mistress: the one calling the shots in a Dominant/submissive relationship; Master is the male title, Mistress is the female. Also known as "Top", "Dominant" or "Dom".

Mouth-Soaping: a common punishment for a naughty boy, employed in many fetishes.

OTK: short for "over the knee", a favorite position for many spanking enthusiasts.

Pantywaist: a derogatory term which is often a buzzword, or turn-on, for some fetishists who enjoy being humiliated.

Paraphilia: a powerful, persistent sexual interest in fetishes that revolve around an object or act. The Diagnostic Manual of Mental Disorders (DSM IV) classifies sexual cravings that are atypical, extreme and out of the norm as a paraphilias or sexual disorders. The author defines fetish as a paraphilia or "disordered" only when imposed upon a non-consenting adult, law-breaking or interfering with day-to-day activity.

Rimming: licking a circle around (i.e. "rimming") the anus with one's tongue. Refer to the *Ass and Anal Play* chapter.

Safety Word: a code word decided upon before fetish play which will immediately stop the action if it becomes too intense or painful. Also known as "safe word".

Scene: a fetish encounter or occurrence, can also describe a trend or interest, as in "the S/M scene". Often used synonymously with "session".

Session: a fetish enactment, often with a paid Dominatrix or Mistress. The establishment where paid fetish sessions take place is often referred to as a "session house." Sometimes used interchangeably with "scene" (above) but sessions are generally paid encounters when scenes are generally not.

Sexual Role Playing: the activity where couples don costumes and wigs, or plan "chance" encounters in public places as a way to spice up bedroom activity.

Sissy Baby: a male Adult Baby who enjoys dressing up as a female infant. See chapter on *Adult Babies and Infantilism* for details.

Slave: another word for "submissive", "sub" or "bottom".

S/M: short for sadomasochism, the phenomenon where one partner enjoys inflicting pain upon the other, who, in turn, enjoys receiving it. Also an abbreviation for Slave/Mistress. Formerly known as S&M. Discussed in several chapters, including *Dominant and Submissive Roles, FemDom Domestic Disciplinary Relationships* and *Female Sexual Dominance*.

Smothering: similar to "face-sitting" (above) but with the additional dimension of actually cutting off the male's air supply for brief periods of time by placing the buttocks or vagina over his face.

Spanko: spanking fetishist, as referred to in the spanking community.

Sploshing: deriving sexual satisfaction from the act of rubbing, pouring or having foods thrown at you.

Sub: short for submissive (below).

Submissive: a male who gets sexual satisfaction by being dominated by a female. Generally spelled with a lower-case "s" to connote subservience.

Subspace: a state of mind where the person being spanked experiences a form of euphoria. See the chapter on *Spanking*.

Swingers club: a place where couples go to "swing" or swap partners with other couples.

Switch: someone who enjoys both spanking and being spanked or being the Dominant as well as the submissive.

Tickle Torture: tickling someone to the extreme point where it becomes almost unbearable.

Top: another word for Dominant (above).

Trampling: the act of walking upon or stomping upon someone to give them sexual pleasure. For more, see the chapter on *Foot Fetish*.

Voyeurism: getting an erotic charge from spying on people engaged in intimate behaviors such as undressing, sexual situations, or other activities thought to be private in nature.

Water Sports: refers to urination play; someone who enjoys water sports likes being urinated on or having someone urinate on them.